UML 2 Certification Guide

Morgan Kaufmann OMG Press

Morgan Kaufmann Publishers and the Object Management Group™ (OMG) have joined forces to publish a line of books addressing business and technical topics related to OMG's large suite of software standards.

OMG is an international, open membership, not-for-profit computer industry consortium that was founded in 1989. The OMG creates standards for software used in government and corporate environments to enable interoperability and to forge common development environments that encourage the adoption and evolution of new technology. OMG members and its board of directors consist of representatives from a majority of the organizations that shape enterprise and Internet computing today.

OMG's modeling standards, including the Unified Modeling Language™ (UML®) and Model Driven Architecture® (MDA), enable powerful visual design, execution and maintenance of software, and other processes—for example, IT Systems Modeling and Business Process Management. The middleware standards and profiles of the Object Management Group are based on the Common Object Request Broker Architecture® (CORBA) and support a wide variety of industries.

More information about OMG can be found at http://www.omg.org/.

Forthcoming Morgan Kaufmann OMG Press Titles

UML 2 Certification Guide: Fundamental and Intermediate Exams
Tim Weilkiens and Bernd Oestereich

Real-Life MDA: Solving Business Problems with Model Driven Architecture
Michael Guttman and John Parodi

Architecture Driven Modernization: A Series of Industry Case Studies
Bill Ulrich

UML 2 Certification Guide

Fundamental and Intermediate Exams

Tim *Weilkiens*
Bernd Oestereich

AMSTERDAM • BOSTON • HEIDELBERG • LONDON
NEW YORK • OXFORD • PARIS • SAN DIEGO
SAN FRANCISCO • SINGAPORE • SYDNEY • TOKYO

ELSEVIER

Morgan Kaufmann Publishers is an imprint of Elsevier

MORGAN KAUFMANN PUBLISHERS

Publisher	Denise E. M. Penrose
Publishing Services Manager	George Morrison
Senior Editor	Tim Cox
Assistant Editor	Mary E. James
Project Manager	Marilyn E. Rash
Cover and Interior Design	Chen Design
Composition and Illustrations	Integra
Copyeditor	Joan M. Flaherty
Proofreader	Daniel Stone
Indexer	Kevin Broccoli
Interior printer	Sheridan Books
Cover printer	Phoenix Color Corp.

Morgan Kaufmann Publishers is an imprint of Elsevier.
500 Sansome Street, Suite 400, San Francisco, CA 94111

This book is printed on acid-free paper.

Library of Congress Cataloging-in-Publication Data
Weilkiens, Tim
 UML 2 certification guide / Tim Weilkiens and Bernd Oesterreich.
   p.   cm. [UML 2.0 zertifizierungvorbereitung. English]
 Includes bibliographical references and index.
 ISBN-13: 978-0-12-373585-0 (alk. paper)
 ISBN-10: 0-12-373585-8 (alk. paper)
1. Electronic data processing personnel—Certification.   2. Computer software—Development—
Examinations—Study guides.   3. UML (Computer science)—Examinations—Study guides.
I. Oesterreich, Bernd.   II. Title.
 QA76.3.W4622 2006
 005.1'17–dc22   2006032920

ISBN 13: 978-0-12-373585-0
ISBN 10: 0-12-373585-8

For information on all Morgan Kaufmann publications, visit our
Web site at www.mkp.com or www.books.elsevier.com

Printed in the United States of America
06 07 08 09 10   5 4 3 2 1

Working together to grow
libraries in developing countries

www.elsevier.com | www.bookaid.org | www.sabre.org

ELSEVIER   BOOK AID International   Sabre Foundation

For Ben

CONTENTS

LIST OF METAMODELS

FOREWORD

The Unified Modeling Language (UML) is one of the biggest success stories in the information technology (IT) industry. Once used solely as a way to sketch the possible requirements or operations of an IT system, UML is now used in a variety of ways by people with very different backgrounds; for example, by

- business planners, as a language to specify the planned operation of a business process, perhaps in concert with a business process language such as the Business Process Modeling Notation (BPMN).
- consumer device engineers, as a way to outline the requirements for an embedded device and the way it is to be used by an end user.
- software architects, as an overall design for a major stand-alone software product.
- IT professionals, as an agreed-on set of models to integrate existing applications.
- database professionals, to manage the integration of databases into a data warehouse, perhaps in concert with a data warehousing language such as the Common Warehouse Metamodel (CWM).
- software developers, as a way to develop systems that are flexible in the face of changing business requirements and implementation infrastructure.

These are just a few examples of how UML is used; there are many more. Since the creation of the UML standard in 1997, the language has even been extended into a full systems engineering language (SysML) to solve the integrated development problems of systems development professionals.

Clearly, there's some utility and expressibility in a language that has many dozens of implementations, both open-source and closed, and that has found its way into every major (and most not-so-major) integrated development environment. That's not enough for a language to be successful, however; an entire ecosystem is needed to make a standard like UML successful. One needs to be able to find, train, and evaluate modeling professionals to know that one's projects will actually be carried out on time, on budget, and within other constraints. This means that change must be instilled in the IT organization.

It's wonderful that the UML standard and related standards (e.g., the Meta Object Facility, MOF, and XML Metadata Interchange, XMI) allow tools to share models and diagrams; this means that developers can choose and easily implement their own tool chains, integrating the right reverse-engineering tool with the right model display tool with the right code generator. But all this technical infrastructure is pointless unless the human dimension is covered too. Development teams that rely on UML, from the business analysts to the architects to the systems analysts to the programmers, must learn to speak the lingo.

The OMG's standards specifications (found at http://www.omg.org/) define the norms, but more is needed to ensure team builders that they are hiring, building, and delivering quality to their internal and external customers. In 2003, the Object Management Group teamed up with the UML Technology Institute to deal with this issue; they developed the OMG-Certified UML Professional (OCUP) program. The OCUP program defines UML expertise at three professional levels (Fundamental, Intermediate, and Advanced) and tests ability against those measures in a fair, unbiased, worldwide testing program. The OCUP UML Intermediate test taken in Bangalore is equivalent to the OCUP UML Intermediate test taken in Paris; passing that test clearly marks the test-taker as a leader in the field—someone who understands the need for expertise in modeling and who has taken the time and effort to improve his or her development expertise.

This ground-breaking book is focused on preparing you to pass the OCUP Fundamental and Intermediate tests. This allows you to show yourself, your peers, and your employer that you understand the value of modeling to the creation of quality systems that are delivered faster, better, and cheaper. The authors of this tome have proved their mettle not only by passing both tests themselves but also by teaching UML expertise in classroom and conference settings that has led to remarkably high OCUP test-passing rates.

You have taken the right first step to prepare yourself to show what you know; and this book will help you pass the tests and earn the certification!

Richard Mark Soley, Ph.D.
Chairman and Chief Executive Officer
Object Management Group, Inc.

FOREWORD

The Unified Modeling Language (UML) can be used like any other natural language. It is spoken in several ways.

Some people use UML slang to sketch a model to communicate with colleagues or to store some notes. Others speak a UML dialect. They use some vocabulary that is not formally defined, but which is easy to use, pragmatic, and a lot of people understand the right thing.

Most software developers speak pragmatic UML. Not perfect—some special words are rarely or never used. Sometimes the blur of their models leads to misunderstandings. However, generally speaking, it works well.

Some people are real UML virtuosos. So to speak the Goethe's, Schiller's, and Lessing's of the UML. They know every detail of the Unified Modeling Language and know how to use it.

Today it is a must for a software developer to communicate with UML. Surely it is more important to know how to use UML instead of knowing each vocabulary or every grammar rule of the UML. However, just like in natural languages, you can battle your way with basic knowledge of language formalism. Although the content is correct and good, a missing knowledge of language formalism can lead to misunderstandings, wrong or laborious models.

If you would like to use UML professionally, you should know the language well. The three UML certification levels define the level of language knowledge. The Fundamental level makes sense for all UML users. This book prepares you for it and the Intermediate level. That second level is important for every developer who is more than a simple UML user, such as architects, instructors, coaches, tool vendors, senior developers, MDA developers, and so on.

For these people, UML diagrams are not simple pictures for communication and documentation purposes. A UML diagram is a view of a formally defined model. That is the content of the Intermediate certification. It is only this formal foundation that turns the Unified Modeling Language into something powerful. In contrast to natural languages like Swedish or German, UML is understandable for computers. And in contrast to programming languages, such as C++, Java, C#, and Co, UML is easy to read by humans: A picture is much more expressive than a thousand words.

Developers who know this level can clearly, concisely, and unambiguously communicate sophisticated and complex facts. Their models are less mistakable and have less margin for interpretation. Finally, they can work more effectively and efficiently.

This book focuses on preparing you to pass the OCUP Fundamental and Intermediate examinations and shows you, your peers, and your employer that you understand the value of modeling for the creation of quality software that can be delivered better, faster, and cheaper.

The authors have proved their mettle not only by passing the tests themselves, but by teaching UML expertise in classroom settings that have led to remarkably high test-passing rates, just weeks after the OCUP Program became available worldwide. You have taken the right first step to prepare yourself to show what you know—and this book is the right tool to get you there!

Ivar Jacobson

PREFACE

WHY THIS BOOK?

NOT AN INTRODUCTION TO UML

It is a lot easier to work your way through this book than through the UML specifications. This book is *not* meant to give you an introduction to UML. Rather, working through this book requires you to have fundamental UML knowledge. There are other books to familiarize yourself with the UML basics (see References in the appendix).

This book systematically covers the topics relevant to the test. It is designed to prepare candidates well for the Fundamental and Intermediate UML certification exams. It prepares you exactly but exclusively for these tests. The Advanced level will be addressed in the second edition of the German book. (This translation is based on the first edition.)

COVERAGE MAP

The OMG publishes a coverage map (see *http://www.omg.org/uml-certification/UML_ Exams_Coverage_Map.pdf*), which indicates the topics and areas the test covers.

We, the authors of this book, have experience with the test. In fact, Tim has served as a beta tester in the OMG test program. In Germany, oose GmbH was the first company to offer preparatory courses. Within one month of starting the Fundamental test program in Germany, 60 candidates took the test, and only one failed. Before the test, we interviewed the candidates to get an idea of their experience and knowledge. After the test, we asked them what they had found particularly difficult and how they would improve their preparation.

All these findings, and more, have found their way into this book. Note, however, that we don't know all the questions that can come up in the test. And even if we knew them, we wouldn't pass them on because it would make the test and the certificate worthless.

This is one of the reasons why it won't be sufficient to merely consume this book, and learning everything by heart would be just as wrong. This book, however, will help you to better understand the topics that the test addresses so that you will know the material and will succeed on the test regardless of the way the questions are asked.

PREREQUISITES

This book is intended to specifically prepare candidates to take the UML certification exams at the Fundamental and Intermediate levels. As such, it requires the knowledge of certain general basics of UML and object orientation.

Just as the Intermediate section of the test builds on the Fundamental section, the Intermediate section of this book assumes that you are familiar with the material from the Fundamental section.

WHAT MOTIVATED THIS BOOK?

Since the launch of the UML certification program in early 2004, we have gained extensive experience with the tests and proper preparations; we have helped several hundred candidates pass the test. Henceforth, the demand for our test preparations for the Fundamental and Intermediate exams has continually increased.

Our candidates' success and the ever-increasing demand encouraged us to write this book based on our sound training documentation and the feedback from people who have used our materials to prepare for the UML certification tests. This book includes the topics recommended by OMG for the Fundamental and Intermediate levels and additionally considers important practical experience.

It is our desire to make test preparation as easy as possible for you. Who, after all, likes to cram for tests? Exactly. So we left out lengthy explanations of material that would not be required or useful in preparing yourself for the tests. Finding out, compiling, and representing the relevant material in an easy-to-understand way were our goals.

HOW TO USE THIS BOOK

We present the material in this book in an arrangement that mimics the OCUP examination. We address the topics and subtopics that appear on the tests and do so in a certain scheme: Definition, Notation and Semantics, Metamodel, and Checklist. The checklist at the end of each topic presents hands-on test-type questions for you to answer, to help you make sure that you have understood the section's material.

New or important terms introduced in the text are highlighted in *italics*. In the *margins* are numbered references that match the number of the questions in the checklists; if you find any question difficult, you can use those numbers to find the section that you need to review. In the text you will see small round symbols with a combined letter-number name—for example, MI . These symbols refer to the metamodel in the figure that's being discussed.

Chapter 2, *OCUP Fundamental*, represents the preparatory material for the Fundamental test and Chapter 3, *OCUP Intermediate*, discusses and explains the test material for the Intermediate exam. Each one contains many figures and examples.

Although Chapters 2 and 3 represent self-contained preparatory material for each of the two test levels covered in this book, Chapter 3 builds on the Fundamental material dealt with in Chapter 2. Where material in Chapter 3 refers to the Fundamental test, you will find marginal comments in emphasizing this fact.

Since every discipline has its particular lingo, we have prepared a glossary of terms specific to UML, which you will find in the appendix. These terms and definitions are divided into a Fundamental and an Intermediate section and correspond to the original definitions from the UML specification. The appendix also contains a list of typical Fundamental exam questions (not the real ones, though), and the correct answers at the end of the section. Finally, the appendix includes a list of references for further reading.

ACKNOWLEDGMENTS

We would like to acknowledge the people who have made this book possible. In particular, they include Christa Preisendanz, Tim Cox, Marilyn Rash, our colleagues from oose Innovative Informatik GmbH, and our customers who did the UML certification.

We thank Bran Selic, Conrad Bock, and all other members of the UML RTF for their great work for the UML.

We also wish to thank Richard M. Soley and Ivar Jacobson for their forewords.

UML 2 Certification Guide

CHAPTER ONE

INTRODUCTION

This chapter is a small road map about UML and this book. It presents a self-contained overview of UML and its history, the UML metamodel and compliance levels, and a brief description of the three levels of the UML certification program.

1.1 WHAT IS UML?

The Unified Modeling Language (UML) is a language and notation system used to specify, construct, visualize, and document models of software systems. UML covers a wide range of applications and is suitable for technical (concurrent, distributed, time-critical) systems and so-called commercial systems; for example, socially embedded information systems.

By design, UML is not a methodology. Although the initiators and authors of UML recognize the significance of methodologies, they consider them distinct from language and notation systems. A methodology considers the specific framework and conditions of an application domain, the organizational environment, and many other things. UML can be used within various methodologies and can form the basis for various approaches because it provides a defined set of modeling constructs together with uniform notation and semantics.

1.1.1 THE THREE AMIGOS

By the beginning of the nineties, a large number of books on object-oriented (OO) software modeling had been published, and a large number of graphical notations had been introduced. It took a few years until the wheat separated from the chaff and a modeling standard eventually emerged. The decisive progress came about in 1995 when Grady Booch and Jim Rumbaugh announced the combining of their concepts into a *Unified Method*. Soon their Unified Method became the

Unified Modeling Language, a term that clearly indicates a language that comprises semantics and a uniform notation rather than a methodology or approach to object-oriented software development. Booch and Rumbaugh were soon joined by Ivar Jacobson, and the three have henceforth been called the "Three Amigos" in the world of software engineering and information technology (IT).

Because the books written by Booch, Rumbaugh, and Jacobson were very popular and enjoyed a large market share, by the time the UML was born, the majority of professionals were well acquainted with the work of the three pioneers. Thus, when UML appeared, it was eagerly received and soon became a quasi standard among software professionals, Eventually, UML Version 1.1 was submitted to the Object Management Group (OMG) for standardization and accepted in 1997. Since then, the UML has been further developed by the OMG. Later, the ISO (International Organization for Standardization) also accepted UML as a standard.

1.1.2   THE OBJECT MANAGEMENT GROUP

The Object Management Group, an international industry organization of which all important IT companies are members, further developed and standardized UML. OMG's member companies cooperate in maintaining and implementing the UML standard. The group's members include large international corporations such as IBM, Hewlett-Packard, Sun Microsystems, Telelogic, Boeing, Adobe, and DaimlerChrysler, as well as innovative medium-sized companies such as the German companies PROSTEP AG, b + m Informatik, and oose GmbH.

1.1.3   THE HISTORY OF UML

UML versions 1.2 through 1.5 contained several corrections and extensions (see Figure 1.1). Version 2.0 represents a fundamental review of UML, in which the specification and the metamodel, as well as the extent of coverage, have been extensively redesigned. In June 2003, corresponding submissions for UML 2.0 had been conclusively selected and accepted by the OMG. UML Version 2.0 was officially published in August 2005. Current information about UML, including the official specification, is available at *http://www.omg.org/uml/*.

UML is extremely diverse and integrates interesting ideas and concepts of many contributors. In addition to the ideas of Booch, Rumbaugh, and Jacobson, it includes, for example, state diagrams of Harel (Harel 1987). The more recent versions of UML bear only a light imprint of the Three Amigos now; instead, they carry the characteristics of many collaborators, including Bran Selic, Conrad Bock, and James Odell.

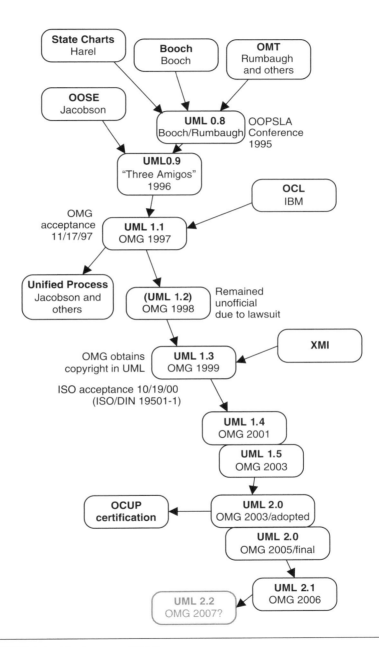

FIGURE 1.1   The history of UML.

1.1.4   UML COMPLIANCE LEVELS

The official UML specification is a complex volume of more than one thousand pages of small type. However, UML is divided into the following compliance levels:

Level 0, Foundation: Fundamental structural and behavioral elements.

Level 1, Basic: Simple diagrams.

Level 2, Intermediate: Improved diagrams and constructs (e.g., parallelism in activity diagrams).

Level 3, Complete: All other and more advanced constructs (e.g., streaming in activity diagrams).

This division is intended to help tool developers to gradually, or selectively, implement UML 2.0.

1.1.5   UML SUBSPECIFICATIONS

UML Version 2.0 has been formally divided into the following subspecifications:

Infrastructure: Core of the architecture, profiles, and stereotypes.

Superstructure: Static and dynamic model elements.

Object Constraint Language (OCL): A formal language used to describe expressions on UML models.

Diagram Interchange: The UML interchange format for diagrams.

1.1.6   THE METAMODEL OF UML 2.0

The UML 2.0 language is largely defined in a so-called metamodel. The reason for the prefix *meta* is that the language resides one abstraction level above the model that a UML user models. Now, the metamodel might seem confusing and illogical at first because the metamodel is a UML class model that describes UML. In other words, UML is defined in UML.

Remember that UML is a language and is similar to human languages such as English and German. How is the English language defined? Right! In the English language. When you use a dictionary to look up the meaning of an English word, the definition is in English, of course. The same is true with any language, including the Unified Modeling Language. You can find each word of UML as a

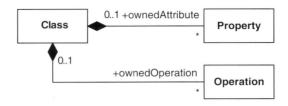

FIGURE 1.2 Simplified section of the metamodel.

class in the metamodel. Figure 1.2 shows a simplified section of the metamodel. You can see three elements—*class, property*, and *operation*—and that a class can have an arbitrary number of properties (attributes) and an arbitrary number of operations.

Defining UML. When defining a formal language like UML, we would quickly hit the limits of the expressive means that class models provide. For this reason, the UML specification describes formal constraints (mostly in OCL), and text comments for each element let you specify the semantics in more detail.

Note that not all model elements of UML are contained in the UML metamodel; in fact, only a minimum subset (of the class modeling) is required. In turn, this set is described in its own model, the *meta-metamodel*.

This means that we have a metamodel and a meta-metamodel. Of course, we also have the models of UML users—your models—which include yet another model, the model of objects based on your model. So in total, we have four models; hence, the four-layer architecture of UML (Figure 1.3).

You can easily imagine that the metamodel of UML is very large. For structuring purposes, it is therefore divided into many *packages*. Each of these packages comes up in this book over and over again because all of them represent the granularity of the exam topics.

The UML certification exam is a pure language test, which means that knowledge of the metamodel of UML is tested. In addition to elements such as *Class*, which UML users are familiar with, the metamodel includes many abstract classes that are not used on the users' modeling level (if they were, they would have to be instantiated, which abstract classes won't, as we know). The abstract concepts are also an integral part of the UML certification. One of the major benefits of abstract classes is that they are normally simple.

1.2 THE UML CERTIFICATION PROGRAM

In 2004, OMG introduced qualification standards for individuals in the form of a three-level certification program based on UML 2.0 called the OMG-Certified UML

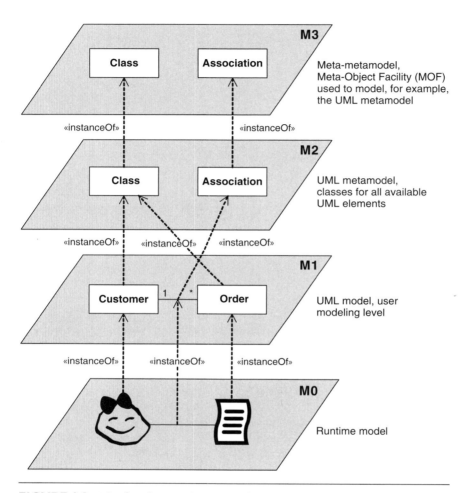

FIGURE 1.3   The four-layer architecture of UML.

Professional (OCUP) certification program. This certification program ensures that UML users, trainers, consultants, tool developers, and other interested parties can acquire a uniform UML understanding and a minimum qualification. For further information, visit *http://www.omg.org/uml-certification/index.htm*. The certification program consists of three levels—Fundamental, Intermediate, and Advanced. Each level has its own examination, testing progressively more complex concepts and more challenging usage of the UML 2.0 specification.

Each certification level builds on the preceding one: that is, you can obtain a higher certificate only if you have passed the next lower test level. This means that it is not possible to pass only the Advanced test to obtain the Advanced certificate.

The certification questions asked in the tests are based on the adopted UML 2.0 Specification UML2.0cert. Meanwhile, there is a final Specification for UML Version 2.0 as well as a successor, UML 2.1 [UML2.0 and UML2.1, respectively]. However, there are only minor changes with regard to the certification. Once you have passed the Fundamental test, you can tackle the Intermediate certification as your next major target. The three certification exams are structured and organized in the same way, but the topics are different, of course, and the questions increase in difficulty from one level to the next.

1.2.1   FUNDAMENTAL LEVEL

The first level examines fundamental UML knowledge, including basic notions on class diagrams, activity diagrams, interaction diagrams, and use case diagrams, as well as various elements such as standard stereotypes and primitive types. These basics include not only the elements visible to UML users, but also abstract UML concepts, such as Element—the base class for all UML classes in the metamodel. This level is suitable for regular UML users.

1.2.2   INTERMEDIATE LEVEL

The second level of the test for certification emphasizes a deeper knowledge of activity diagrams and interaction diagrams. Moreover, it adds composition structure diagrams, basic notions on component and deployment diagrams, state diagrams, the action model, and the profile extension mechanism. This level is suitable for UML users who do extensive work in it.

1.2.3   ADVANCED LEVEL

The third and highest level of test deals with advanced knowledge of class diagrams, such as association classes and metatypes, composition structure diagrams, component diagrams, activity diagrams, action modeling, deployment diagrams, and protocol automatons. In addition, this level covers the topics: the Object Constraint Language, the UML 2.0 architecture (including infrastructure and the Model-Driven Architecture [MDA]), information flow modeling, models, and templates. This level is suitable for advanced UML users (e.g., designers of executable models, MDA architects, profile designers, and UML tool developers).

1.2.4   PREREQUISITES AND REGISTRATION

Registration and cost. To take one of the three tests, you need to register with a Prometric Test Center and pay the test fee in advance. The fee is currently $200 (U.S.). Specific professional prerequisites (study, preparatory courses) are not required.

Identification. Each test candidate has to report at the test site and identify himself or herself 30 minutes before the test begins. Two kinds of identification are required, one of which must have a picture (e.g., driver's license, student identification) and a signature.

Fail-and-repeat waiting period. Candidates who fail the test have to wait at least 21 days before they can repeat the test. A maximum of three attempts within 12 months is allowed. Specific professional prerequisites (study, preparatory courses) are not required.

The three certification levels build on top of each other—that is, you will obtain a higher certificate provided that you have successfully passed the next lower test level. This means that it is not possible to only pass the Advanced test to obtain the Advanced certificate.

Once you have passed the Fundamental test you can tackle the Intermediate certification as your next major target. While the two certification exams are identical in the way they are structured and organized, the topics are different, mostly being more difficult in the Intermediate certification.

1.2.5   EXAMINATION PROCEDURE

We will briefly review what you need to know about taking the test, but you should also review the FAQ page at OMG's UML Certification website (*http://www. omg.org/uml-certification/frequently_asked_questions.htm*), which has a great deal of useful information.

Multiple-choice test. To obtain the certificate, you have to take a computer-based test. This test consists of a number of multiple-choice questions and you will have to answer all questions within a given time.

The test room is monitored electronically by video, or personally by a test assistant. You can bring nothing into the testing room, not even paper and pens. The test center provides a way for you to make notes, which have to be handed in at the end of the test. A participant who disregards, or breaks, any of these rules is automatically deemed to have failed the test. There are, of course, rules and controls for the test center operators also to ensure fairness and equity.

Prometric testing center. You can take the test for UML certification in any authorized Prometric Test Center. To take a test, you simply register. To find the nearest testing site, visit *www.2test.com*.

The test fee, which is not refundable, must be paid prior to the scheduled test. Once you have registered and paid the fee for a test, you will not get a refund if you arrive late or don't show, regardless of the reason.

On the day of the test, you will be briefly shown how to the use the testing software and will have an opportunity to run a small example to familiarize yourself with the test procedure. Then the real test starts.

Content of test. The Fundamental test is comprised of 80 questions, which have to be answered in a total time allowance of 90 minutes. The Intermediate test has 70 questions that need to be answered in 90 minutes. Each question appears on a separate screen, It is usually a good idea to answer the questions in the order they appear, but you may skip questions and go back and answer them later. You can browse forward and backward through the questions and can annotate any question with a marker. From within a callable overview, you can see the questions that you haven't answered and those that you have flagged with markers.

The test questions are drawn from a large pool and they are freshly chosen and combined for each test, so that each test is unique. The questions are secret and unknown even to the test center. The testing language is English.

Test results. At the end of the test, the candidates can see their results on their screens. In addition, they will be given a printout of their test results by the test center. Successful candidates will receive a colored official certificate by mail several weeks later.

1.3 EXAM PREPARATION

If you are very familiar with the current UML version, for example, have more than one year of practical experience, and have had a look or two at the official specifications, you will have a good chance of passing the Fundamental test at first go. The test is not trivial though.

Beyond good UML knowledge. The test is not trivial, however. Good knowledge of UML alone is not necessarily sufficient to pass the test for certification. The test includes a number of questions that are irrelevant in practice, and they are not all addressed, or addressed well, in textbooks. The main problem appears to be that the test examines UML exclusively as a language. Everything you need for practical use of UML—everything that belongs to the methodology, which is normally much more interesting—is not part of the test. Compare this to a situation where you study a foreign language; to prepare properly for the test, you have to deal with grammar, though grammar is not normally thrilling reading and certainly not the most exciting part of learning and using a language.

Many candidates have reported, after the test, that knowing UML well and passing the test are two totally different things. For this reason, it is very helpful and meaningful to prepare yourself well—for example, by studying the official UML specification. Because the specification is a very extensive and complex work, however, it would be an arduous task to wend your way through the entire document.

SUMMARY

Now, before dedicating ourselves to the exam topics, we want to note something important: *UML is used for much more than developing software.* In fact, business process modeling and systems engineering are also domains of UML. This means that UML has constructs that cannot be mapped directly to programming languages. If you wear programming language glasses while studying UML, you will lose sight of these constructs or overlook them, which means that you won't understand them. We suggest you take these glasses[1] off before you continue reading.

LIVE REFERENCES

- Homepage of the German book—http://www.uml-zertifizierung.de
- Object Management Group—http://www.omg.org/uml/; http://www.omg.org/uml-certification/; and/or http://www.omg.org/uml-certification/UML_Exams_Coverage_Map.pdf
- Other information about tools, books, news, and more
  - http://www.uml-sig.de
  - UML information in German—http://www.oose.de/uml
  - Tools list in English and German—http://www.oose.de/umltools
  - English UML portal—http://www.uml-forum.com

---

[1] If you wear reading glasses, use them by all means!

2

CHAPTER TWO
OCUP FUNDAMENTAL

2.1 GENERAL BASICS

This chapter discusses all basic and diagram-specific fields of knowledge for the Fundamental test except the basics of behavior, which are described in Chapter 3.

2.1.1 EXAMINATION TOPICS

The Fundamental test covers the following miscellaneous basic topics:

- Primitive types
- Basic notions of UML modeling
  - Diagrams
  - Stereotypes
  - Glossary
- Basic notions of UML behavior

This topic area constitutes 10 percent of the test.

2.1.2 DATATYPES

The topic area "miscellaneous basic notions" covers only the primitive data types predefined in UML. The more general set of data types, which are discussed in this section, belongs to the topic area "class diagrams" (see Section 2.2).

Definition and Examples

UML distinguishes between the following data types: *2.1.2.1*

- Simple data types *(DataType)*—A simple data type is a type with values that have no identity (e.g., money, banking information); that means two instances of a datatype with the same attribute values are indistinguishable.
- Primitive data types *(PrimitiveType)*—A primitive data type is a simple data   *2.1.2.2*
  type without structures (see D2 in Figure 2.2). The algebra that belongs to that type is described outside UML; for example, the addition of integers is not modeled as an operation of a primitive data type. UML itself defines the following primitive data types:
  - Integer: (Infinite) set of integers: $(\ldots, -2, -1, 0, 1, 2, \ldots)$ Boolean: true, false
  - UnlimitedNatural *(Infinite)* set of natural numbers $(0, 1, 2, \ldots)$—The symbol for infinite is the asterisk (*). This data type is used, for example, in the metamodel to define multiplicities.
- Enumeration types—Enumeration types are simple data types with values that originate from a limited set of enumeration literals (see D3 in Figure 2.2). Examples are marital status and form of address.

The labels shown in Figure 2.1 are UML keywords, not stereotypes (discussed   *2.1.2.3*
later in this chapter). A simple data type and a primitive data type have nothing to do with a class, except that they share a common superclass, *Classifier*, as in the metamodel, DI, in Figure 2.2.

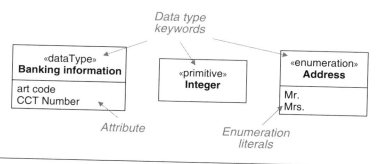

FIGURE 2.1   Examples of data types.

Metamodel

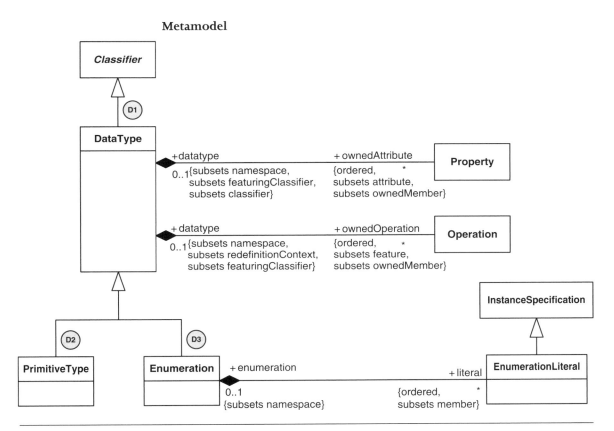

FIGURE 2.2   The metamodel of data types.

2.1.3   OVERVIEW OF DIAGRAMS

There is no official UML diagram overview or diagram grouping. Although UML models and the repository underlying all diagrams are defined in UML, the definition of diagrams (i.e., special views of the repository) are relatively free.

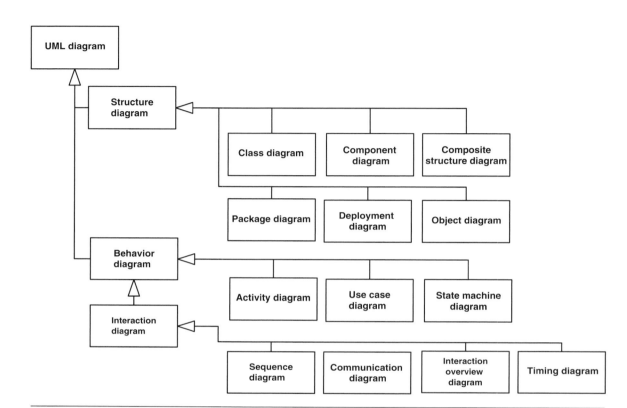

FIGURE 2.3   Overview of the UML diagrams.

In UML a diagram (see Figure 2.3) is actually more than a collection of notational elements. For example, the package diagram describes the package symbol, the merge relationship, and so on. A class diagram describes a class, the association, and so on. Nevertheless, we can naturally represent classes and packages together in one diagram.

The basic notation for diagrams is shown in Figure 2.4 and a use case diagram is shown in Figure 2.5. A diagram consists of an area within a rectangle and a header in the upper left corner. The diagram header shows the diagram type (optional), the diagram name (mandatory), and parameters (optional).

2.1.3.1

2.1.3.2

For example, the diagram type is *interaction* for sequence diagrams and *class* for class diagrams. The parameter field is important for parameterized models.

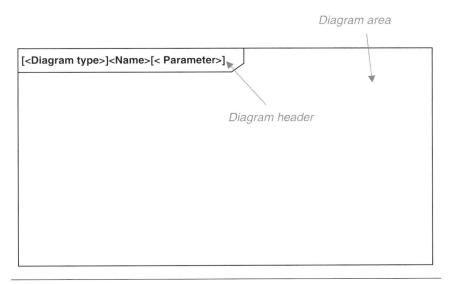

FIGURE 2.4   Basic notation for diagrams.

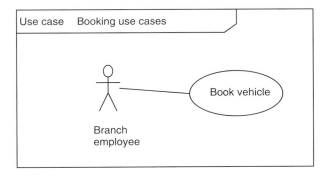

FIGURE 2.5   Example of a use case diagram.

CHECKLIST: DIAGRAMS

☐ 2.1.3.1.   What information is shown in the diagram header?

☐ 2.1.3.2.   How does the basic graphical representation of a diagram, including diagram header, look?

2.1.4   STEREOTYPES

The *concept* of stereotypes is not part of the fundamental exam. The mechanism in UML 2.0 is formally not trivial at all. Only the predefined standard stereotypes of the Basic level are part of the exam. However, at the very least it is helpful to understand the most important aspects of the concept of stereotypes.

Definition

Stereotypes are formal extensions of existing model elements within the UML metamodel, that is, *metamodel extensions*. The modeling element is directly influenced by the semantics defined by the extension. Rather than introducing a new model element to the metamodel, stereotypes add semantics to an existing model element.   *2.1.4.1*

Notation and Semantics

Stereotypes classify the possible uses of a model element. This classification has nothing to do with the modeling of metaclasses. Instead, certain common characteristics are attributed to one or several model elements.

Multiple stereotyping. Several stereotypes can be used to classify one single modeling element. Even the visual representation of an element can be influenced by allocating stereotypes. Moreover, stereotypes can be added to attributes, operations, and relationships. Further, stereotypes can have attributes to store additional information.

Notation. A stereotype is placed before or above the element name (e.g., class name) and enclosed in guillemets («, »). The characters « and », sometimes referred to as angled quotes, should not be mistaken for doubled greater-than, ≪, or smaller-than, ≫, characters.

Not every occurrence of this notation means that you are looking at a stereotype. Keywords predefined in UML are also enclosed in guillemets.   *2.1.4.2*

Graphical symbols. As an alternative to this purely textual notation, special symbols can be used. The stereotypes «*entity*», «*boundary*», and «*control*» in Figure 2.6 are good examples.

In addition, tools are free to use special color marking or other visual highlighting.   *2.1.4.3*

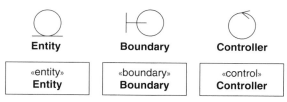

Entity   **Boundary**   **Controller**

| «entity» **Entity** | «boundary» **Boundary** | «control» **Controller** |

FIGURE 2.6   Visual and textual stereotypes.

UML Standard Stereotypes		
Stereotype	**UML Element**	**Description**
«call»	Dependency (usage)	Call dependency between operations or classes.
«create»	Dependency (usage)	The source element creates instances of the target element.
«instantiate»	Dependency (usage)	The source element creates instances of the target element. *Note*: This description is identical to the one of «create».
«responsibility»	Dependency (usage)	The source element is responsible for the target element.
«send»	Dependency (usage)	The source element is an operation and the target element is a signal sent by that operation.
«derive»	Abstraction	The source element can, for instance, be derived from the target element by a calculation
«refine»	Abstraction	A refinement relationship (e.g., between a design element and a pertaining analysis element).
«trace»	Abstraction	Serves to trace of requirements.
«script»	Artifact	A script file (can be executed on a computer).
«auxiliary»	Class	Classes that support other classes («focus»).
«focus»	Class	Classes contain the primary logic. See «auxiliary».
«implementationClass»	Class	An implementation class specially designed for a programming language, where an object may belong to one class only.
«metaclass»	Class	A class with instances that are, in turn, classes.
«type»	Class	Types define a set of operations and attributes, and they are generally abstract.
«utility»	Class	Utility classes are collections of global variables and functions, which are grouped into a class, where they are defined as class attributes/operations.
«buildComponent»	Component	An organizationally motivated component.
«implement»	Component	A component that contains only implementation, no specification.
«framework»	Package	A package that contains Framework elements.
«modelLibrary»	Package	A package that contains model elements, which are reused in other packages.
«create»	Behavioral feature	A property that creates instances of the class to which it belongs (e.g., constructor).
«destroy»	Behavioral feature	A property that destroys instances of the class to which it belongs (e.g., destructor).

FIGURE 2.7   UML standard stereotypes (selection).

CHECKLIST: STEREOTYPES

☐ 2.1.4.1.   What is a stereotype? Does it define a new metamodel element?
☐ 2.1.4.2.   Are all keywords stereotypes?
☐ 2.1.4.3.   Which standard stereotypes does UML recognize, and what do they mean?

2.2 CLASS DIAGRAMS

This chapter covers all exam-specific topics about class diagrams.

2.2.1   EXAMINATION TOPICS

The topics discussed in this section refer to the following areas of the metamodel:

- Package: *Classes::Kernel*
- Package: *Classes::Dependencies*
- Package: *Classes::Interfaces*

This topic area constitutes 30 percent of the test.

2.2.2   BASIC CONCEPTS

Definition

The basis of UML is described in the *Kernel* package of the metamodel. As we
know from many object-oriented programming languages, such as Java, most class
models have a *superclass*, from which all other elements are directly, or indirectly,
specialized. This is also the case with UML. The superclass is called Element and has
the ability to own other elements, which is shown by a composition relationship
in the metamodel (see Figure 2.8). And that's the only ability an element has.

    Of course, there is no notation for an element because you would never use
the element construct in UML models. If we wanted to do that, we would have
to create an object of the class Element, which can't be done because the class is
abstract.

2.2.2.1

Relationship. Next comes a fundamental concept used to interconnect elements.
A *relationship* is an abstract concept to put elements in relation to one another
(see Figure 2.9). Again, similar to Element, there is no other property or semantics.
Both the properties and the semantics are added later by abstract or concrete
subclasses. As you might have guessed, there is no notation for Relationship either.

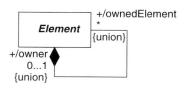

FIGURE 2.8   The basic UML class.

FIGURE 2.9 The basic Relationship class.

2.2.2.2   **Supplier and client.** The Relationship concept is specialized by the concept of a
2.2.2.3   directed relationship, as shown in Figure 2.10. The set of related elements is
divided into a set of source and a set of target elements. In many relationships,
one element offers something and another element wants something. The former
is called a *supplier* and the latter is a *client*. This is expressed in one direction.

Note that we are still far up in the metamodel. Accordingly, we are dealing with
abstract and rather simple concepts. If you'd like to see something substantial at
this point, you can look forward to the next element. In addition to the elementary
abstract concepts, up here, there is a very concrete element: the *comment* (see
Figure 2.11). *Comments* and *notes* are terms often used synonymously.

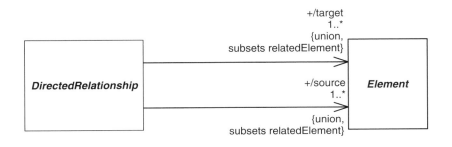

FIGURE 2.10 Directed relationships.

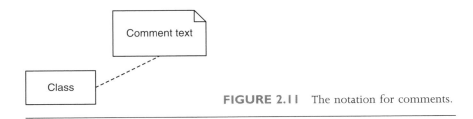

FIGURE 2.11 The notation for comments.

Comment. A comment can be annotated to any UML model element. In the meta-model, you can see that the *Comment* class is directly associated with the *Element* base class.

2.2.2.4

CHECKLIST: BASIC CLASS DIAGRAM CONCEPTS

☐ 2.2.2.1.   What is the top base class of the metamodel called?
☐ 2.2.2.2.   How are directed relationships defined?
☐ 2.2.2.3.   Can directed relationships have more than one source or target element?
☐ 2.2.2.4.   Can a comment be appended to any UML element?

Metamodel[1]

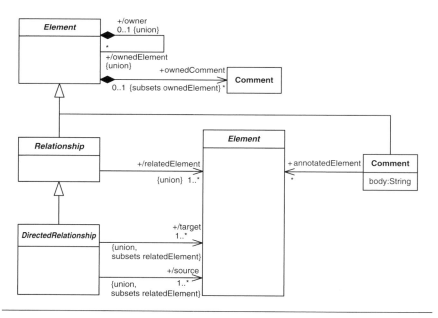

FIGURE 2.12   The basic metamodel concepts.

---

[1]   Elements of the same name in a metamodel diagram designate the same model element. They are shown more than once for layout reasons.

2.2.3   NAMESPACES

Definition

A *named element* is an element that can have a name and a defined visibility (*public, private, protected, package*), as commonly known from OO and programming languages) (see NE2 in Figure 2.15. The name of the element and its visibility are optional (see NE1 in Figure 2.15).

A *namespace* is a named element that can contain named elements. Within a namespace, named elements are uniquely identified by their names. In addition, they have a qualified name, resulting from nested namespaces; see, for example, the class *Customers::CorporateCustomers::Insurance* in Figure 2.13. The qualified name of a named element can be derived from the nesting of the enclosing namespaces (NE1 in Figure 2.15).

A *packageable element* is a named element that can belong directly to a package. For example, an operation cannot belong to a package, but a class may. The visibility statement is mandatory for a packageable element (see NE3 in Figure 2.15).

2.2.3.1   The act of importing an element is called *ElementImport* and is a relationship between a namespace and a packageable element that resides in another namespace (see NI in Figure 2.16 on page 28). The referenced element can then be addressed directly by its (unqualified) name. In addition, an optional alias name can be specified.

2.2.3.2   The act of importing a package is called *PackageImport*; it is semantically equivalent to the import of a single element from that package. Naturally, we cannot specify an alias name here.

Notation and Semantics

The visibilities are stated as follows:

$+$ = public
$-$ = private
$\#$ = protected
$\sim$ = package

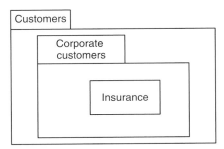

FIGURE 2.13 Nested namespaces.

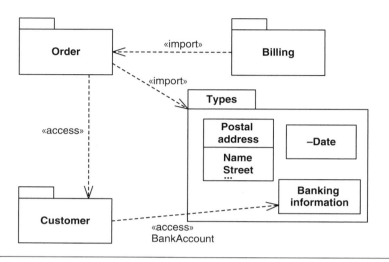

FIGURE 2.14 Example of element and package import relationships.

We have the following import options:

«import»: The visibility is *public*; see, for example, the postal address for Order in Figure 2.14. The public import is a transitive relationship; that is, if A imports B and B imports C, then A is indirectly importing C too.

«access»: The visibility is *private*, not public. You can see an example in Figure 2.14: Customer is visible in Order but not in Billing. The private import is not transitive.

2.2.3.3

Figure 2.14 shows several element and package import relationships. We can draw the following conclusions from this diagram:

- *Date* is a private element in the package *Types*.
- *Postal Address* and *Banking Information* are visible in the *Order* package (package import). *Date* is not visible in *Order* because elements with private visibility cannot be imported.
- A public import is transitive. For this reason, both the *Postal Address* and the *Banking Information* are visible in the *Billing* package.
- The elements of the package *Customer* are visible in the *Order* package (private package import) but not in the *Billing* package.
- The *Banking Information* in the *Customer* package is visible by the name *BankAccount* (alias).

Metamodel

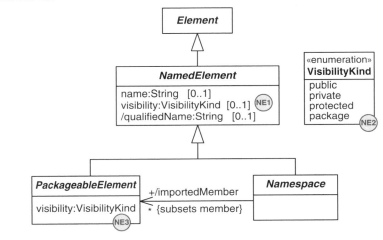

FIGURE 2.15   The metamodel for NamedElement.

2.2.4   TYPED ELEMENTS

Definition

2.2.4.1   A *typed element* is a named element that can have a type. For example, attributes and parameters are typed elements.

2.2.4.2   A *type* specifies a set of values for a typed element. For example, simple data types and classes are types.

Both the type and the typed element (Figure 2.17) are abstract classes in the metamodel. Other than that, they have no properties.

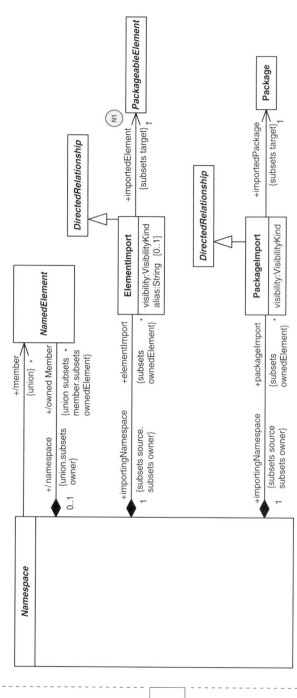

FIGURE 2.16   The metamodel for namespaces.

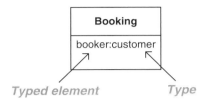

FIGURE 2.17 Example showing a type and a typed element.

Metamodel

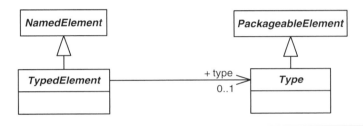

FIGURE 2.18 The metamodel for typed elements.

2.2.5   MULTIPLICITIES

Definition

2.2.5.1   A *multiplicity element* is the definition of an interval of positive integers to specify allowable cardinalities. A *cardinality* is a concrete number of elements in a set.

A multiplicity element is often simply called *multiplicity*; the two terms are synonymous.

2.2.5.2   The terms *multiplicity* and *cardinality* are also often used synonymously, which is wrong. The example in Figure 2.19 shows how the two terms differ.

The notation for multiplicity is either a single number or a value range. A value range is written by stating the minimum and maximum values, separated by two dots (e.g., 1..5). In addition, you can use the wildcard character ∗ (asterisk) to specify an arbitrary number of elements. You are probably familiar with that symbol. It is the symbol for "infinite" used for the primitive data type *UnlimitedNatural*.

See Table 2.1 for examples of multiplicities.

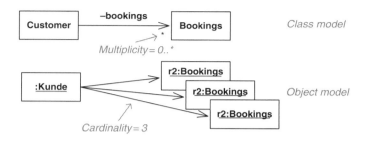

FIGURE 2.19   Example of multiplicity and cardinality.

TABLE 2.1   Examples of Multiplicities

0..1	Zero or one.
1	Exactly one (shortcut for 1..1).
*	Zero to an arbitrary number (shortcut for 0..*).
1..*	One to an arbitrary number.
5..3	<u>Invalid</u>; the lower value must be equal or smaller than the upper value.
−1..0	<u>Invalid</u>; all values must be positive.
3+5..7+1	Generally meaningless, but valid; the lower or upper value, respectively, is defined by a value specification (see Ⓜ️ in Figure 2.20).

CHECKLIST: MULTIPLICITIES

☐ 2.2.5.1.   What value range is described by a multiplicity?
☐ 2.2.5.2.   What is the difference between multiplicity and cardinality?

Metamodel

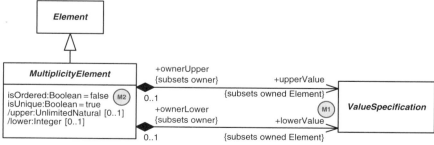

FIGURE 2.20   The multiplicity metamodel.

2.2.6   VALUE SPECIFICATION

Definition
A *value specification* indicates one or several values in a model.

Semantics
Examples for value specifications include simple, mathematical expressions, such as $4 + 2$, and expressions with values from the object model, *Integer::MAX_INT*-1.

2.2.6.1   In addition, there are language-dependent expressions defined by a language statement and the pertaining expression in that language (*opaque expression*), such as an OCL or Java expression. The language statement can be omitted if the language is implicitly defined by the expression or context (see **EI** in Figure 2.23).

2.2.6.2   The metamodel for value specifications looks rather complex at first sight. Don't be deceived; it's just a class model used to create tree-type expressions. The composite pattern serves as the metamodel's basis (see Figure 2.21).

Figure 2.22 shows the object model for the expression $1 + 1$ as an example.

CHECKLIST: VALUE SPECIFICATION
☐ 2.2.6.1.   What is a language-dependent expression?
☐ 2.2.6.2.   What does a complex metamodel eventually express?

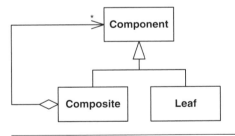

FIGURE 2.21   The composite pattern.

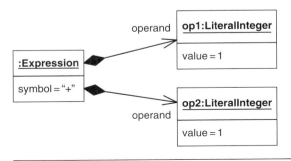

FIGURE 2.22   Object model for 1+1.

Metamodel

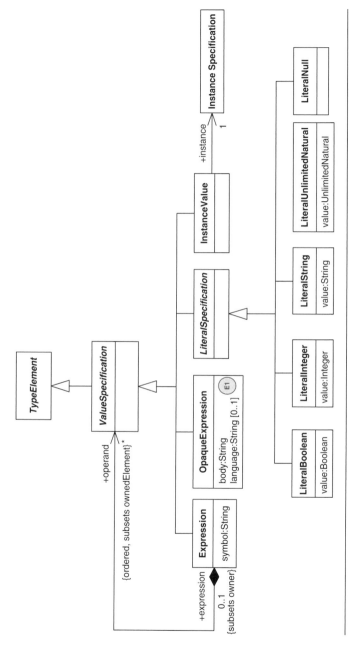

FIGURE 2.23 The metamodel for value specifications.

2.2.7   CONSTRAINTS

Definition

A *constraint* is an expression that constrains the semantics of an element, and it must always be true. This can be a formal expression (OCL) or a semiformal or human-language formulation.

Notation and Semantics

Constraints are written between curled brackets. They can be written directly after a textual element or within a comment symbol. Constraints can have names.

The syntax for constraints is defined as follows:

2.2.7.1   `'{' [<name> ':'] < Boolean expression> '}'`

2.2.7.2   The `xor` constraint is predefined in UML and can be graphically written between associations.

Figure 2.24 shows examples of constraints.

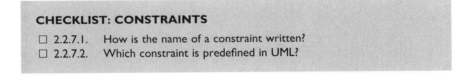

CHECKLIST: CONSTRAINTS
- ☐ 2.2.7.1.   How is the name of a constraint written?
- ☐ 2.2.7.2.   Which constraint is predefined in UML?

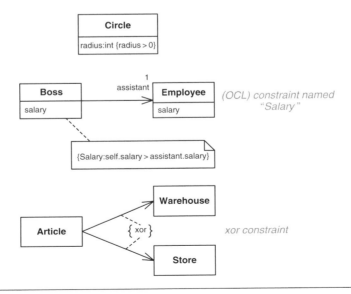

FIGURE 2.24   Examples of constraints.

Metamodel

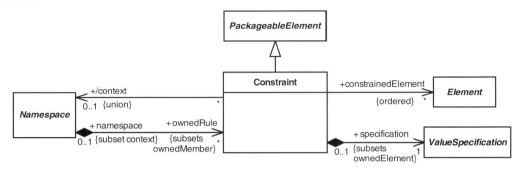

FIGURE 2.25 The metamodel for constraints.

2.2.8   INSTANCE SPECIFICATION

Definition

An *instance specification* represents a concrete instance in the modeled system (see
Figure 2.26). The terms *instance* and *object* are used synonymously. A *slot* represents
values for a structure element of an instance specification, such as an attribute
value of an object.

2.2.8.1

Notation

An instance specification can be incomplete, which means that you don't have to
specify all values of the attributes of the pertaining class.

Figure 2.26 shows notation for instance specifications.

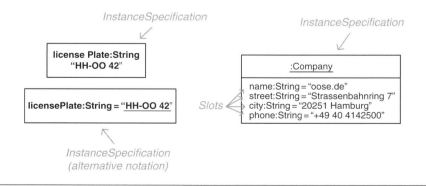

FIGURE 2.26 Notations for instance specifications.

Metamodel

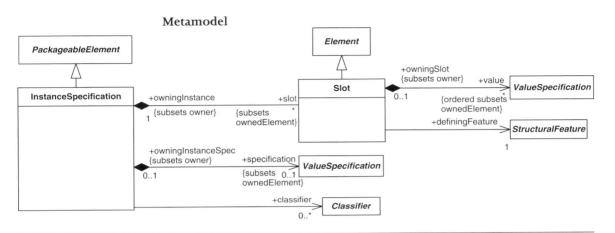

FIGURE 2.27 The metamodel for instance specifications.

CHECKLIST: INSTANCE SPECIFICATIONS

☐ 2.2.8.1. How does a slot differ from an instance specification?

2.2.9   CLASSIFIER

Definition

A *classifier* is an abstract base class that classifies the instances with regard to their *features.*

A classifier is a namespace and a type, and it can be generalized (i.e., inherited; see ⓒ2 in Figure 2.32).

Notation and Semantics

2.2.9.1 Concrete classifiers in the UML metamodel include, for example, class, component, and use case (see Figure 2.28).

A classifier associates a set of features (ⓒ3 in Figure 2.32). Concrete features are operations and attributes.

Though the metamodel class *Classifier* is abstract, which means that the UML user won't see it as a modeling element, a notation is nevertheless defined in the specification. This notation is inherited by the subclasses and used by them. Note, however, that some of the notation will eventually be overwritten.

The standard notation for Classifier is a rectangle that contains the name with the name of the subclass in guillemets above it (see Figure 2.29).

Each subclass introduces notation variants. For example, the name of the concrete metamodel class («class») is normally omitted. A use case is generally represented in the pure ellipse notation, and so on.

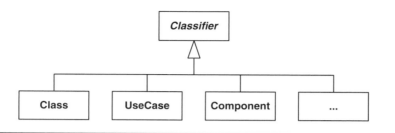

FIGURE 2.28　A classifier and a set of concrete subclasses (simplified).

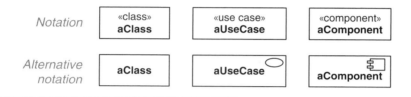

FIGURE 2.29　Examples of the notation of Classifier subclasses.

A classifier is abstract if its description is incomplete. This means that no instances can be created. Abstractness is a feature of classifiers (see cɪ in Figure 2.32).

The names of abstract classifiers (for instance, those shown in Figure 2.30) are written in italics. Optionally, you can add the property string {abstract}.

In addition to the notation area for the name (these areas are called *compartments* in UML lingo), there may be others, for example, for attributes and operations (see Figure 2.31).

CHECKLIST: CLASSIFIER

☐ 2.2.9.1.　What subclasses does a classifier have?

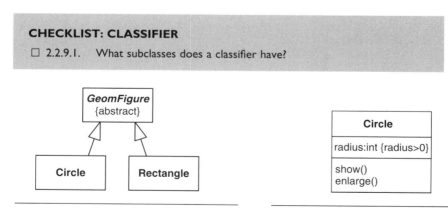

FIGURE 2.30　An abstract class called GeomFigure.

FIGURE 2.31　A class with compartments for name, attributes, and operations.

Metamodel

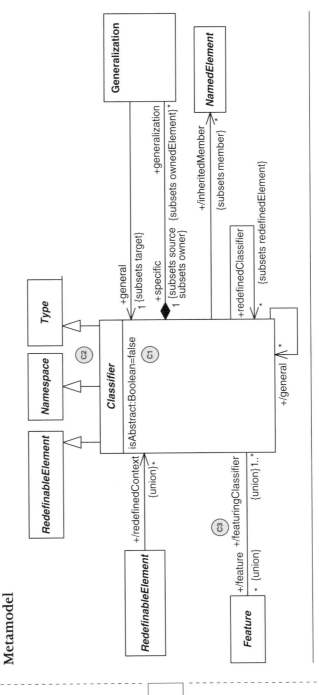

FIGURE 2.32 The classifier metamodel.

2.2.10   FEATURES

Definition

A *feature* describes a structural or behavioral characteristic of a classifier's instances (see Figure 2.33).

2.2.10.1

A *structural feature* is an abstract metaclass, which describes a typed structure of an instance of a classifier. A common example of a structural feature is the *property* attribute. To prevent a structural feature from being changed, you can specify that it be {readonly}. Accordingly, a changeable structural feature can be specified with {unrestricted}.

A *behavioral feature* is an abstract metaclass, which means that an instance of a classifier can respond to requests by calling certain behavior. More specifically, parameters can be passed and returned. A behavior can also throw an exception. An operation is a common example of a behavioral feature.

A *parameter* is the specification of an argument that is passed by a behavioral feature or returned by this behavioral feature. A parameter has a type ((P3) in Figure 2.34), a multiplicity, and a direction. You can optionally state a default value and a name.

The direction of a parameter is specified by use of the keywords in, out, inout, or *return* (ParameterDirectionKind; see (PI) in Figure 2.34), depending on what you want to do with the data (see the explanation in the following table). The default value *in* is assumed if no direction is stated ((P2) in Figure 2.34). Table 2.2 lists the meanings of direction keywords.

2.2.10.2

Notation

The syntax of a parameter looks like this:

```
[direction] name : type [multiplicity] [= default] [{property
string}]
```

The property string for a parameter can be one of the values known for properties, such as {ordered} and {nonunique}.

TABLE 2.2   The Meaning of the Direction Keywords

In	The caller passes the parameter value to the behavior.
Out	The behavior passes the parameter value to the caller.
Inout	The caller first passes the parameter value to the behavior, which returns it to the caller.
Return	Similar to *out*, except that *return* explicitly specifies the return values of the behavior.

Metamodel

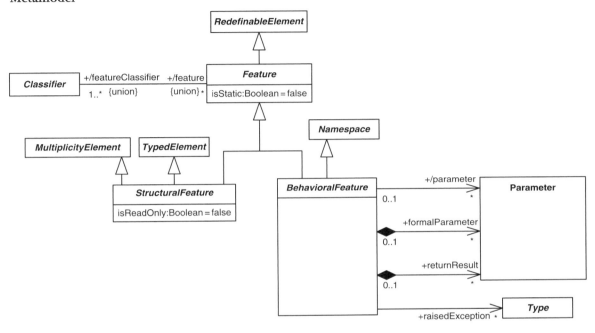

FIGURE 2.33 The metamodel for features.

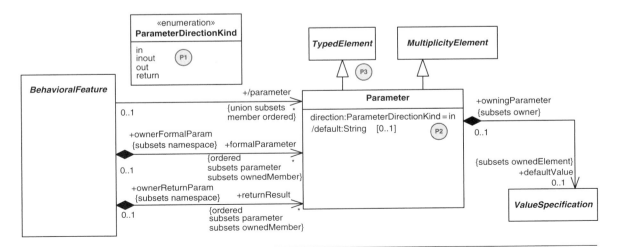

FIGURE 2.34 The metamodel for parameters.

CHECKLIST: FEATURES

☐ 2.2.10.1. How are a feature, a structural feature, and a behavioral feature related?
☐ 2.2.10.2. What direction statements can be used for parameters?

2.2.11   OPERATIONS

Definition

An *operation* is a behavioral feature of a classifier, which specifies name, type, parameters, and constraints for the call of a behavior.

In addition to the features an operation inherits from its superclass *Behavioral Feature*, the operation can

- have preconditions and postconditions and a body condition (OP1 in Figure 2.35); specify whether it will change the state of the pertaining instance (*isQuery*; see OP4 in Figure 2.35); and
- have a type (see OP2 in Figure 2.35).

Notation and Semantics

The syntax for operations is described somewhat imprecisely in the UML specification (UML20cert). In fact, the syntax given in the specification appears not to be totally correct, and the examples used in the specification are different from those in the notation. Based on the current state of discussion, the notation should look like this:

```
[visibility] name ( parameter list ) [: type] [{property string}]
```

where `parameter list` is a list of parameters, separated by commas.

Type of operation.. It may appear strange that an operation can have a type (OP2 in Figure 2.35). It is the type of the return parameter, provided there is exactly one return parameter. In this case, the parameter type can be written behind the parameter list to specify the type of operation.   *2.2.11.1*

Moreover, {query} can be used to specify a property value for the operation. This characterizes an operation that has no side effects, that is, an operation that does not change the state of the object and other objects such as get() operations.

The preconditions and postconditions, as well as the invariants, are denoted   *2.2.11.2*
similarly to constraints (OP1 in Figure 2.35). The precondition must always be   *2.2.11.3*
true before the operation is executed. The postconditions have to be true after the execution, and the body condition has to be true during the execution. If an exception occurs during operation execution, the postconditions must no be true. The difference between body condition and postcondition is that the invariant can

be overwritten (redefined) by inheritance; a postcondition merely lets you add postconditions. The latter is also true for a precondition.

Examples

```
getPosition(return x : int, return y : int)
enlarge(byFactor : Real) : GeomFigure
+addPhone(phone : String)
deposit(in amount : Amount):Amount
#release():contractStatus
"create"create()
```

CHECKLIST: OPERATIONS

☐ 2.2.11.1.　What is the type of an operation?
☐ 2.2.11.2.　Explain pre-, post-, and body condition.
☐ 2.2.11.3.　What happens to the conditions if an exception occurs?

Metamodel

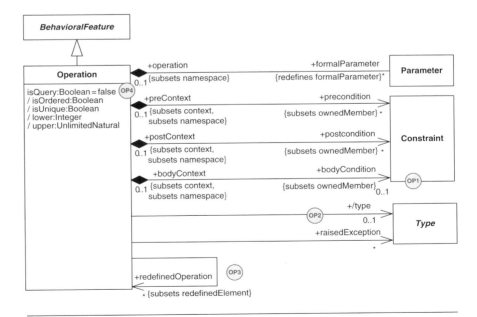

FIGURE 2.35　The metamodel for operations.

2.2.12   PROPERTIES

Definition

A *property* is a special structural feature that if it belongs to a class, is an attribute. However, it can also belong to an association. But more about this later.   *2.2.12.1*

Notation and Semantics

An *attribute* is a (data) element that is equally contained in every object of a class and that is represented by an individual value in each object. In contrast to objects, attributes have no identity outside the object to which they belong. Attributes are fully under the control of the objects of which they are part.

The UML metamodel does not have a metaclass for attributes. An attribute is a role that a property can take on.

In contrast to UML 1.x, UML 2.0 no longer strictly separates attributes and   *2.2.12.2*
association ends. This means that the representation of an attribute in a class and its representation as a navigable association are the same (see Figure 2.36). In both cases, the class *Customer* owns the property *bookings*.

Each attribute is described at least by its name. In addition, you can define a type, a visibility, an initial value, and so on. The full syntax is as follows:

```
[visibility][/]name[:type][multiplicity][=initial
value][{property string}]
```

where

- visibility is indicated by:
  - + public: It can be seen and used by all.
  - −private: Only the class itself can get hold of private attributes.
  - # protected: Both the class itself and its subclasses have access.
  - ~package: Only classes from the same package can access these attributes.
- / symbolizes a derived attribute.
- multiplicity is in square brackets (e.g., [1..*]).
- default value specifies the initial value of the attribute.
- property string indicates a modifier that applies to the attribute
  - {readonly}: The property can be read but not changed.   *2.2.12.3*
  - {union}: The property is a union of subsets.
  - {subsets <property>}: The property is a subset of <property>.
  - {redefines <property>}: The property is a new definition of <property> (overwritten by inheritance).
  - {ordered}, {unordered}: An ordered or unordered set.
  - {unique}, {nonunique}, or {bag}: A set may or may not contain several identical elements.
  - {sequence}: An ordered list (array; identical elements are permitted).
  - {composite}: The property is an existence-dependent part. and others.

If the multiplicity is greater than 1, then the attribute represents a set. Additional information can be specified for the order (*isOrdered*) and uniqueness (*isUnique*); for properties of multiplicity, see ⓜ₂ in Figure 2.20. Depending on the combination of these two pieces of information, we obtain different collection classes, as shown in Table 2.3.

2.2.12.4   A particularity of properties concerns matters relating to ownership, which you can recognize in the navigational direction of the association. Figure 2.37 uses the example from Figure 2.36 to show ownership of properties. You can see that the property *bookings* belongs to the *Customer* class, which means that it is an attribute of *Customer* (navigation from *Customer* toward *Booking*).

But what about the property *booker*? The class *Booking* knows nothing about this property (see navigational direction). To understand better, let's have a look at the relevant UML repository, that is, the object model for the UML metamodel. Figure 2.38 shows that *Customer* and *Booking* are objects of *Class* and the properties *booker* and *bookings* are objects of the class *Property*; and you can see an anonymous object of the class *Association*.

2.2.12.5   The classes are the types of the properties (see also Figure 2.18). The association knows each of the two properties as an association end (*memberEnd*). The association describes a set of *tuples* whose values refer to typed instances. Moreover, you can

TABLE 2.3   Order and Uniqueness

IsUnique	isOrdered	Collection Class
Yes	Yes	Ordered set {ordered}
Yes	No	Set (default)
No	Yes	Ordered list {sequence}
No	No	{bag}

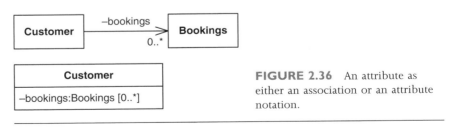

FIGURE 2.36   An attribute as either an association or an attribute notation.

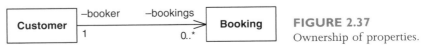

FIGURE 2.37
Ownership of properties.

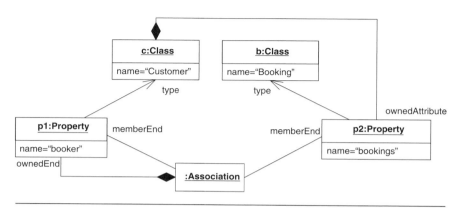

FIGURE 2.38 UML repository for Figure 2.37.

see that the property *bookings* belongs to the class *Customer* (attribute). The property *booker* belongs to no class, but to the association.[2]

The navigatability of the association in the notation shows the ownership.

Examples

```
name : String = 'unknown'
birthDate : Date
radius : Integer = 25 {readonly}
/age : Integer {age = today - birthDate}
-versionNo : Integer
time : DateTime::Time
dynamArray[*] {ordered}
name : String[1]
firstName : String[0..1]
firstNames : String[1..5]
```

CHECKLIST: PROPERTIES

☐ 2.2.12.1. What do a property and an attribute have in common?
☐ 2.2.12.2. How do an attribute and an association relate?
☐ 2.2.12.3. What property strings can a property have?
☐ 2.2.12.4. Who owns a property?
☐ 2.2.12.5. Explain the meaning of "tuple" in the context of an association

---

[2] This situation cannot be mapped in conventional programming languages.

Metamodel

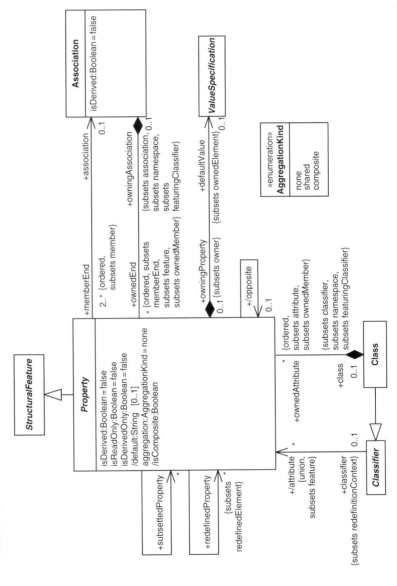

FIGURE 2.39 The metamodel for properties.

2.2.13   ASSOCIATIONS

Definition

2.2.13.1

An *association* describes a set of tuples of typed instances.

The *multiplicity* of an association specifies how many objects of the opposite class an object can be associated with. If this number is variable, we state a range, that is, the minimum and maximum values. A minimum of 0 means that the relationship is optional (the relationship exists, nevertheless, but the number of elements is 0).

Notation and Semantics

Roles and constraints. An association is represented by a straight line between the participating properties (see Figure 2.40). At least two properties participate in an association (see (Ass3) in Figure 2.51 on page 53).

Association name. Each association can be given a *name* that should provide clues about the relationship. The name can also identify a *reading direction* within a small filled triangle. The reading direction refers only to the name and not at all to the navigatability of the association. At either end of the association, *role names* can be added to describe in more detail what roles the objects have within the relationship. These roles are the names of properties (for example, attributes), which belong to the association or to one of the participating classes.

In addition to role names, you can add visibility information to either end of the association. For example, if an association end is declared private (−), then the object itself (i.e., the operations of this object) can use the association, but neighboring classes have no access. Since a role represents a property, it can be fitted with everything a property can do.

Associations are generally implemented in programming languages such that the participating classes obtain corresponding attributes. In the example shown in Figure 2.40, the class *Customer* would obtain an attribute, *account*, to reference an object of the class *CustomerAccount*, and the class *CustomerAccount* would get a private attribute, *bpos*, with a collection object (or a subclass thereof), which references the *BookingPosition* objects. Many modeling tools use the role names of a relationship for the corresponding attributes that are generated automatically.

FIGURE 2.40   An association/composition with names, reading direction, multiplicities, role names, and visibility information.

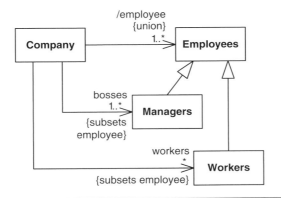

FIGURE 2.41 Example of {union} and {subsets} property strings.

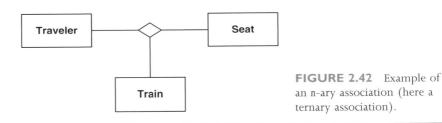

FIGURE 2.42 Example of an n-ary association (here a ternary association).

Property strings. Properties can have the property strings {union} and {subsets <property>}. Figure 2.41 shows a simple example of these strings. The attribute *employee* in the class *Company* is a derived union, which means that you will also find the corresponding subsets in the class model. In this example, they are specified in the same diagram. The attributes *bosses* and *workers* are subsets of *employee*, jointly representing the union.

N-ary assoication. An association can have more than two ends (by the way, fewer than two is invalid; see Ass3 in Figure 2.51). Figure **??** represents a ternary association. The diamond-shaped symbol is a rhombus, commonly used as a connection point to distinguish an association from intersecting lines. An n-ary association is subject to formal limitations. For instance, an aggregation or composition would be invalid in this example.

Association generalization. Since associations are special classifiers (see Ass5 in Figure 2.51), they can be generalized or inherited. The notation is shown in Figure 2.43. There are formal rules for generalizing associations. One rule says that the number of association ends has to remain equal and the corresponding

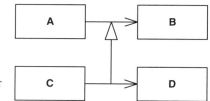

FIGURE 2.43 The notation for association generalizations.

classes have to be compliant to one another. This means that they either are identical or have a direct or indirect generalization relationship. Another rule is that when specializing an association, the multiplicity of the superassociation can be restricted but not expanded. Figure 2.44 is an example of how an association can be generalized.

An *aggregation* is an association expanded by the semantically noncommittal comment that the participating classes have no equal-ranking relationship; instead, they represent a whole-parts hierarchy. An aggregation is used to describe how something whole is logically composed of its parts.

2.2.13.2

A *composition* is a strict form of aggregation, where the existence of its parts depends on the whole. The whole is the owner of its parts. It describes how something whole is composed of individual parts.

2.2.13.3

An aggregation or composition is a property of the metamodel class *property* (i.e., a property of the property). The type is an enumeration called *AggregationKind* with the literals *none*, *shared*,[3] and *composite* (see Ass4 in Figure 2.51). This means that, formally, neither aggregation nor composition is a form of relationship of its own.

Similarly to an association, an aggregation is represented by a line between two classes and a small rhombus. The rhombus is placed at the aggregate side (i.e., the whole). It virtually symbolizes the container object, which is used to collect and

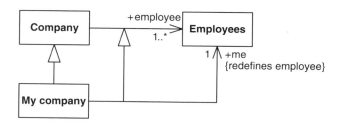

FIGURE 2.44 Example of an association generalization.

----

[3]   Here *shared* refers to aggregation.

FIGURE 2.45   A rhombus symbolizes an aggregation.

hold the individual parts (see Figure 2.45). Otherwise, all notation conventions valid for associations apply to aggregations, too.

In Figure 2.46, the example *Corporation-Department-Employees* shows that a part (in this case *Department*) can, in turn, be an aggregate.

Similarly to an aggregation, a composition is shown as a line between two classes and a small rhombus at the side of the whole (see Figure 2.47). In contrast to aggregations, however, the rhombus for a composition is filled.

Compositions. If we define a class as part of several compositions, as in the example shown in Figure 2.48, then this means that both cars and boats have engines, but a specific *Engine* object always belongs only to one *Car* or one *Boat*. The decisive characteristic of a composition is that the aggregated parts are never shared with other objects. In our example of aggregations in Figure 2.46 (but not in Figure 2.48!), there can be an *Engine* object that concurrently belongs to a *Car* object and a *Boat* object.

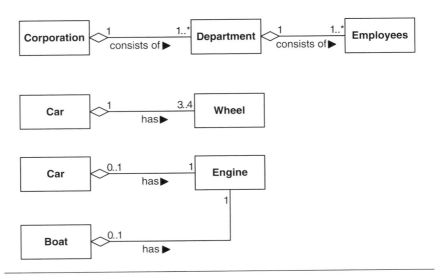

FIGURE 2.46   Examples of aggregations.

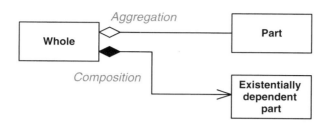

FIGURE 2.47 Example showing an aggregation and a composition.

FIGURE 2.48 Compositions don't share instances.

If a variable multiplicity for the parts is specified (e.g., 1..*), then they don't have to be created together with the aggregate; they can be created later. From the time of their creation, however, they normally belong immediately to the whole. Similarly, they can be destroyed before the aggregate at any given time; however, generally the latest they are destroyed is when the aggregate is destroyed. An aggregate can be changed at runtime. For example, the engine could be removed from the car and installed in a boat.

The internal structure of a classifier can be described in a *composition structure diagram*. This diagram type is new to UML 2.0 and not part of the Fundamental certification examination. For this reason, we limit this discussion to a simple example so you get an idea of this diagram type (see Figure 2.49). At first sight, the diagram can be easily mistaken for a communication diagram (see Figure 2.110).

Navigation option. A *directed association* is an association that lets you navigate from one of the participating association roles to the other.

A directed association is denoted like a regular association. It differs from the latter in that it has an open arrowhead at the side of the class to which we can navigate (i.e., in navigation direction). Theoretically, however, both multiplicity and role names can also be denoted at the side to which we cannot navigate. In this case, multiplicity and role names designate a property that belongs to the association rather than to a class.

Navigation exclusion. We can explicitly exclude a navigation direction. To exclude a navigation direction, we put a small cross to the side of the class that shouldn't be navigated to (i.e., the association line is crossed out at this side).

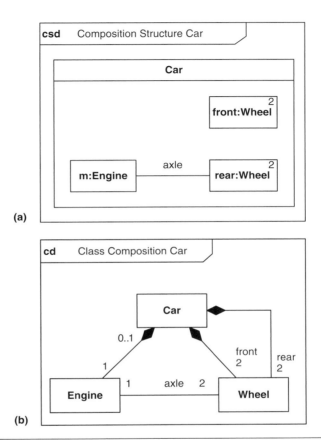

FIGURE 2.49 (a) A composition structure diagram and (b) the pertaining class diagram with compositions.

The navigation exclusion is new to UML 2.0. UML 1.x used only the open arrowhead, or only a line, so that there had been two notation forms for three cases: navigable, not navigable, and not specified. Accordingly, the representation was somewhat blurred. In contrast, UML 2.0 lets us use a different notation form for each of the three cases: open arrowhead, cross, or line only. However, people normally stick to their habits, so that the specification contains three possible forms of interpretation for navigability:

2.2.13.4

1. *All arrows and crosses* means that all navigation options are explicitly denoted.
2. *No arrows and crosses* means that there is no statement on navigability. In particular, there is no way to tell the difference between some kind of

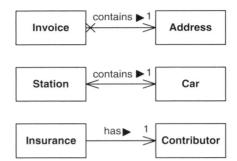

FIGURE 2.50 Defining association directions.

navigation that may be present and some kind of unspecified navigation.

3. *Arrows only for associations with a navigation direction* means that there is no unspecified navigability, that is, no arrow has a meaning equal to the cross representation. This interpretation introduces a lot of blur with regard to associations that have no arrow representation. According to this interpretation, such an association would have navigability in any direction. The same representation would in this case also represent navigability in no direction. However, this is rarely the case. The third option is the common interpretation of the UML metamodel diagrams.

Unidirectional and bidirectional relationships. Figure 2.50 shows a number of different associations. In this example, the relationship is unidirectional so *Invoice* can access *Address*, but *Address* doesn't know what invoices it is associated with so that it cannot access them. In contrast, the definition between *Car* and *Station* is bidirectional so that you can navigate in both directions.

Reading direction versus navigation direction. Note also that the navigation direction (the arrow on the association line) is independent of the specified reading direction (filled triangle, e.g., "contains"). The navigation direction tells us whether an object can access another object. The reading direction is used to understand the association name (e.g., "invoice contains address" instead of "address contains invoice").

CHECKLIST: ASSOCIATIONS
- [ ] 2.2.13.1. What does an association describe?
- [ ] 2.2.13.2. What are the semantics of an aggregation?
- [ ] 2.2.13.3. What are the semantics of a composition?
- [ ] 2.2.13.4. What are the forms of interpreting the navigability?

Metamodel

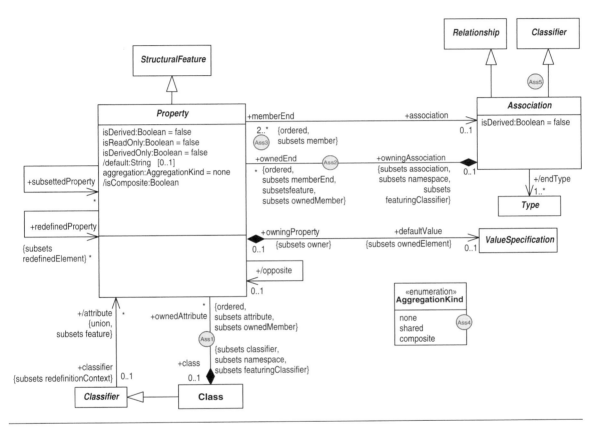

FIGURE 2.51 The metamodel for associations.

2.2.14 CLASSES

Definition

A *class* describes a set of instances that have the same features, constraints, and semantics. A class is a special classifier.

Notation and Semantics

2.2.14.1   Classes are represented by rectangles that carry just the name of the class or the class name plus attributes and operations. These three compartments (class name,

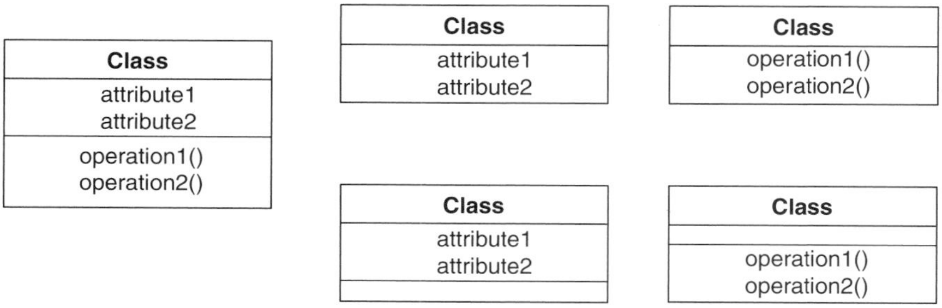

Class
attribute1
attribute2
operation1()
operation2()

Class
attribute1
attribute2

Class
operation1()
operation2()

Class
attribute1
attribute2

Class
operation1()
operation2()

FIGURE 2.52 Notation variants for attributes and operations.

attributes, and operations) are separated by a horizontal line. This notation stems from the classifier superclass. A class name normally begins with an uppercase letter and is often a substantive (noun) in singular form (collection classes and similar classes may be written in plural).

Attributes are listed at least with their names and can also have information about their types, an initial value, property strings, and constraints (see Figure 2.52).

Operations are also listed with at least their names; additional information can be their parameters, types, and initial values as well as property strings and constraints.

Instances are never created from an *abstract class*. An abstract class is intentionally incomplete, thus forming the basis for other subclasses that can have instances.

An abstract class is represented like a regular class, but the name of the class is set in italics. Optionally, we can add the property string {abstract} below the class name. Otherwise, things like attributes, operations, and constraints can be part of the class.

CHECKLIST: CLASSES

☐ 2.2.14.1.   What is the superclass of *Class* in the UML metamodel?

Metamodel

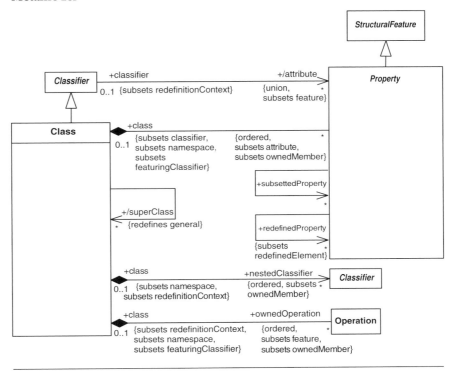

FIGURE 2.53   The metamodel for Class.

2.2.15   GENERALIZATION

Definition

A *generalization* is an abstraction principle applied to hierarchically structure the semantics of a model.

A generalization is a relationship between a general classifier and a special classifier, where the special classifier adds more features (*specialization*) and behaves in a way compatible to the general classifier.

Notation and Semantics

A generalization or specialization classifies features hierarchically; features with general meanings are allocated to general classifiers and special features are allocated to classifiers that are *subclassifiers* of general classifiers. The features of *superclassifiers* are passed on to their subclassifiers; subclassifiers inherit from their superclassifiers. Accordingly, a subclassifier has the features specified for it and

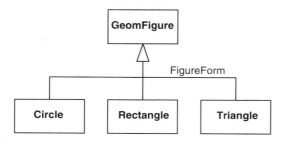

FIGURE 2.54 The notation for generalization.

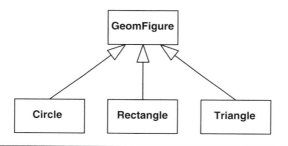

FIGURE 2.55 The notation for a generalization set called FigureForm.

the features of its superclassifiers. Subclassifiers inherit all features of their super-classifiers, and they can enhance them by adding features or can overwrite them.

In UML, overwriting (redefining) features is controlled by the metamodel class *RedefinableElement*. All metamodel classes that are subclasses of *RedefinableElement* can be overwritten in a generalization relationship. The overwriting element stores a reference to the overwritten element. For attributes, this relationship also transpires in the notation, namely, by the property string {redefines <property>}.   *2.2.15.1*

A generalization is specified by a special arrow, which points from the special element to the general element (see Figure 2.54). The generalization arrows are often put together in one single arrow, as you can see in Figure 2.55. Note, however, that the two representations are not equal. The summarized arrows represent a *generalization set*, which is among the exam topics for Advanced certification.   *2.2.15.2*

CHECKLIST: GENERALIZATION

☐ 2.2.15.1.   What is a redefinable element?
☐ 2.2.15.2.   In what direction does the generalization arrow point?

Metamodel

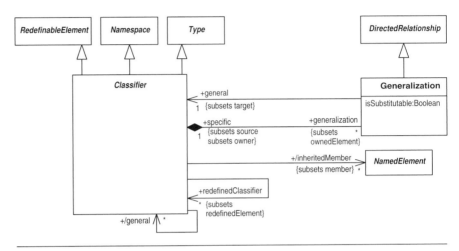

FIGURE 2.56 The metamodel for generalizations.

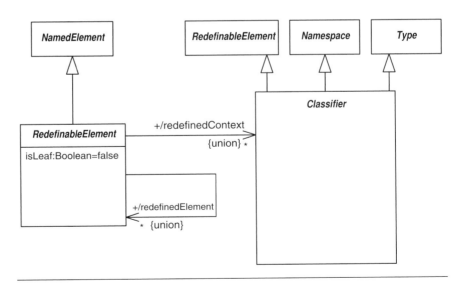

FIGURE 2.57 The metamodel for redefinable elements.

2.2.16   PACKAGES

Definition

A *package* is a collection of model elements that can be of arbitrary types and that are used to structure the entire model in smaller, easily manageable units. Packages can contain all elements that are derived from *PackageableElement* (see Ⓟ2 in Figure 2.64 on page 63).

A package defines a namespace; that is, the names of the elements a package contains have to be unique (see Ⓟ3 in Figure 2.64). Every model element can be referenced in other packages, but it can belong to only one (home) package. Packages can contain packages (see Ⓟ1 and Ⓟ3 in Figure 2.64).

2.2.16.1

Notation and Semantics

Packages can contain various model elements, for example, classes and use cases. They can be structured hierarchically, which means that they can, in turn, contain other packages.

A model element, such as a class, can be used in several packages, but every class has its home package. All other packages would merely mention it by stating its qualified name, which would look like this:

```
package name::class name
```

This causes *dependencies* to form between the packages involved; a package uses classes of another package.

In Figure 2.58 a package is represented in the form of a folder. The name of the package appears within this folder symbol. If model elements were shown within the symbol, then their names would appear on the folder tab; otherwise, they would appear within the large rectangle. Stereotypes can be denoted beyond the package name.

Member notation. Figure 2.59 shows another notation form for packages and their nesting. The relationship denoted by a crossed-out circle, grouped in a tree-type arrangement, at the Contract side can be read as "contains" or "consists" (Figures 2.58 and 2.59) and is identical with regard to the package nesting. The member notation is not limited to packages. It can be used to represent the hierarchical structure of other elements, such as classes residing in a package.

Generalization versus package merge. UML 1.x allowed us to generalize packages. Since the introduction of UML 2.0, the *merge* relationship is used to this end.

2.2.16.2

A *package merge* is a relationship between two packages, where generalization and redefinition are used to merge the content of the target package with the

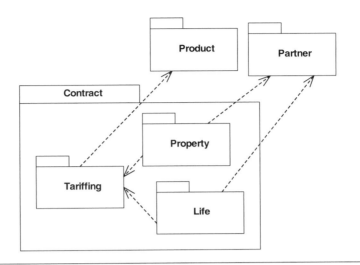

FIGURE 2.58   A package model (using the "insurance" example).

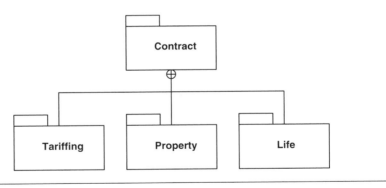

FIGURE 2.59   Alternative notations for package structures.

content of the source package. One important assumption of this merge is that equally named elements in different packages are based on the same concept. Our discussion of transformation will show why this assumption is important.

2.2.16.3   Figure 2.60 shows a simple package merge. The content of package P is merged into package R. This merging is based on formally defined rules, which can

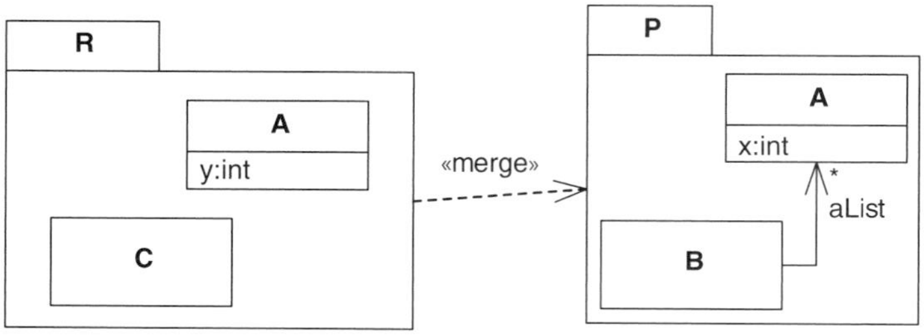

R

A

y:int

C

«merge»

P

A

x:int

*
aList

B

FIGURE 2.60   Example of a package merge.

optionally be automated and executed by a UML tool. The merging rules are as follows:

1. The merge relationship is converted into a package import relationship. Among other things, this means that private elements are not included in the package merge.
2. A new (empty) classifier is created in the source package for each classifier in the target package that does not exist in the source package. Then a generalization relationship for equally named classifiers in the target package is defined between all classifiers in the source package. All features of the superclassifier are redefined in the respective subclassifier. The consequence is that all features are owned by the subclassifier; that is, the classifier in the source package.
3. Generalization relationships between classifiers in the target package are transferred to the corresponding classifiers in the source package.
4. Next, a subpackage by the same name is created in the source package for each subpackage in the target package, unless it already exists. Subsequently, a package merge relationship is defined between the equally named subpackages of both the source and the target packages. This guarantees a recursive application of the process to subpackages.
5. Package and element import relationships from the target package are transferred to the source package.
6. Finally, all elements from the target package that cannot be generalized are copied to the source package and equipped with the same relationships to the other elements.

If we apply these transformation rules to the example shown in Figure 2.60, we obtain the results shown in Figure 2.61. You can see that the package merge relationship is actually a shortcut notation.

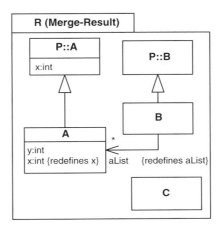

FIGURE 2.61 The merge result for the example in Figure 2.60.

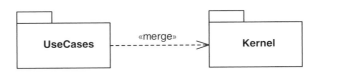

FIGURE 2.62 Package merge in the UML metamodel.

The package merge relationship is used intensively to structure the Unified Modeling Language's metamodel. For example, there is a package merge relationship between the use case package and the kernel package (see Figure 2.62). The *UseCases* package defines the class *Classifier*, among other things. Its property is essentially limited to be able to own use cases.

The *Kernel* package also has a Classifier class—the one we introduced earlier. These properties are merged with the properties of the class *UseCases::Classifier* (see the metamodel for use cases in Figure 2.122 on page 108).

Another example from the UML metamodel is the package structure of the activity model. The granularity of this model's specification is extremely fine to ensure that it supports a wide range of UML tools, from simple analysis tools to tools for complex and executable activity models.

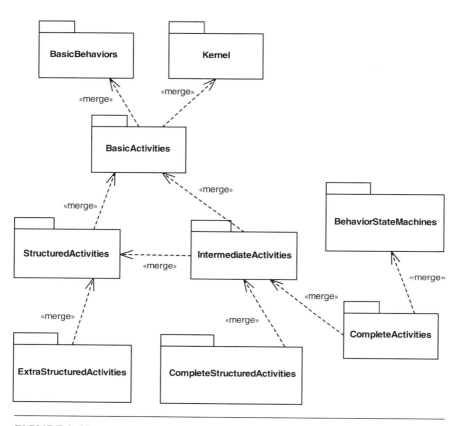

FIGURE 2.63 Merge relationships in the UML activity model.

Figure 2.63 shows the package structure. The exam topics of the Fundamental certification include only the *BasicActivities* package.

CHECKLIST: PACKAGES

☐ 2.2.16.1. What does the generalization relationship have to do with packages?

☐ 2.2.16.2. What additional semantics for grouping property does a package have?

☐ 2.2.16.3. How does the package merge work?

Metamodel

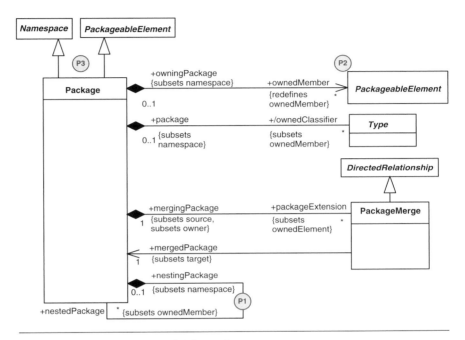

FIGURE 2.64 The metamodel for packages.

2.2.17   DEPENDENCIES

Definition
A *dependency* is a relationship between one (or several) source elements and one (or several) target element(s).

2.2.17.1   The target elements are required for the specification or implementation of the source elements. That means that the source elements are incomplete without the target elements.

Notation and Semantics
2.2.17.2   A dependency is represented by a dashed arrow, where the arrow points from the dependent element to the independent element. In addition, the type of dependency can be specified by using a keyword or stereotype (see Figure 2.67).

   The rare case where a dependency relationship (see Figure 2.65) has several source elements or target elements is shown in Figure 2.66. You will find this situation in the metamodel near the AB2 marker in Figure 2.72.

Dependencies can have different causes, as in the following examples.

- A package depends on another package. The cause can be, for example, that a class in one of the two packages depends on a class in the other package.
- A class uses a specific interface to another class. If this interface is changed, then changes are also required in the class that uses this interface.
- An operation depends on a class, for example, when the class is used in an operation parameter. A change to the class of this parameter may require a change to the operation itself.

FIGURE 2.65 Notation for a dependency relationship.

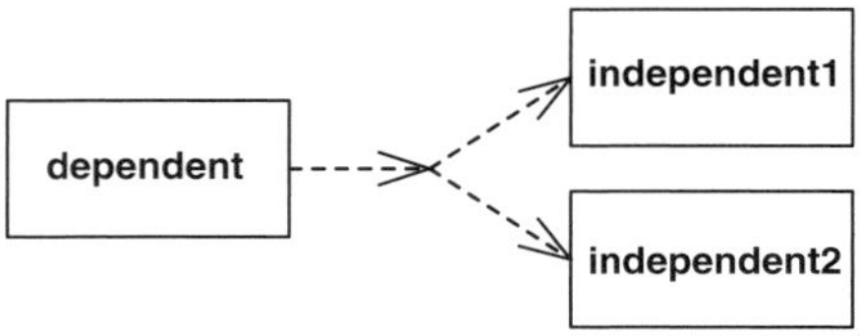

FIGURE 2.66 Notation for several target elements (suppliers).

Keyword/Stereotype	Description
«call»	Stereotype to usage relationship. The call relationship is defined and specified from one operation to another operation, so that the source operation calls the target operation. The source element can also be a class. This would then mean that the class contains an operation that calls the target operation.
«Create»	Stereotype to usage relationship. The dependent element creates instances of the independent element. The create relationship delined between classifiers.
«derive»	Stereotype to abstaction relationship. The dependent element is derived from the independent element.
«instantiate»	Stereotype to usage relationship. The dependent element is creates instances of the independent element. The create relationship is defined between classifiers.
«permit»	Keyword for permission relationship. The dependent element is permitted to use private of this independent element.
«realize»	Keyword for realization relationship. The dependent element implements the independent element (e.g.,interface or an abstact element).
«refine»	Stereotype to abstaction relationship. The dependent element resides on a more concrete semantic level than the independent element.
«trace»	Stereotype to abstaction relationship. The dependent element leads to the independent to trace semantic dependencies (e.g., from a class to a request, or from a use case to a class).
«use»	Keyword for usage relationship. The dependent element uses the independent element for its implementation.

FIGURE 2.67 Various types of dependency relationship.

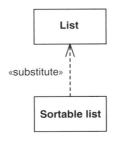

FIGURE 2.68   Notation for a dependency relationship.

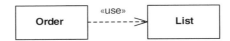

FIGURE 2.69   Notation for several target elements (suppliers).

2.2.17.3   An *abstraction relationship* is a special dependency relationship between model elements at various abstraction levels. The relationship is written similarly to a dependency relationship with the keyword "abstraction". The relationship is typically used with a stereotype. UML defines the following default stereotypes: «derive», «trace», and «refine».

Moreover, an abstraction relationship always has a *mapping rule*, specifying how the participating elements relate to one another. This information can be formal or informal (see **ABI** in Figure 2.72).

Regardless of the direction the arrow points in, an abstraction relationship can also be bidirectional, depending on the stereotype and the mapping rule (e.g. the «trace» relationship).

2.2.17.4   A special abstraction relationship is *realization*, a relationship between an implementation and its specification element.

2.2.17.5   A *substitution* relationship (Figure 2.68) is a special realization relationship. It specifies that instances of the independent element can be substituted by instances of the dependent element at runtime, for example, when the elements implement the same interfaces.

2.2.17.6   A *usage* relationship (Figure 2.69) is a special dependency relationship. It differs from a dependency relationship in that the dependency is limited to the implementation and it doesn't apply to the specification. This means that the dependent element requires the independent element for its implementation.

More specifically, there can be no usage relationship between interfaces but there can be a dependency relationship.

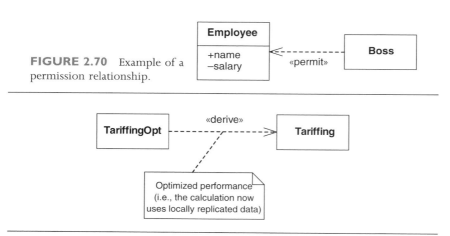

FIGURE 2.70 Example of a permission relationship.

FIGURE 2.71 Use of «derive» for an optimization (abstraction relationship).

A *permission* relationship[4] is a special dependency relationship that allows the dependent element to access the independent element. In the example shown in Figure 2.70, the class *Boss* obtains the right to access the class *Employee*. This means that the class *Boss* can access the private attribute *salary* of *Employee*.

Figure 2.71 shows a design class and its optimized implementation. Attaching a comment with an appropriate explanatory text to the refinement relationship is often very helpful.

2.2.17.7

CHECKLIST: DEPENDENCY RELATIONSHIPS

☐ 2.2.17.1. In what context is the term "incomplete" used for a dependency relationship?
☐ 2.2.17.2. In which direction does the arrow point that indicates the relationship between dependent and independent elements?
☐ 2.2.17.3. What is an abstraction relationship?
☐ 2.2.17.4. What is a realization relationship?
☐ 2.2.17.5. What is a substitution relationship?
☐ 2.2.17.6. What is a usage relationship?
☐ 2.2.17.7. What is a permission relationship?

---

[4] The permission relationship was removed in the final UML 2.0 specification [UML2.0]; however it is still part of the certification test.

Metamodel

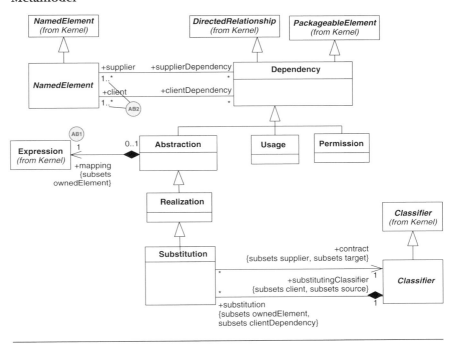

FIGURE 2.72 The metamodel for dependencies.

2.2.18 INTERFACES

Definition

2.2.18.1   *Interfaces* are special classifiers (see ⑬ in Figure 2.79) that use a set of features to specify a selected part of the externally visible behavior of model elements (mainly classes and components).

2.2.18.2   An *implementation*[5] relationship is a special realization relationship (see ⑪ in Figure 2.79) between a classifier and an interface. The classifier implements the features specified in the interface.

Notation and Semantics

Interfaces are denoted the way that classifiers are denoted except that they carry the keyword «interface».

-----

[5]   Implementation was renamed in the final UML 2.0 specification [UML2.0]; it became InterfaceRealization.

UML distinguishes between supplied and required interfaces. A *supplied* interface is provided by a model element for use by another element. A *required* interface is an interface requested by another model element.

Interfaces specify not only operations, but also attributes. Accordingly, interfaces can have associations to other interfaces or classes (see ⑫ in Figure 2.79 on page 71).

If a classifier wants to implement an interface, it has to implement all operations defined in that interface. With regard to the attributes defined in the interface, the implementing classifier has to behave as if it owned these attributes. In the simplest case, it actually implements the attributes. However, it is also sufficient, for instance, to supply just the pertaining *get()* and *set()* methods.

A classifier can implement several interfaces and also contain other properties. In other words, an interface generally describes a subset of a classifier's operations and attributes.

There is a special realization relationship between the implementing classifier and the interface called *implementation relationship*[6] (using the «realize» keyword).

Supplied interface. An implementation relationship is expressed by a special arrow (see Figure 2.73). Another notation to represent the implementation of an interface uses a small empty circle connected to the classifier that supplies the interface by a line (see Figure 2.74). This symbol is supposed to express a ball (in UML 1.x it is also called lollipop). The name of the interface appears above the circle.

When using the arrow notation, we have a way to read the operations and attributes required by the interface. When using the shortcut notation, in contrast,

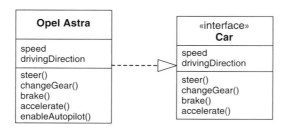

FIGURE 2.73   The class Opel Astra implements the Car interface (arrow notation).

---

[6]   The UML 2.0 specification [UML2.0cert] does not clearly state whether the dashed arrow with the keyword «realize» should be used for the implementation relationship or whether the dashed generalization relationship should be used instead as in UML 1.x. We assume the latter because this variant is better suited for practical work.

FIGURE 2.74 The class Opel Astra implements the interface Car (plug notation).

FIGURE 2.75 The class RacingDriver requests the interface Car (socket notation).

we can see only the name of the interface; we can't see the operations and attributes it requests.

Required interface. For a required interface, the requiring element has a usage relationship with the interface. Again, there is a shortcut notation, this time using a semicircle on a stick to represent a socket (see Figure 2.75).

2.2.18.3   The notation for interfaces is summarized in Figure 2.76. The shortcut notation on the left is also known as *ball-socket notation*.

Since interfaces are special classifiers, all relevant rules apply to them; for example, generalization can be used (see Figure 2.77). An interface can extend several other interfaces, which means that it can have several superinterfaces.

Example

Figure 2.73 shows that the class *Opel Astra* implements the interface *Car*. The interface *Car* requests four operations—*steer()*, *changeGear()*, *brake()*, and *accelerate()*—and two attributes— *speed* and *drivingDirection*. The class *Opel Astra* meets the requirements for this interface because it has the four required operations and the two attributes, among other things.

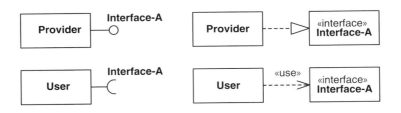

FIGURE 2.76 Alternative notations for interfaces and the use and supply of interfaces.

FIGURE 2.77 Extending interfaces.

Figure 2.78 shows the implementing class *Jaguar* to the interface *LuxuryCar*, which is an extension of the interface *Car*. The user *RacingDriver* requests the interface *Car*. This means that he or she can use both the *Opel Astra* and the *Jaguar*. In contrast, the *Manager* requests the interface *LuxuryCar*. He or she can use the *Jaguar* but not the *Opel Astra* because the latter doesn't meet all requirements, such as adjusting the seat heating.

The definition of interfaces is helpful in explicating and reducing the linkage between classes. In our preceding example, the interface user *RacingDriver* depends only on four special operations of the class *Jaguar*. All other operations of the class *Jaguar* could be changed without impairing the class *RacingDriver*. This is a piece of information we would otherwise have gained only by intensively studying the class *Jaguar*.

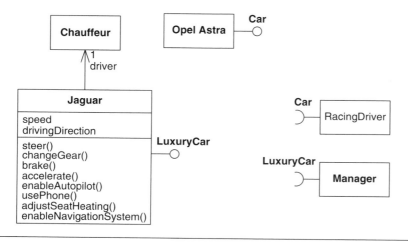

FIGURE 2.78 Example of the implementation of interfaces.

Metamodel

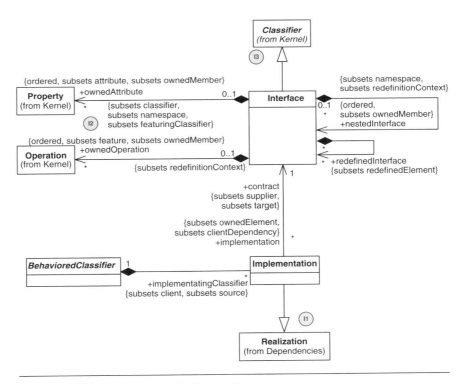

FIGURE 2.79   The metamodel for interfaces.

2.3 BEHAVIOR BASICS

This section discusses the basics for the representation and description of general behavior in UML to the extent relevant for the Fundamental OCUP examination.

The following sections describe special aspects of behavior in the context of specific diagram types.

2.3.1   EXAMINATION TOPICS

The section "Behavior Basics" refers to the package *CommonBehaviors::BasicBehaviors* in the UML 2.0 specification. This topic is part of the General Basics area (see Section 2.1) and it constitutes 10 percent of the test.

2.3.2   INTRODUCTION

The process of modeling behavior involves a description of flows, time dependencies, state changes, the processing of events, and similar things. UML is object-oriented, which means that behavior is nothing that exists independently, but always concerns specific objects. The *responsibility for a behavior* can always be put down in detail to an object.

In UML the description of behavior refers to the *behavior of a classifier*, where four variants of behavioral descriptions are available:

- State and protocol automatons (state machines)
- Activities and actions
- Interactions
- Use cases

In the metamodel, the packages used in Figure 2.80 show these descriptions.

The package *CommonBehaviors* defines the fundamental concepts used to describe behavior and corresponding relations with structural elements. Every behavior results from the actions of at least one object and causes the participating objects to change their states.

We distinguish between two forms of behavior.   *2.3.2.1*

Executing behavior: This behavior is directly connected to an object that processes this behavior (*host*) and to another object that caused this behavior (*invoker*). The execution of this behavior is triggered by calling a behavioral feature of an object, where this call is made by another object or an event or by creating a new object.

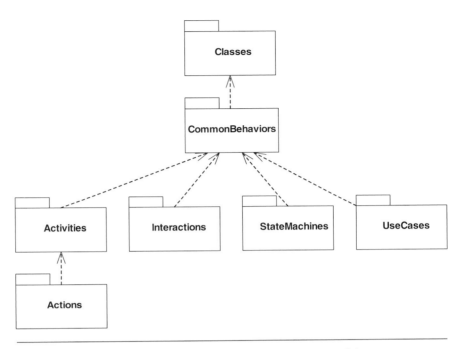

FIGURE 2.80   Packages for dynamic modeling in the metamodel.

Emergent behavior: This behavior refers to the interactions among different participating objects. It is an abstraction and summary of the behavior of several single objects or a set of objects. This form of behavior doesn't give a clue as to which objects trigger or process what.

<table>
<tr><td>2.3.2.2</td><td></td></tr>
<tr><td>2.3.2.3</td><td></td></tr>
</table>

2.3.2.2
2.3.2.3   Behavior can be defined directly and independently as a class. The item *Behavior* in Figure 2.81 is a specialization of *Class*. Moreover, a behavioral description can be defined within another classifier that owns this behavior. This other classifier (*BehavioredClassifier*) forms the context for the behavior (the *BehavioredClassifier* is the context of *Behavior*). This means that *Behavior* can access the structural and behavioral features of the context classifier. A *BehavioredClassifier* can own several behaviors, but each of these behaviors would then have exactly one context.

2.3.2.4   Similarly to the way classifiers can own a behavior and act as the context for this behavior, operations (behavioral features) can own behavior. In this case, the behavior is the implementation of the operation, and the operation is the specification of the behavior. The *context* is identical to that of the classifier, which owns this operation.

CHECKLIST: BEHAVIOR BASICS

☐ 2.3.2.1.   What forms can behaviors have?
☐ 2.3.2.2.   Can behavior be defined independently as a class?
☐ 2.3.2.3.   Can a classifier own behavior?
☐ 2.3.2.4.   What is the context of a behavior?

Metamodel

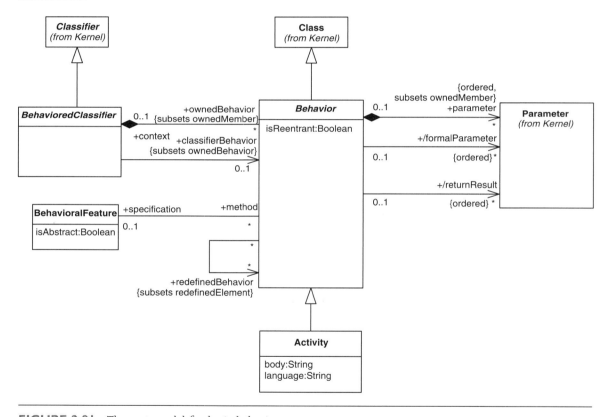

FIGURE 2.81   The metamodel for basic behavior.

2.3.3   THE CALL MODEL

Behavior in UML is event oriented by definition. The execution of behavior (see   *2.3.3.1*
Figure 2.82) is always triggered by an event. The occurrence of an event can

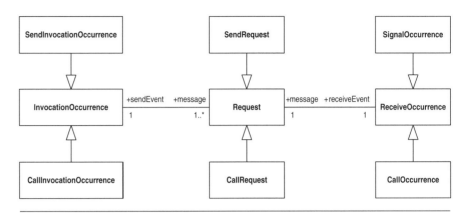

FIGURE 2.82   The notational model for executing behavior.

trigger the execution of behavior. In turn, new events may happen during each execution of behavior. Two particular events occur always: the *start occurrence* and the *termination occurrence*.

2.3.3.2   When a behavior call is triggered by the receipt of a message rather than by an
2.3.3.3   operation call, then this form of request is described by using *signals*. Signals can
2.3.3.4   be arranged in a specialization hierarchy (see Figure 2.83). *Exceptions* are a special
form of signals. Only active objects can receive signals. Signals always represent an asynchronous call behavior. The receiver of a signal is responsible for selecting the behavior to be executed.

CHECKLIST: THE CALL MODEL

☐ 2.3.3.1.   How is the execution of behavior triggered?
☐ 2.3.3.2.   What is the Request object?
☐ 2.3.3.3.   What are the two ways to invoke behavior?
☐ 2.3.3.4.   Is the sender or the receiver responsible for selecting the behavior
           to be executed?

2.3.4   BEHAVIOR PARAMETERS

A behavior can have an arbitrary number of *parameters*. Upon calling a behavior, the input parameters are made available to that behavior. The output parameters are filled with values when the behavior terminates.

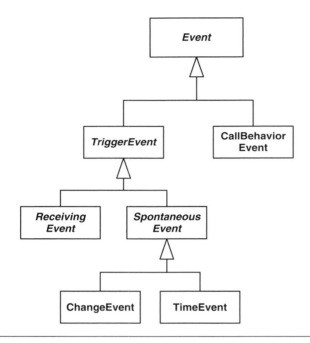

FIGURE 2.83   Event hierarchy.

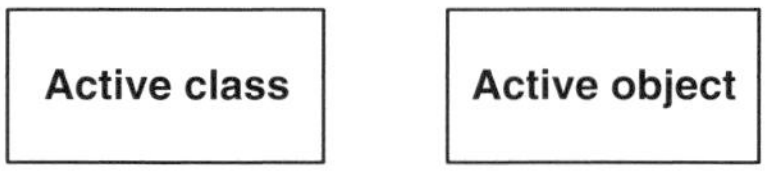

FIGURE 2.84   Notations for active class and active object.

Active class	Active object

The attribute *is Reentrant* can be used to define whether the behavior may be called several times concurrently or whether one call to the behavior has to be terminated before another call for the same behavior can be made.

The attribute *isActive* can be used to define whether instances of *BehavioredClassifier* can have their own control flows. If they are permitted to own control flows, they are also called *active objects*. Active objects respond to events autonomously and independently of other objects. (See Figure 2.84.)

2.3.4.1

If an object is not active, then its behavior is executed with other objects in a common control flow. In this case, we can state how concurrent calls to a behavior should be handled:

Concurrent: Concurrent calls are executed independently of one another and concurrently.

Sequential: There is no coordination of concurrent calls, and the participating instances have to police the situation themselves.

Guarded: With concurrent calls, only one behavior is called at a time; all others are blocked until the first behavior terminates. Deadlocks have to be handled by the developer.

CHECKLIST: BEHAVIOR PARAMETERS

☐ 2.3.4.1. How can behaviored classifiers be defined as active objects?

2.4 ACTIVITY DIAGRAMS

This section is dedicated to the representation and description of special behavior that occurs in activity diagrams. We discuss these topics to the extent relevant for the Fundamental test.

2.4.1 EXAMINATION TOPICS

The topics in this section refer to the following metamodel areas:

- Package: *Activities::BasicActivities*
  - Nodes
  - Edges (flows)
  - Actions (basics only)
  - Control nodes

This topic area constitutes 20 percent of the test.

Definition

2.4.1.1 An *activity* describes the sequence of actions based on control models and object flow models. An activity contains edges and activity nodes—special actions (see **AI** in Figure 2.88).

2.4.1.2 An *action* is an abstract class in the metamodel. The specific subclasses are also defined in UML. They are described in the so-called *Action Semantics*. Though this section had been introduced in UML Version 1.5, it was integrated in activity models in UML 2.0 for the first time.

Notation and Semantics

An activity is represented by a rectangle with rounded corners. Within the rectangle there are the nodes and edges of the activity. The name of the activity appears at the top left of the rectangle.

An activity is derived from *Class* across several generalization levels. For example, you can see the superclass *Activity* from the package *BasicBehaviors* in (A2) of Figure 2.88. This superclass is derived from *Behavior* and is a behavior of *Class*. This tells us in particular that activities themselves can also be generalized.

Just like any behavior in UML, an activity can also have parameters. Objects incoming to or outgoing from an activity model are referred to as the *parameters* of that activity. These objects are placed on the rectangle of the activity and additionally listed beneath the activity's name, including their types.

The example in Figure 2.85 shows an activity for the production of six-packs. The activity has two parameters: one input parameter called *Produced Bottles* in the state [empty] and the output parameter *New Six-Pack*. The exact declaration of the activity parameters appears on the top left directly beneath the activity's name.

www.eclipse.org. You can see in Figure 2.85 that this activity has various kinds of nodes and edges. The rounded rectangles are actions. The small rectangles near the actions are called *pins*. They supply the input or output parameters for the actions.

2.4.1.3

The keywords «precondition» and «postcondition» can be used within an activity to define preconditions and postconditions for it. A *precondition* describes the state required upon the activity's entry and a *postcondition* describes the state that has to prevail when the activity exits.

Decision. In our example with the six-pack production, the readily produced empty bottles pass from the activity entry parameter to the first action, *Fill Bottles*. This

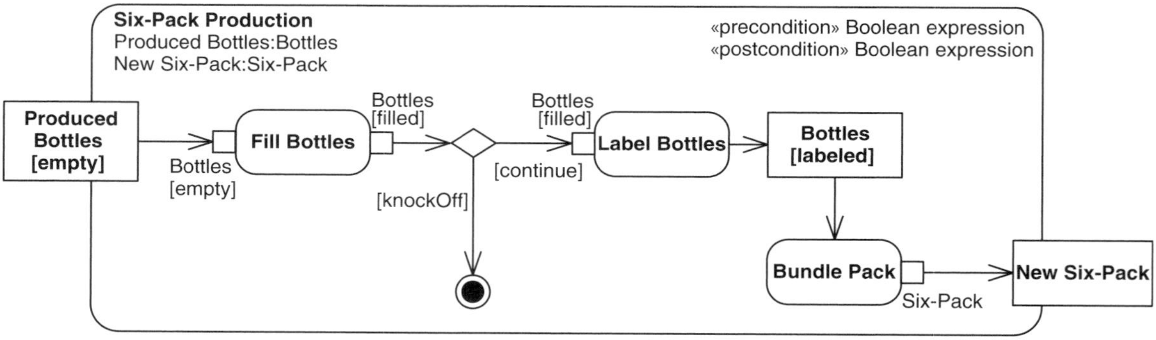

FIGURE 2.85 Example of an activity.

action results in bottles in the [filled] state. Following the action is a *decision node* (the rhombus symbol). At the end of the day, the activity end node is reached and the entire activity is terminated. Otherwise, it continues with the next action, *Label Bottles*. Notice that this time the output pin *Bottles [labeled]* is written differently. This notation is possible when the output pin, and the input pin of the next action, are identical. Finally, the pack is bundled, and the activity can return a new six-pack.

We will discuss each of the nodes and edges and the semantics in more detail soon.

Predefined actions. As mentioned before, the kinds of action are predefined in UML. Examples of actions include the following:

- Calling a behavior (e.g., another activity)
- Calling an operation
- Sending and receiving signals
- Creating, deleting, and changing objects

A good example of a specific action is *CallBehaviorAction*. This action calls another behavior. For example, this can be another activity or a state machine. In our example in Figure 2.85, it is just *CallBehaviorActions*. Another example for an action is *CreateObjectAction*.

Knowledge of each of these actions, including their input and output parameters and semantics, is part of the Intermediate and Advanced certification levels, so we will not discuss them further here.

2.4.1.4　**ActivityEdge.** The edges in an activity (*ActivityEdge*) are divided into control flow edges and object flow edges (*ControlFlow* and *ObjectFlow*, respectively; see Aka2 in Figure 2.93). You will understand how they differ in a moment. Both edge types are equal as far as the notation—a straight line with an open arrowhead.

Connector edge. It can easily happen in activity diagrams that you will have to draw an edge across the entire diagram. To ensure easy reading of the diagram, we could introduce connectors. A *connector* is used to split an edge, and it's only a notational means and doesn't influence the underlying model. A connector is represented by a circle containing an optionally selectable name. Notice that the element always occurs in pairs. You can see a connector, *A*, in Figure 2.86. This means that there may be no other connector by the same name in this diagram.

Nodes. Figure 2.87 uses a simplified section from the UML metamodel to show different types of activity node.

2.4.1.5　In Figure 2.87, the left branch shows the actions, the middle branch shows the *object nodes*, and the right branch shows the *control nodes*. You can see that most of

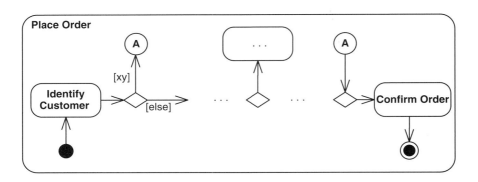

FIGURE 2.86 Notation for connectors.

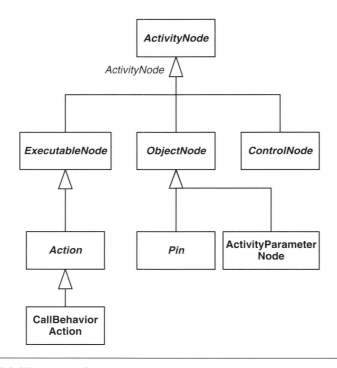

FIGURE 2.87 Types of activity node.

the metamodel classes used here are abstract. You have already seen the concrete subclasses for actions. With the object nodes, the classes *InputPin* and *OutputPin* are concrete subclasses for the abstract metamodel class *Pin*. Concrete control nodes are *DecisionNode*, *MergeNode*, *ActivityFinalNode*, and *InitialNode*.

Practice

Activity diagrams can be used for graphical representations of the kinds of flows that are, for instance, described in use cases. Natural languages are normally used to describe extremely simple flows in an easily understandable way. In contrast, activity diagrams allow you to represent even very complex flows that include many exceptions, variants, jumps, and iterations, and still remain clear and understandable.

Metamodel

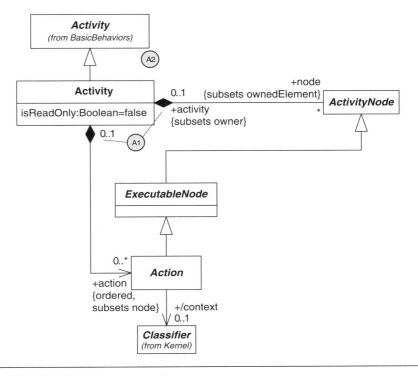

FIGURE 2.88 The metamodel for activities.

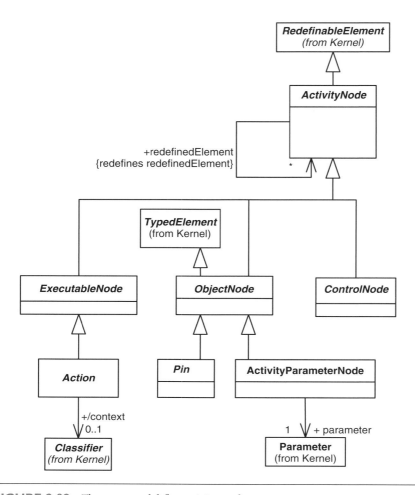

FIGURE 2.89 The metamodel for activity nodes.

CHECKLIST: ACTIVITIES

- ☐ 2.4.1.1. What does an activity represent?
- ☐ 2.4.1.2. What does an action represent?
- ☐ 2.4.1.3. What are pins?
- ☐ 2.4.1.4. What kinds of edge are there?
- ☐ 2.4.1.5. What kinds of activity node are there?

2.4.2 TOKEN FLOW

Notation and Semantics

The semantics of an activity is based on a *token flow*. More specifically, control tokens or object tokens flow between nodes over edges. Rather than flow randomly, however, these flows obey the following elementary rules:

2.4.2.1
- An action can start only if tokens are available at all incoming edges (implicit synchronization; and semantics).

2.4.2.2
- When an action terminates, a token is made available at all outgoing edges (implicit splitting; and semantics).
- A token flows from one action to the next if
  - ○ the token is made available at the outgoing action;
  - ○ the leading action is ready to take the token;
  - ○ and the rules allow the edge to accept the token flow.

An edge can specify rules that control the token flow. Most of these rules are part of the Intermediate and Advanced certification levels. You can see one way to use these rules in the metamodel (see Aka1 in Figure 2.93). Every edge has a condition referred to as a *guard* that has to be true in order to be able to transport tokens. The default value is *true*.

There are two types of edge: control flow edges and object flow edges (see Aka2 in Figure 2.93). Their notation is identical, and both can be allocated exclusively by their context.

Control flow. Figure 2.90 shows two independent sections from an activity that uses control flows. There is no object flow, though, since the edges are directly connected with actions. This also means that no pins or activity parameters are involved.

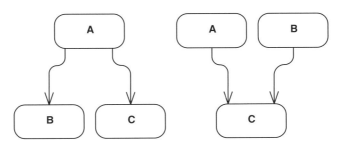

FIGURE 2.90 The and semantics for control flows.

Implicit splitting. In the left section, once action *A* terminates, a control token is made available at both outgoing edges. This means that, after action *A*, actions B and C start concurrently.

Implicit synchronization. In contrast, action C in the right section doesn't start until tokens are available at both incoming edges; that is, actions *A* and B have to terminate first.

Object flow. Things with an object flow look similar to those with a control flow. Figure 2.91 shows the preceding situation, but this time with object flows. You can see that the actions have input and output pins. Otherwise, the same rules apply.

With object flows, however, there is one exception. The and semantics actually applies only to incoming and outgoing edges of actions. For an object flow, the source or the target of an edge is not an action, but an object node. So the or semantics applies, as shown in Figure 2.92. Notice the subtle but important difference from Figure 2.91. In the left section, the action has only one output pin, which means that the action supplies one object token. Outgoing from that pin are two edges. Which one of these edges the object token will select is not defined. This means that the model behavior cannot be anticipated. To make the model predictable, we could use conditions at the edges. However, an explicit decision node is generally preferred.

Things are a little more complicated on the right side. Actions *A* and B each supply an object token. But action C has only one input pin. In this case, action C would be called twice. This is generally not a behavior the modeler would like to see here.

Of course, the token flow can also be influenced by other means. In addition to actions and object nodes, there are control tokens that can be used to influence the token flow.

2.4.2.3

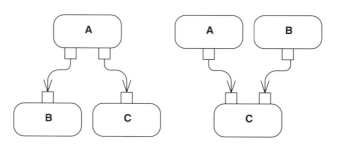

FIGURE 2.91   The and semantics for object flows.

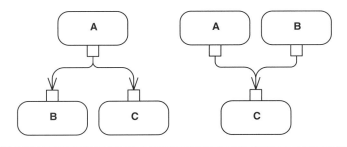

FIGURE 2.92 The or semantics for object flows.

CHECKLIST: TOKEN FLOW

☐ 2.4.2.1. What prerequisite must be met for an action to execute?
☐ 2.4.2.2. At which outgoing edges are tokens made available when an action terminates?
☐ 2.4.2.3. When does the or semantics apply to object flows?

Metamodel

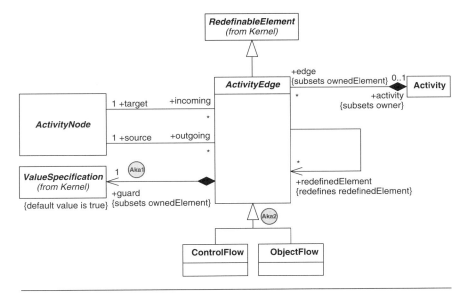

FIGURE 2.93 The metamodel for activity edges.

2.4.3   CONTROL NODES

Definition

A start node, called *InitialNode*, is a point of departure for an activity's flow.

An activity's end node is called *ActivityFinalNode* and causes the defined flow to terminate—that is, all actions and token flows within that activity will terminate.

A *DecisionNode* is a control node with one or several outgoing edges, at which decisions are made based on certain conditions, i.e., at which of the continuing edges the token flow should continue.

A *MergeNode* is a control node, at which each of several incoming token flows leads immediately to a common outgoing token flow.

Some of you will miss splitting and synchronization (with the black bar notation) at this point. In fact, these control nodes are used in UML 2.0, but they are part of the Intermediate certification level, so we won't discuss them here.

Notation and Semantics

An *InitialNode* is represented by a filled circle (see Figure 2.94). It has outgoing edges, but no incoming edges. When calling an activity, a control token is placed on each initial node. This means that when an activity has several initial nodes, there will be several concurrent flows immediately after the activity has been called.   *2.4.3.1*

Several outgoing edges of an initial node have semantics. A control token is made available at each outgoing edge. It is not mandatory for an activity to have an initial node. For example, there is no initial node in Figure 2.97.   *2.4.3.2*

A final node is also represented by a filled circle, but it additionally has an outer ring. It has at least one incoming edge, but no outgoing edges. The entire

FIGURE 2.94   Notation for initial and final nodes.

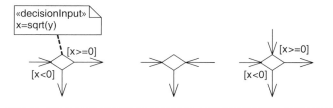

FIGURE 2.95   Example for decision and merge.

activity terminates as soon as a token reaches a final node, regardless of how many other tokens are still within the activity.

2.4.3.3   Several incoming edges that have only one of them must transport a token. As soon as a token is made available at one of the edges, the final node is activated and the activity terminates. It is not mandatory for an activity to have a final node. For instance, there is no final node in Figure 2.97.

In the metamodel you will notice something striking: between the abstract class *ControlNode* and the class *ActivityFinalNode*, there is yet another level with the abstract class *FinalNode* (see Ak2 in Figure 2.96). The reason is that there is another variant, in addition to activity final nodes: *FlowFinalNode*. This variant terminates only the current token, not the entire activity. *FlowFinalNode* is a topic of the Intermediate certification level, so we won't discuss it further here.

A *DecisionNode* is represented by an empty rhombus, which has one incoming edge and several outgoing edges. As soon as a token is supplied over the incoming edge, the guards at the outgoing edges are evaluated. The sequence of evaluation is not defined. As soon as a condition is true, the token traverses the respective outgoing edge.

2.4.3.4   A decision can also define a behavior (see Ak1 in Figure 2.96). Every token arriving over the incoming edge is passed to the behavior before the guards are evaluated. For example, the behavior could be a complex calculation. The result of such a calculation can be accessed in the individual guards, so that the calculation doesn't have to be repeated every time a guard is being evaluated. The behavior must not have side effects, which means that no values in the object model may be changed. The notation for behavior is a note symbol with the keyword «decisionInput» (see Figure 2.95).

Similarly to a decision node, a *MergeNode* is also represented by an empty rhombus, except that a merge has several incoming edges and one outgoing edge.

The only purpose of a merge node is to connect incoming edges to one outgoing edge. Nothing is calculated, and nothing is expected.

Decision and merge can be combined, and the rhombus symbol for this combination has several incoming and several outgoing control flows. Notice that the implicit sequence is important: first the merge and then the decision.

CHECKLIST: CONTROL NODES

☐ 2.4.3.1.   How many incoming edges can an initial node have?
☐ 2.4.3.2.   What do several edges outgoing from one initial node signify?
☐ 2.4.3.3.   What do several edges incoming into one final node signify?
☐ 2.4.3.4.   What is the meaning of behavior (decision input) that can be defined by a decision?

Metamodel

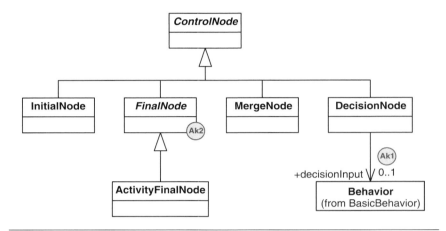

FIGURE 2.96 The metamodel for control nodes.

2.4.4 OBJECT NODES

Definition

An *ObjectNode* specifies that an object or a set of objects exists within a flow at a certain point in time. Object nodes can be used in activities to serve as incoming or outgoing parameters (activity parameter nodes) or as incoming or outgoing parameters of actions (pins).

Similarly to a control flow, an *object flow* is a special edge, except that object tokens are transported over it.

Notation and Semantics

An object flow is used to express that the objects involved are required by action nodes or are created or modified by them. An action won't start until the required objects are present. At the end of an action, the new or modified objects will be made available.

Activity parameters are represented by rectangles, including the name of the object and optionally the object state within square brackets (see Figure 2.97).

An activity can have an arbitrary number of activity parameters. When an activity is called, object tokens are present at all input parameters. This means that if there is more than one input parameter, there will be concurrency in the activity from the start.

An initial node is normally not required when there are input parameters.

2.4.4.1

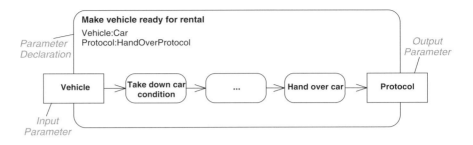

FIGURE 2.97 The notation for activity parameters.

2.4.4.2   When an activity terminates, there are object tokens at all output parameters. If the corresponding object does not exist, then a *null* (*or zero*) *token* is created and can then be used for any object type.

2.4.4.3   A *pin* is always allocated to an action (see ⟨Ap2⟩ in Figure 2.103 in the next section). We distinguish between *input pins* and *output pins*. An action can have an arbitrary number of pins (see ⟨Ap1⟩ in Figure 2.103).

Pins are represented by small squares leaning against the outer margin of an action node. The object's name and its state are written beneath the pin.

The bottom part in Figure 2.98 suppresses the object flow; it shows only that there is an object flow without giving details. This can be useful, for instance, when we want a view of a complex activity model where we are interested in the flow sequence and the object flow is secondary.

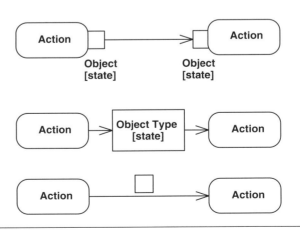

FIGURE 2.98 Various notations for pins.

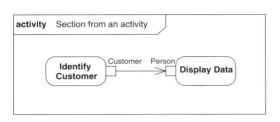
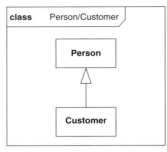

FIGURE 2.99 Various object types.

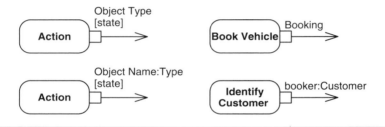

FIGURE 2.100 Labeling object nodes.

Regarding labeling pins, the object types and object states of output pins and their partner input pins don't have to be identical, as you can see in Figure 2.99. But it should be easy to derive the object type at the input pin from the incoming object types.

2.4.4.4

You can add the object type and the name of the object with the type to an object node (see Figure 2.100).

States of objects do not have to be modeled. The notation for object states is merely a way to emphasize such things in case they are important.

It is not mandatory for an input pin to have incoming edges, or for an output pin to have outgoing edges. An output pin without continuing edges expresses that the pertaining action has an output parameter which, however, doesn't play a role in the activity's further flow. If pins are not connected to edges, you have no way of telling input pins and output pins apart. This is why small arrows are added to the pin notation in such cases (see Figure 2.101).

A special form of input pins is the *value pin* (see **Ap3** in Figure 2.103). The notation adds a *value specification*, describing a value in the model, next to the pin (see Figure 2.102). Value pins are used, for example, to model constants in activities.

FIGURE 2.101 Input pins and output pins without edges.

FIGURE 2.102 Example for a value pin.

CHECKLIST: OBJECT NODES

☐ 2.4.4.1.   What happens at the input parameters of an activity when that activity is called?
☐ 2.4.4.2.   What happens at the output parameters of an activity when that activity is terminated?
☐ 2.4.4.3.   How many pins can an action have?
☐ 2.4.4.4.   When may pins be modeled alternatively as large rectangles with incoming and outgoing edges?

Metamodel

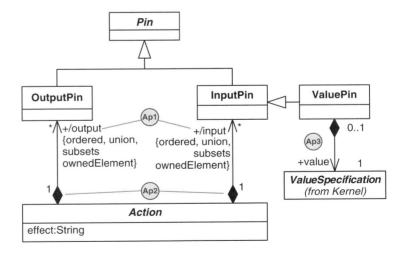

FIGURE 2.103   The metamodel for pins.

UML Version Notes

The UML versions up to, and including, 1.x defined activity diagrams as a mix of state diagrams, Petri nets, and event diagrams, which caused all kinds of theoretical and practical problems. One of the most important novelties in UML 2.0 is a completely new definition of activity diagrams. The following changes have occurred:

- The single steps within a flow are no longer called *activities*, but *actions*.
- A set of steps, which is eventually a flow diagram or a partial flow, is now called an *activity*.
- Activity diagrams now have semantics similar to that of Petri nets.

In the UML versions, up to, and including, 1.x, each incoming transition started a flow step, but there is now an implicit synchronization; that is, all incoming object flows and control flows have to be present in order for an action to start.

Similarly, an action node is exited only provided that all outgoing edges can fire. In UML 1.x it was exactly the opposite: when several outgoing edges (which were then called "transitions") had been written, you had to use appropriate conditions to ensure that only one single edge could fire. The new version waits until all conditions for all outgoing edges are met before firing.

Several new elements have been introduced:

- Activities can have object nodes in the form of input and output parameters.
- You can define preconditions and postconditions for activities.
- The initial and final states are now called *InitialNode* and *FinalNode*.
- You can now use connectors to simplify the representation of control flows that travel long distances in a diagram.

2.5 INTERACTION DIAGRAMS

This section is dedicated to the representation and description of behavior in interaction diagrams to the extent relevant for the Fundamental test.

2.5.1   EXAMINATION TOPICS

The topics described in this section refer to the following metamodel areas:

- Package: *Interactions::BasicInteractions*
  - ○ Interactions
  - ○ Lifelines
  - ○ Messages

This topic area constitutes 20 percent of the test.

2.5.2   INTERACTIONS

Definition

An *interaction* describes a series of messages that a selected set of participants exchange within a situation limited in time. UML 2.0 defines four diagrams to represent interactions:

> *Sequence diagrams* emphasize the sequence in which messages are exchanged.

> *Communication diagrams* emphasize the relationship between the participants.

> *Timing diagrams* emphasize the state changes of the participants relative to the time and the messages exchanged.

> *Interaction overview diagrams* present the order of interactions in an activity-like notation. Sequence diagrams are relevant mainly to the Fundamental certification level.

Notation and Semantics

The most important aspect in sequence diagrams is the time of messages. The participants are represented by a rectangle and a vertical dashed line. The rectangle and the line together are called *lifeline*. Messages are represented by arrows between lifelines. The time runs from top to bottom, showing the time of message flows.

2.5.2.1   The sequence diagram in Figure 2.104 shows an interaction with three lifelines. Note that the entire diagram represents one interaction, and that one interaction is not just a single exchange of messages.

2.5.2.2   **Connectable elements.** Readers familiar with the sequence diagrams of UML 1.x will notice that the name in the header of the lifeline is not underlined. The reason is that in UML 2.0 lifelines represent *connectable elements* (see 🔵 in Figure 2.114) rather than objects.

Connectable elements are important in the Intermediate and Advanced certification levels in connection with composition structure diagrams. It is sufficient here to understand that they describe instances located in the classifier to which the interaction belongs. So it's not a bad idea if you think of the lifelines as objects of the specified types, as in UML 1.x, when reading the sequence diagrams given in this book.

Multiobjects. The header of a lifeline shows (optionally) the element name, together with the pertaining classifier, in the usual declarative notation (i.e., *name : type*). A lifeline always represents exactly one element. *Multiobjects* known from UML 1.x are not permitted. Of course, a lifeline can represent an element from a multivalued property. If you need only one specific element, you have to state a selector (see Figure 2.105 and IL2 in Figure 2.114).

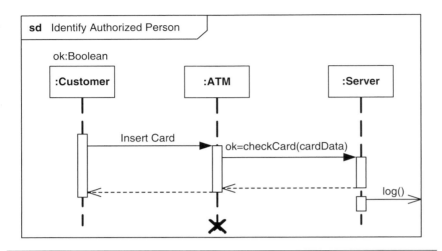

FIGURE 2.104 Simple example of a sequence diagram.

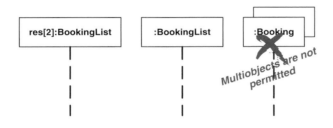

FIGURE 2.105 Lifelines and set types.

The header of a lifeline can also show the keyword *self*. In this case, the lifeline   *2.5.2.3*
represents an instance of the classifier to which the interaction belongs.

Execution occurrence. When messages are exchanged between lifelines, then a   *2.5.2.4*
behavior in the participating elements has to be executed. This behavior is represented by oblong rectangles on the lifelines. The rectangles represent the *execution
occurrence*. The beginning and the end of an execution occurrence are defined by
event occurrences. In other words, the sending and receiving of messages determine the beginning and the end of an execution occurrence (see ⒠ and ⒠₄ in
Figure 2.116 on page 103).

The transmission of a message is denoted by arrows. In this respect, UML uses   *2.5.2.5*
different types of message, which are represented by different arrow notations.
Figure 2.106 shows various kinds of message with their notation forms.

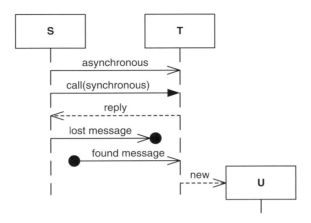

FIGURE 2.106   Notation forms for various message types.

Synchronous messages have a filled arrowhead. "Synchronous" means that the caller waits until the called behavior terminates. The reply message following a synchronous call is represented by a dashed line and an open arrowhead.

Asynchronous messages have an open arrowhead. "Asynchronous" means that the caller doesn't wait, but continues immediately after the call. Accordingly, there are no reply arrows on asynchronous calls.

Lost messages are denoted by an open arrowhead pointing to a filled circle. The circle is not connected with a lifeline. The sender of a lost message is known, but the receiver is not.

Found messages are denoted by an open arrowhead. The line originates from a filled circle. The circle is not connected with a lifeline. The receiver of a found message is known, but the sender is not.

Create messages. A message that creates a new instance is represented by a dashed line and an open arrowhead. The lifeline belonging to the instance begins only at this position in the diagram; that is, the arrow points to the header of the lifeline.

The message is denoted on the message arrows. The syntax is as follows:

```
[attribute =] name [(arguments)] [:return value] | '*'
```

where

attribute can be a local variable of the interaction or an instance of a lifeline. The attribute allocation is used only for synchronous messages with return values.

name is the name of the called message or the name of the signal sent. The sending of a signal is always asynchronous.

arguments is a list of parameter values, separated by commas, that are passed to the message. The syntax of an argument is one of the following:

    [parameter=]value

or

    attribute=output parameter[:output value]

or

    '_'

The dash is used when the value is unknown and when it doesn't play a role for the interaction.

The notation with the output parameter is used for parameters with the direction out, inout, or return. The first syntax is used for parameters with the direction in. The name of the parameter can be optionally added to the parameter value for better understanding. Here are examples of messages:

    message(4,-,2, "HelloWorld!")
    x=calculate(17,bpos):42
    message(arg=2003)

Instead of the message you can specify simply an asterisk (*). It's a kind of joker for any message.

Local attributes, which can be used to serve as loop counters or similar things, are declared in the top left corner of the diagram. For example, Figure 2.104 uses the local attribute *ok*.

In addition to creating objects (*object construction*), sequence diagrams can also represent the removal of objects (*object destruction*). The destruction of an object is represented by a cross on the lifeline. The UML 2.0 specification refers to the

2.5.2.6

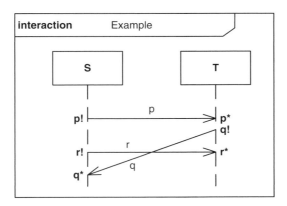

FIGURE 2.107 Example of sequences.

destruction as a stop. A *stop* is a special event occurrence (see ⬤IE2 in Figure 2.116 at the end of this section).[7]

2.5.2.7

2.5.2.8   Event occurrences that arise immediately upon sending and receiving messages are more important than a stop for the certification. Sending is an event, as is receiving (see ⬤INI in Figure 2.115). These events are used to define the semantics of an interaction that can be described by two sets. One set contains the valid sequences of send and receive events. The other set contains invalid sequences. All remaining sequences are irrelevant for the interaction.

2.5.2.9   Figure 2.107 shows an interaction with two lifelines and three (asynchronous) messages, p, q, and r. A send event in this example is denoted by an exclamation mark and a receive event is denoted by an asterisk. Note that this is not a UML notation. A valid sequence for the interaction in Figure 2.107 is, for example, $< p!, p^*, q!, r!, r^*, q^* >$. Many modelers will probably be surprised about something particular at first: there can be more than one valid sequence in one interaction. Another interaction in our example is $< p!, r!, p^*, q!, r^*, q^* >$.

2.5.2.10   Only two simple rules have to be observed in order to determine valid sequences:

1. Before a receive event, there must always be the pertaining send event first.
2. The sequence along one lifeline is relevant. In contrast, the position of one event relative to an event on another lifeline is insignificant. In Figure 2.107, for example, though event r! comes after event q!, r! can nevertheless happen first.

---

[7] The stop event is renamed in the final UML 2.0 specification [UML2.0] to DestructionEvent; however the certification still uses the old name.

General ordering. As a modeler, you can use a *GeneralOrdering* relationship to influence the sequence of events. General ordering is a relationship between two events, bringing these events into a time sequence (see IE3 in Figure 2.116 on page 103). This relationship is drawn as a dotted line between a centered filled triangle, showing the direction between the two events involved. The triangle points to the later of the two events.

2.5.2.11

Figure 2.108 adds a GeneralOrdering relationship to our example. This causes the sequence $< p!, p^*, q!, r!, r^*, q^* >$, valid in our previous example, to become invalid because event r! has to occur before p^*.

Found and lost messages play a particular role in this environment. One event of each type is missing: the receive event in the lost message and the send event in the found message. As you can see in the metamodel (IN2 in Figure 2.115 on page 103), this categorization of messages is also derived (i.e., it can be derived from the IN1 associations in Figure 2.115).

The exchange of messages can cause the states of instances represented by lifelines to change. This can be denoted by state invariants (see I2 in Figure 2.113 on page 102). A *StateInvariant* is denoted by a state symbol on the lifeline, or directly by a constraint, or a constraint in a note symbol. The notation forms are shown in Figure 2.109.

2.5.2.12
2.5.2.13

State invariants are evaluated immediately prior to the next event occurrence. The invariant has to be met for a sequence to be valid.

Structure of interactions. In closing we will briefly describe the general structure of interactions. The metamodel class *Interaction* owns the elements *Message* and *Lifeline* by composition. The abstract superclass of *Interaction* and other elements, such as *EventOccurrence*, is *InteractionFragment*. The entire structure of an interaction is formed by means of the composite pattern (see " I1 " in Figure 2.112 on page 101).

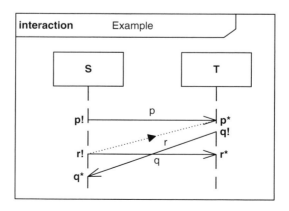

FIGURE 2.108 Example of a GeneralOrdering relationship.

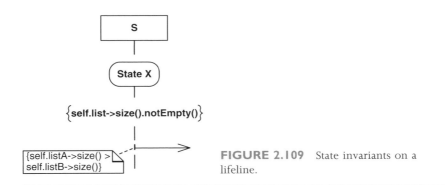

FIGURE 2.109 State invariants on a lifeline.

CHECKLIST: INTERACTION DIAGRAMS

☐ 2.5.2.1.   What is an interaction?
☐ 2.5.2.2.   What does a lifeline represent?
☐ 2.5.2.3.   What does *self* mean in a lifeline?
☐ 2.5.2.4.   What is an execution occurrence?
☐ 2.5.2.5.   What types of message are there?
☐ 2.5.2.6.   What is a stop?
☐ 2.5.2.7.   What events are triggered by an exchange of messages?
☐ 2.5.2.8.   How is the semantics of an interaction defined?
☐ 2.5.2.9.   How many valid event sequences can an interaction have?
☐ 2.5.2.10.   What rules determine valid event sequences?
☐ 2.5.2.11.   What does the *GeneralOrdering* relationship express?
☐ 2.5.2.12.   What is a state invariant?
☐ 2.5.2.13.   How are state invariants denoted?

2.5.3   COMMUNICATION, TIMING, AND INTERACTION OVERVIEW DIAGRAMS

Sequence diagrams and the interaction model are relevant mostly for the Fundamental exam. Nevertheless, you should at least have a look at the other three interaction diagrams.

Communication diagram. The communication diagram corresponds to the collaboration diagram of UML 1.x. It has been renamed because the name "collaboration diagram" was found to be misleading. UML also uses a model element called *collaboration*, which has nothing to do with collaboration diagrams.

Figure 2.110 shows clearly that the communication diagram emphasizes the relationships of the participants rather than the time sequence of the exchange of messages as in sequence diagrams.

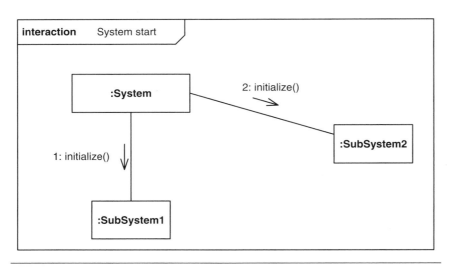

FIGURE 2.110   Example of a communication diagram.

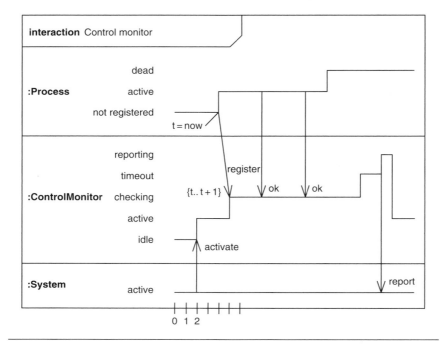

FIGURE 2.111   Example of a timing diagram.

At first sight, the communication diagram can easily be mistaken for a composition structure diagram (see Figure 2.49), particularly if you are not yet familiar with the new UML 2.0 notation.

Timing diagram. The timing diagram is another view on the interaction model. It emphasizes timing aspects; in particular, the state change of the lifelines at specific times. The states are state invariants in the interaction model. See Fgures 2.111 and 2.112.

Interaction overview diagram. This diagram looks like an activity diagram. However it is an interaction diagram that uses the same notation. The nodes are interactions or interaction uses. The diagram specifies the executing order of interactions. Figure 2.113 hows an interaction overview diagram.

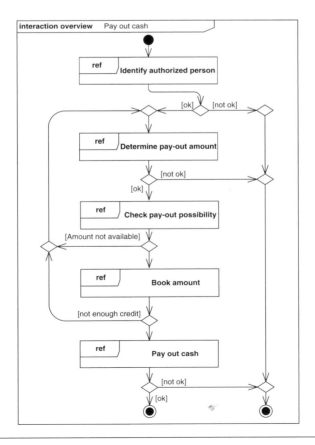

FIGURE 2.112 Example of an interation overview diagram.

Metamodel

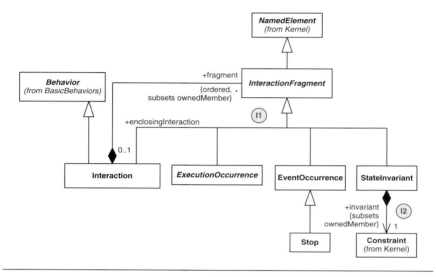

FIGURE 2.113   The metamodel for interactions.

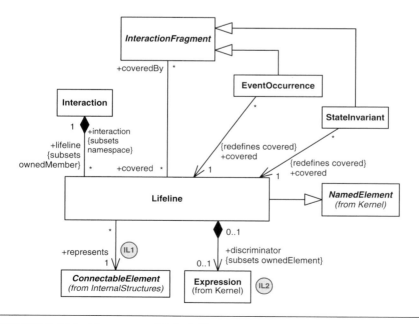

FIGURE 2.114   The metamodel for lifelines.

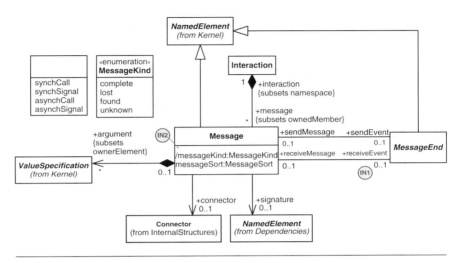

FIGURE 2.115 The metamodel for messages.

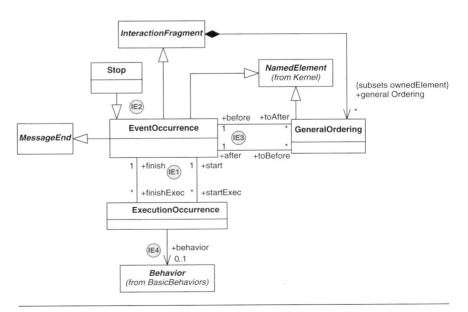

FIGURE 2.116 The metamodel for event occurrences.

2.6 USE CASES

This section discusses the representation and description of behavior in use cases.

2.6.1   EXAMINATION TOPICS

The topics discussed in this section refer to the following areas of the metamodel:

- Package: *UseCases*
  - Actors
  - Include and extend relationships
  - The classifiers of a use case
  - Other use case concepts

This topic area constitutes 20 percent of the test.

2.6.2   USE CASES AND ACTORS

Definition
A *use case* specifies a set of actions that are executed by a system or subject and that lead to a result. This result is normally important for an actor or stakeholder.

An *actor* is defined as a role outside the system or subject of the pertaining use case that interacts with the system in the context of the use case.

Notation and Semantics
A *use case diagram* describes the relationships among a set of use cases and the actors participating in these use cases.

No flow diagrams. Note that a use case diagram itself does not describe behavior or flows. It shows only how the model elements of the use cases relate, and it can be used for requirements analysis and requirements management.

The use case diagram in Figure 2.117 shows two use cases and the participating actors.

Activity diagrams. Although the two use cases suggest a sequence if you read them from top to bottom, the sequence is neither given nor planned in UML. You can try to discern a sequence but you will not find one. So it's wiser not to look for things that aren't there; the diagram merely describes what use cases there are and who participates in them. That's it. See Section 2.4 on activity diagrams to find out how flows and sequences are represented.

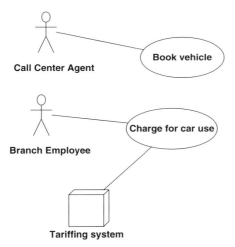

FIGURE 2.117 Example of a use case diagram.

The definition of a use case includes several terms that need some explanation.

2.6.2.1   *System* is not a direct model element of UML. "System" refers to the context of a use case. It describes a classifier in which the actions specified by the use case are executed (see **A4** in Figure 2.6.2 at the end of this section). This classifier can be a class or a component that represents the entire application. In this connection, *use case context, subject, modeling focus,* and *context* are common synonyms for *system*.

Stakeholder is not a model element of UML. It is a general term used to describe a person who has an interest in the system and who is especially interested in the results.

2.6.2.2   Figure 2.118 shows various notations to describe an *actor*. UML uses the stick man as a symbol for actors. The name of the actor appears beneath the symbol. Any user-specific symbol is valid (without using the stereotype mechanism). The block on the right, for instance, is not a symbol used in UML. A block symbol or a similar symbol is widely used for external systems because the stick man is always used to denote human users.

2.6.2.3   An actor in the metamodel is a special classifier (see **A1** in Figure 2.6.2). The actor inherits the second representation from the right from the classifier.

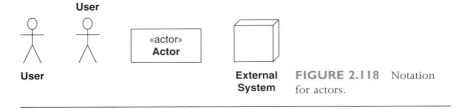

FIGURE 2.118 Notation for actors.

A simple association is used to connect an actor and use cases. That expresses a communication path between the actor and the use case. Similarly to associations in a class diagram, multiplicities are permitted here, too.

2.6.2.4

Multiplicity. The multiplicity on the side of the use case specifies how often this use case may be executed concurrently by the actor. The default multiplicity is 0..1 if nothing is specified.

On the side of the actor, the multiplicity specifies how many actors with the specified roles must or can participate in the use case. The default multiplicity is 1 if nothing is specified.

We don't normally use navigation information, but directed associations are permitted. UML doesn't define the specific semantics of association navigation in the context of use cases. However, it is common for the navigation direction to point from the active to the passive part—that is, to who initiated the communication. Associations between actors are not permitted.

Now, let's have a closer look at use cases. Figure 2.119 shows various notation forms for use cases. The left side shows the standard notation. But it is also permitted to write the name of the use case underneath the ellipse. The advantage of the latter alternative is that the size of the ellipse does not have to scale with the length of the use case name. Interestingly, in contrast to the actor notation, it is not permitted for use cases to write the name above the ellipse.

A use case is a special classifier or, more specifically, a behaviored classifier (see A2 in Figure 2.6.2). The notation on the right in Figure 2.119 is such a case. This representation is suitable, for example, when a large number of extension points have to be defined.

2.6.2.5

The system underlying a use case can be represented in the diagram, as shown in Figure 2.120.

2.6.2.6

In this example, *Booking System* is a component with the stereotype «subsystem». A component is a special classifier. It is not part of the test topics for the Fundamental certification level, but relevant only for the Intermediate level.

In addition to referring to a classifier, a use case can belong to a classifier (see A3 in Figure 2.6.2). This does not necessarily have to be the same classifier.

2.6.2.7

FIGURE 2.119 Notation for use cases.

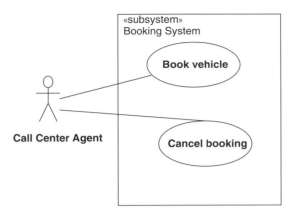

FIGURE 2.120   Use case context.

In the package *UseCase*, the *Classifier* model element is enhanced by the property to own use cases, including a special notation. This means that use cases can be represented in a compartment in addition to the compartments for the name as well as attributes and operations (see Figure 2.121).

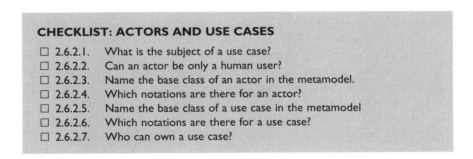

CHECKLIST: ACTORS AND USE CASES

- ☐ 2.6.2.1.   What is the subject of a use case?
- ☐ 2.6.2.2.   Can an actor be only a human user?
- ☐ 2.6.2.3.   Name the base class of an actor in the metamodel.
- ☐ 2.6.2.4.   Which notations are there for an actor?
- ☐ 2.6.2.5.   Name the base class of a use case in the metamodel
- ☐ 2.6.2.6.   Which notations are there for a use case?
- ☐ 2.6.2.7.   Who can own a use case?

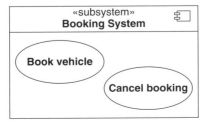

FIGURE 2.121   Example with components and their use cases.

Metamodel

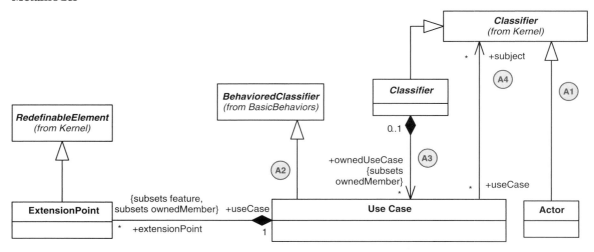

FIGURE 2.122 The metamodel for use cases and actors.

2.6.3 USE CASE RELATIONSHIPS

Definition

An *include* relationship is used to integrate a use case into another use case, thus becoming a logical part of that use case.

In contrast, an *extend* relationship is used to express that a use case will be extended by another use case in certain circumstances, and at a certain point, which is the *extension point*.

Since use cases are special classifiers, they can be generalized. The general rules for generalizations apply. Also, use cases can be abstract.

Notation and Semantics

Parts of use cases that occur identically in several use cases can be swapped into a separate use case, and then an include relationship can be used to integrate the desired part in another use case. This is a smart method to avoid redundant descriptions of identical parts. In contrast to the generalization relationship, no properties are inherited from use case to use case when using the include relationship.

The include relationship is represented by a dashed arrow with open arrowhead, pointing toward the including use case. The keyword «include» is written near the arrow.

2.6.3.1

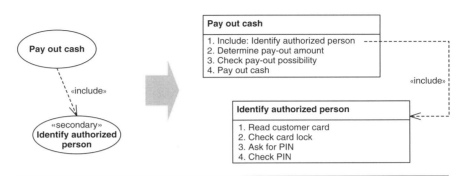

FIGURE 2.123 An include relationship in a use case diagram and its meaning in the use case description (Note: The right side is not UML).

The use case in Figure 2.123 is denoted by the stereotype «secondary». This method is not part of the UML standard and won't come up in the certification exam. However, it is common practice to mark included use cases because they are generally incomplete (use case fragments), so that they are distinguished from the primary (regular) use cases.

2.6.3.2   It is not necessary that an actor be connected to an included use case.

www.eclipse.org. Do you know Eclipse? The concept behind Eclipse can help you understand the functionality of the extend relationship between use cases. The core of Eclipse offers relatively few functions but many extension points at which the functionality can be extended by plug-ins. An Eclipse plug-in connects to an extension point, where it adds new functions. Of course, the core of Eclipse doesn't know anything about plug-ins; it merely defines the extension points.

2.6.3.3   This is exactly the concept the *extend relationship* uses between use cases. In Figure 2.124, use case *A* is extended by use case B at the extension point P under a certain condition. This means that the extend relationship shows the use case to be extended and stems from the use case that describes the behavior of this extension.

2.6.3.4   A use case can define an arbitrary number of extension points (see **AB4** in Figure 2.126 at the end of this section). The Classifier notation (see Figure 2.120) comes in handy when there is a very large number of extension points.

2.6.3.5   The condition for an extend relationship is optional (see **AB2** in Figure 2.126). If no condition is specified, then the extension will always occur.

     The UML notation for extend relationships has changed. While UML 1.x used extend conditions and extension points freely next to the extension arrow, and they are all denoted solidly in a note symbol now.

2.6.3.6   It is not necessary that an actor be connected to the extended use case (B).

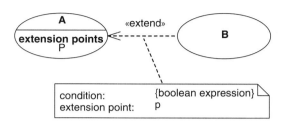

FIGURE 2.124 Notation for the extend relationship.

Examples

Figure 2.125 shows a use case diagram with use cases, actors, and generalization relationships as well as include and/or extend relationships denoted without keywords. Though the diagram doesn't represent a specific situation, we can draw several conclusions from it.

First, use case *A* could be abstract. It is specialized by the use cases C and D so that, for example, *C* with Actor 1 could be concretely executed.

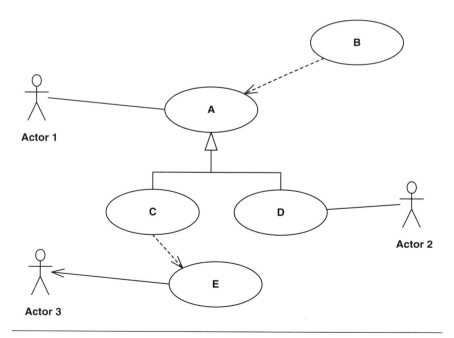

FIGURE 2.125 Example of a use case diagram with use case relationships.

Naturally, you will ask whether the dashed arrows are include or extend relationships. We can find the answer from the diagram.

Use case E has one actor. The association has a navigation direction from the use case to the actor. This means that the actor is passive and does not initiate the use case. If the relationship between C and D were an extend relationship, the triggering actor for use case E would be missing. So it must be an include relationship.

Use case B has no actor. If the relationship between *A* and B were an include relationship, then again, the triggering actor for use case B would be missing. So again, it must be an extend relationship.

USE CASE RELATIONSHIPS

☐ 2.6.3.1. In what direction does the include relationship point?
☐ 2.6.3.2. Does an included use case have to have an actor?
☐ 2.6.3.3. In what direction does the extend relationship point?
☐ 2.6.3.4. How many extension points can a use case define?
☐ 2.6.3.5. Does an extend relationship have to specify a condition?
☐ 2.6.3.6. Does an extended use case have to have an actor?

Metamodel

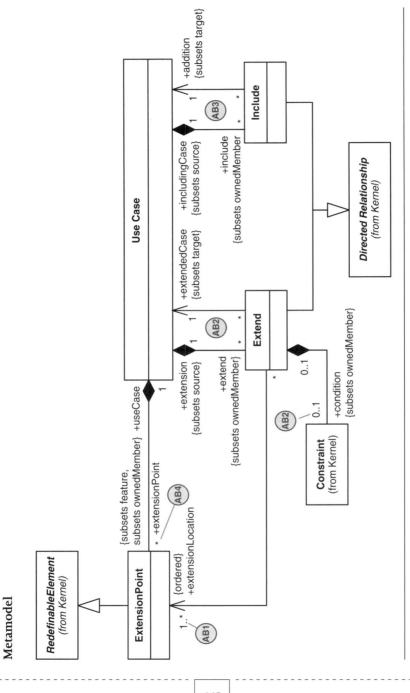

FIGURE 2.126 The metamodel for use case relationships.

112

3

CHAPTER THREE
OCUP INTERMEDIATE

3.1 COMPOSITE STRUCTURE DIAGRAMS

This chapter discusses a diagram form of UML 2.0 that was not around in UML 1x: composite structure diagrams.

A *composite structure diagram* describes the internal structure of things such as classes and components. Because UML is a very extensive language already, so that you may ask, "Why do we need yet another diagram form?"

To answer this question, let's look at the class diagram in Figure 3.1. This class diagram shows the simplified composition of a boat and a car. The boat consists of a propeller and an engine that drives the propeller. The car also consists of an engine, but it is driven by two wheels instead of a propeller. Altogether, the car has four wheels, namely, two front wheels and two rear wheels.

All of this looks pretty logical at first sight. But let's look at the object models in Figure 3.2, which can result from the class diagram in Figure 3.1.

We leave it up to the playful reader to think of more unhappy constellations (e.g., a car with an engine that drives the two left wheels).

How can such a situation be prevented? How can a modeler express which object relationships are valid and which ones are not? UML 1.x allowed us to write constraints in textual form. Formulated in a natural language, however, these constraints won't ensure uniqueness, and though an OCL expression would make them unique, they would be hardly readable. Visualizing structures is a strength of graphical languages, such as UML, versus purely textual languages.

This is where the composite structure diagram comes in handy. And now the name of this diagram form becomes clear. It is a diagram that represents the structure of compositions, that is, it shows the relationships of the parts to the whole.

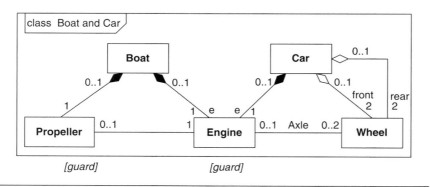

FIGURE 3.1 The Boat and Car class diagram [UML2.0].

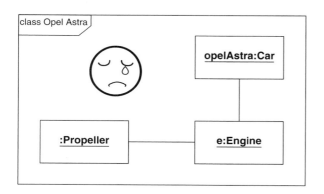

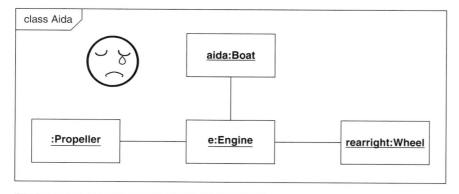

FIGURE 3.2 The Boat and Car object diagrams (unhappy constellation).

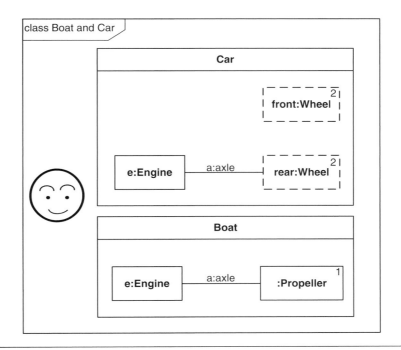

FIGURE 3.3   The Boat and Car composite structure diagram (happy constellation).

In Figure 3.3 we can see the internal composition of the classes *Car* and *Boat*. The car has an engine, *e*, that drives the two rear wheels. In addition, there are two front wheels. In the Boat context, the engine drives a propeller rather than wheels.

The frame line around front:*Wheel* and rear:*Wheel* is dashed because the car associates the wheels only by aggregation and not by composition (see Figure 3.1).

The composite structure diagram is more than a new diagram form; it is also a new model. In a separate chapter, the UML 2.0 specification defines metaclasses and relevant concepts, which are tested on the OCUP examination for the Intermediate certificate.

Figure 3.4 shows the packages of the metamodel in the area of composite structures, which are tested on the examination for the Intermediate certificate.

3.1.1   EXAMINATION TOPICS

The following topics are covered in the Intermediate test:

- Structured classifiers
- Connectable elements, connectors, connector ends, properties

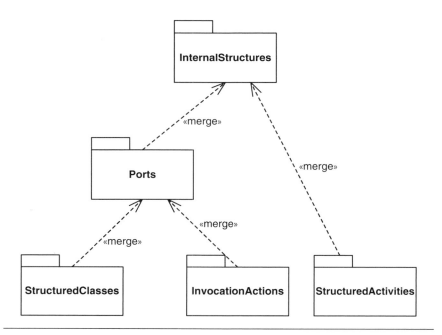

FIGURE 3.4   The package structure for composite structures.

- Ports and classes
- Invocation actions, triggers
- Collaborations
- Variables

This topic area constitutes 15 percent of the test.

3.1.2   STRUCTURED CLASSIFIERS

Definition

A *StructuredClassifier* is an abstract metaclass that represents classifiers with behavior   *3.1.2.1*
that can be described entirely or partly by the interplay of included or refer-
enced instances. Figure 3.5 shows the arrangement of the structured classifier
to the kernel classifier and a special version of the class (from Communication
package).

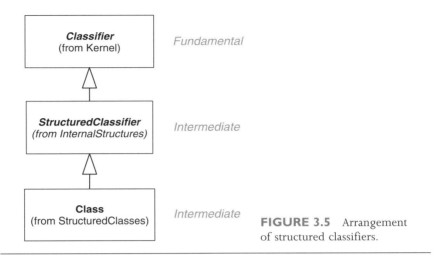

FIGURE 3.5   Arrangement of structured classifiers.

Notation and Semantics

3.1.2.2   The base class of a structured classifier is the classifier from the *Kernel* package. A specific subclass is, for example, the *Class* described in the package *StructuredClasses* in Figure 3.4.

A structured classifier is denoted like a regular classifier. However, it has an additional compartment, and the internal structure is denoted inside that compartment (see Figure 3.3).

3.1.2.3   A structured classifier owns or references properties and connectors. The properties it owns (by way of a composite relationship) are referred to as the *parts* of the structured classifier. In the metamodel (Figure 3.6) the term *part* is merely an association end. But it plays an important role and is used frequently.

CHECKLIST: STRUCTURED CLASSIFIERS

☐ 3.1.2.1.   What distinguishes a structured classifier from a regular classifier?
☐ 3.1.2.2.   Arrange the structured classifier within the generalization hierarchy of the metamodel. Show the immediate base classes and sub-classes.
☐ 3.1.2.3.   Explain the term *part*.

Metamodel

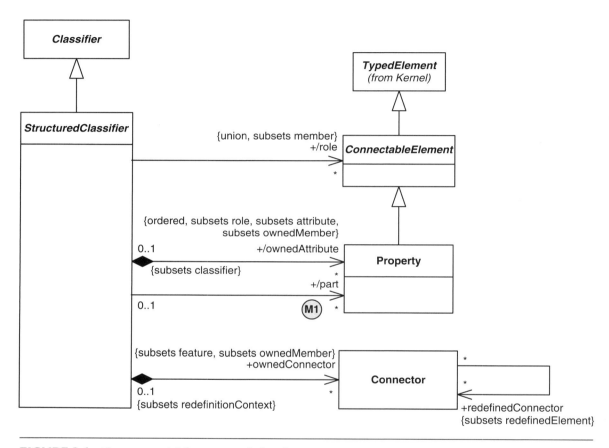

FIGURE 3.6 The metamodel for structured classifiers.

3.1.3 CONNECTABLE ELEMENTS

Definition

A *ConnectableElement* is an abstract metaclass that represents a set of instances that belong to a structured classifier. A connectable element can be attached by use of a connector.

A *connector* specifies a link between connectable elements.

A *connector end* attaches a connector to a connectable element.

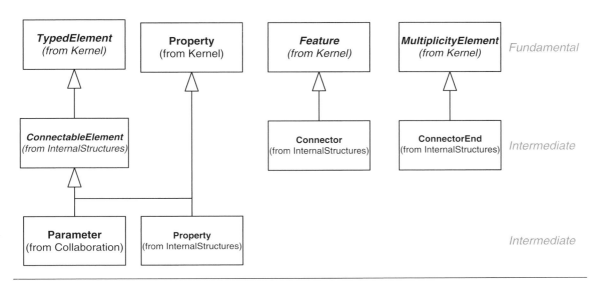

FIGURE 3.7 Arrangement of connectable elements, connectors, connector ends, and properties.

A *property* describes a set of instances that are owned by the instance of a classifier. In the context of composite structure diagrams, the model element from the Kernel package is extended (by use of the PackageMerge relationship) such that it obtains a generalization relationship to a connectable element. (See Figure 3.7.)

A *part* is the relationship for a property that is owned by a classifier through a composite relationship. Note that "part" is not a metamodel class, but an association end in the metamodel.

Notation and Semantics

3.1.3.1   A *ConnectableElement* is an abstract metaclass and has no notation of its own. A specific subclass is *property*. The notation of a property as a connectable element is similar to that of an object. At first, one could be mistaken for the other. A closer look reveals that distinctive difference: in contrast to an object, the name of a property is not underscored. The syntax is as follows:

```
name ':'[classifier]
```

where

- name is the name of the property, and
- classifier is the name of the type.

Stating the classifier in the diagram is not mandatory and can be omitted.

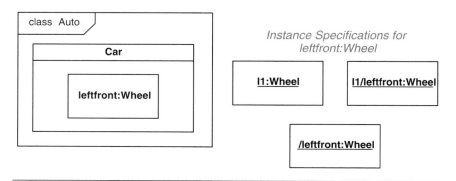

FIGURE 3.8   The syntax used to specify instances.

The multiplicity of the property can be denoted in the upper right corner. In Figure 3.3, for example, *Car* has two rear wheels and two front wheels.

The following syntax is used to specify an instance (Figure 3.8) of a connectable element:

```
{name ['/'role] | '/'role} [':' Classifier [','Classifier] *]
```

where

- `name` is the name of the specified instance,
- `role` is the name of the connectable element, and
- `classifier` is the name of the pertaining classifier.

Note that there can be more than one classifier.

A *connector* can be implemented as an instance of an association, but it can alternatively express that the attached connectable elements are able to communicate.   *3.1.3.2*

The base class is *Feature*. The connector itself is already a concrete class. There are no subclasses.

A *connector end* specifies the role of a connectable element. If a connector is typed   *3.1.3.3*
by an association, then anything that describes the association end can appear at the connector end.

The base class is *multiplicityElement*, while *ConnectorEnd* is a concrete class. There are no subclasses.

The multiplicities at the connector end and the connectable element have an   *3.1.3.4*
impact on the instantiation of the internal structures. We can see in Figure 3.9 that a connector links two properties, and both of them have multiplicity 2. If no multiplicities are stated at the connector ends, then the multiplicity of the respective connectable element is used as default. Figure 3.9 represents the *Star*

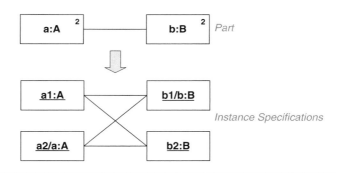

FIGURE 3.9   The Star Connector Pattern [UML2.0].

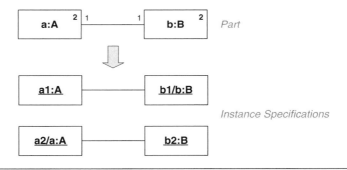

FIGURE 3.10   The Array Connector Pattern [UML2a].

Connector Pattern. Upon instantiation, every *a* is connected with exactly two *b*'s, and vice versa.

We can see that Figure 3.10 states multiplicities at the connector end. This means that every *a* is connected with exactly one *b*, and vice versa, resulting in the *Array Connector Pattern*.

The minimum of a connectable element's multiplicity states how many instances will initially be created; the maximum states how many instances can be created.

3.1.3.5   Note the difference between a part and a connectable element and between an instance specification and a classifier. A connectable element can be a property of the type Classifier. More specifically, it can be an attribute of a class, among other things. The instance specification represents an instance of the property.

The concepts of connectable elements, connectors, and connector ends correspond to the UML 1.x concepts of classifier roles, association roles, and association end roles (see Section 2.10 in UML 1.x for information about collaboration. [UML1]).

Metamodel

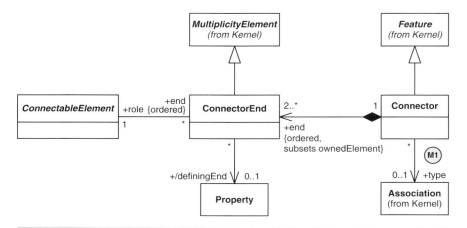

FIGURE 3.11 The metamodel for connectors.

CHECKLIST: CONNECTORS, CONNECTOR ENDS

☐ 3.1.3.1. List the characteristics and specific subclasses of a connectable element.

☐ 3.1.3.2. List the characteristics of a connector.

☐ 3.1.3.3. Explain the relation between a connector end and an association.

☐ 3.1.3.4. Explain the meaning of a multiplicity at a connector end and at a connectable element.

☐ 3.1.3.5. Explain the differences among a classifier, an instance specification, and a part.

3.1.4 PORTS AND CLASSES

Definition

A *port* is a special property of a classifier that specifies a single interaction point between the classifier and its environment or between the classifier and its internal parts.

An *encapsulated classifier* is a special *structured classifier* enhanced by the property to own ports.

A *class* in the context of composite structures is a special class enhanced by the properties to own internal structures and ports.

Figure 3.12 shows ports, encapsulated classifiers, and classes.

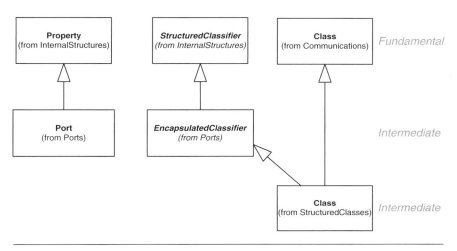

FIGURE 3.12   Arrangement of ports, encapsulated classifiers, and classes.

Notation and Semantics

3.1.4.1

3.1.4.2

A *port* is an interaction point between the pertaining classifier and its environment (see Figure 3.13). This means that requests addressing the classifier are directed to the port, which will then forward the request to the corresponding parts of that classifier. The entire process flows in the opposite direction from requests from the classifier to the environment. If the port forwards requests to the classifier itself rather than to parts of the classifier, then it is referred to as a behavioral port. A *behavioral port* is not a new metaclass, but a property of the port.

3.1.4.3

A port is a special property, which means that the port itself cannot implement interfaces. The interfaces that are allocated to a port are implemented by those classifiers that are the types, or supertypes, of the port. This is why the interfaces of a port are properties derived from that port.

The *ConnectableElement* is a base class of the port (via Property). That means the port can be connected with Connector. If more than one connector is attached to a port, it is a semantic variation point which connector is chosen (all, one, ...).

A port is denoted as a small rectangle on the boundary of the classifier it belongs to. The name and the type of the port are shown next to the rectangle (see Figure 3.14). Within a diagram, this statement is often incomplete (i.e., either without type or without type and name).

The interfaces provided over a port are denoted directly at the port (see Figure 3.15). As many interfaces (provided/required interfaces) as you like can be defined at a port.

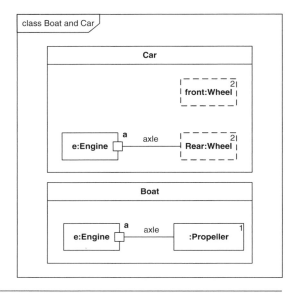

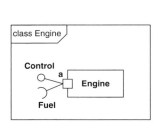

FIGURE 3.13 Ports within a composite structure diagram.

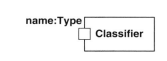

FIGURE 3.14 The notation for a port.

FIGURE 3.15 Interfaces at a port.

A behavioral port is connected to a small ellipse inside the classifier (see Figure 3.16).

Another property of a port, *isService*, is listed in the metamodel. A port is a service by definition. If *isService* is set to *false*, then this means that the port is part of the classifier's implementation and, as such, it is not public. In other words, it doesn't represent a service to the outside. Private ports (isService=false) are not shown on the border of the classifier, but completely inside of it (see Figure 3.17).

Neither the classifier from the Kernel package, nor a structured classifier, knows anything about ports. In order for a classifier to own a port, we have to expand the metamodel. An encapsulated classifier is a specialization of a structured classifier, and it is enhanced by exactly one property, namely, the property to own ports.

3.1.4.4

An encapsulated classifier is an abstract metaclass. A specific specialization is Class (see Figure 3.18).

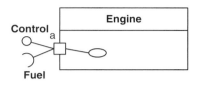

FIGURE 3.16   Example of a behavioral port.

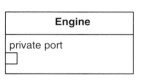

FIGURE 3.17   Private port (isService = false).

Metamodel

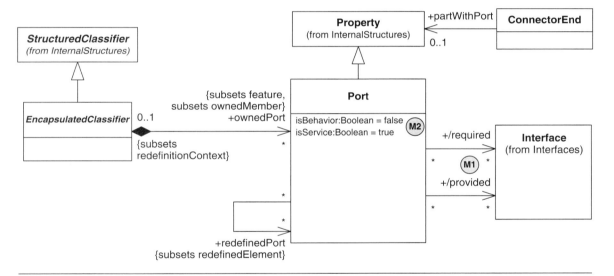

FIGURE 3.18   The metamodel for ports.

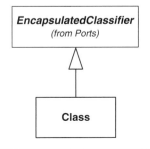

FIGURE 3.19   The metamodel for Class.

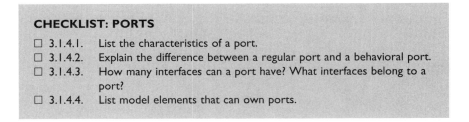

CHECKLIST: PORTS

☐ 3.1.4.1.   List the characteristics of a port.
☐ 3.1.4.2.   Explain the difference between a regular port and a behavioral port.
☐ 3.1.4.3.   How many interfaces can a port have? What interfaces belong to a port?
☐ 3.1.4.4.   List model elements that can own ports.

3.1.5   INVOCATION ACTIONS, TRIGGERS, AND VARIABLES

The port concept has an impact on other areas in the UML 2.0 specification, which will be discussed in this section in the context of composite structures (Figure 3.4).

Definition

An *invocation action* is an action that can call behavior at a port and it can state that a caller be forwarded over a specific port.

A *trigger* can describe the port at which the corresponding event occurred.

A *variable* is extended by the property of the corresponding connectable element. See Figure 3.20 for an illustration of these three terms.

Notation and Semantics

Invocation actions are discussed in detail in Section 3.4.3. For now it is sufficient to understand that it is an action that calls an operation or a behavior, for example, a state machine. The invocation can happen at a port. In this case, the metamodel class *InvocationAction* has to be extended.

3.1.5.1

If an invocation is forwarded over a port, then it is denoted in the form of (via <port>) (see Figure 3.21). This time the "via" notation is not used since it has another meaning in state diagrams (entry/exit points).

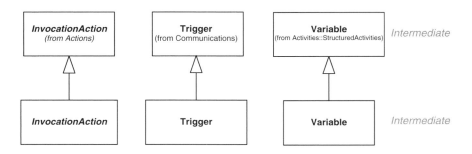

FIGURE 3.20   Arrangement of invocation actions, triggers, and variables.

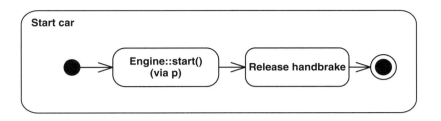

FIGURE 3.21   Invoking an operation via a port.

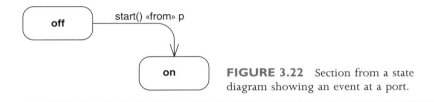

FIGURE 3.22   Section from a state diagram showing an event at a port.

3.1.5.2   Similarly to invocations, triggers can arrive via a port. For this purpose, the metamodel class Trigger is extended (see Figure 3.22).

3.1.5.3   Variables are defined in the context of structured activity nodes in activity models (see Section 3.5.5). They are simply extended by the property of being a connectable element here.

Metamodel

FIGURE 3.23   The metamodel for invocation actions and triggers.

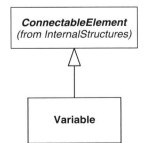

FIGURE 3.24   The metamodel for variables.

3.1.6   COLLABORATION

Unfortunately, collaboration has been leading a shadowy existence in UML. Although the element has existed in UML 1.x, it has been used rarely and only few UML tools support it.

The purpose of collaboration is the modeling of elements that cooperate to implement a certain functionality, for example, the interplay of classes to implement the behavior of a use case. A synonym for *collaboration* is *use case realization*, though this is not the only use for collaboration.

Definition

A *collaboration* is a special structured classifier that describes the structure of elements that jointly implement a certain behavior.

A *collaboration use* describes the use of a collaboration in a specific situation.

A *parameter* in the context of a collaboration is extended by the property of being a connectable element.

See Figure 3.25 for an illustration of these three terms.

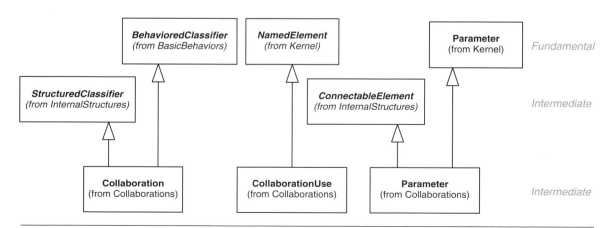

FIGURE 3.25   Arrangement of collaborations, collaboration uses, and parameters.

Notation and Semantics

3.1.6.1   A *collaboration* is a special view of a set of elements with regard to the implementation of a specified behavior. The elements are the properties of the collaboration and, together, assume a certain role with regard to the implementation of the behavior. The connectors contained in the collaboration represent the communication paths between the roles.

Several collaborations can reference the same set of elements. They represent different views of these elements.

A collaboration is denoted as a dashed ellipse. Within the ellipse, there is a compartment for the names and another one for the internal structure (see Figure 3.26).

3.1.6.2   A *collaboration use* (see Figure 3.27) represents the implementation of a pattern
3.1.6.3   described by a collaboration in a specific situation. In this context, *role binding* means that the roles in the collaboration are bound by concrete elements.

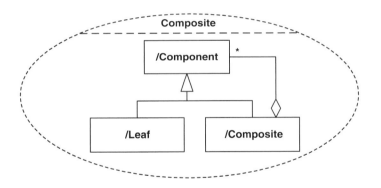

FIGURE 3.26   Example showing the notation for a collaboration.

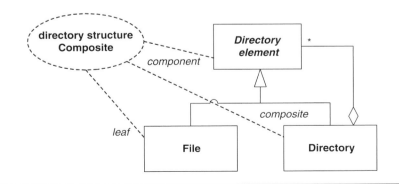

FIGURE 3.27   Notation and example of a collaboration use.

Metamodel

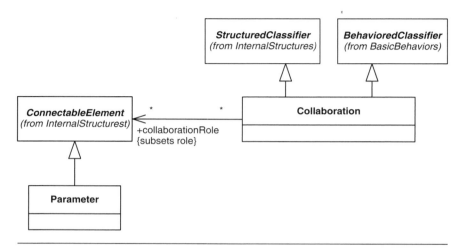

FIGURE 3.28 The metamodel for collaborations.

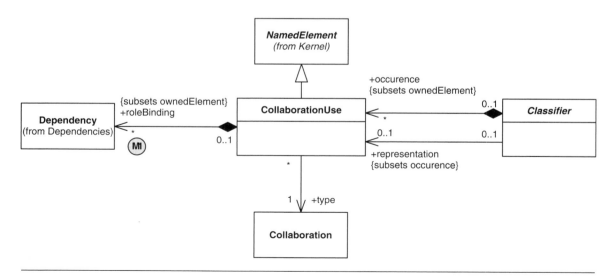

FIGURE 3.29 The metamodel for collaboration uses.

3.2 COMPONENT DIAGRAMS

This section discusses a diagram form and a model that both have been heavily revised for UML 2. UML 1.x and UML 2 had a different understanding of components. You will see that the new definition corresponds to the current general understanding of components. Therefore, the significance of component diagrams for the practice will increase.

3.2.1   EXAMINATION TOPICS

The following issues are covered in the Intermediate test:

- Components
- Connectors
- Realization

This topic area constitutes 15 percent of the test.

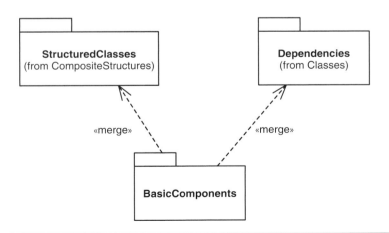

FIGURE 3.30   The package structure for components.

3.2.2 COMPONENTS

The term *component* is one of the "monster words" frequently used in projects but generally not defined in a unique way. In projects that use UML 1.x the problem is complicated because the component definition in UML 1.x deviates from the general understanding of components.

The component definition of UML 1.x has been revised for UML 2, so that components as defined in UML 2 can be used according to the common understanding of components.

Definition

A *component* is a special class that represents a replaceable unit in a system, the parts of which are encapsulated.

A component provides its public functionality over interfaces to the outside. Functionality required from the outside is also defined via interfaces.

A *realization* relationship specifies the classifiers that implement the contract of a component in the form of provided and requested interfaces.

Figure 3.31 illustrates these two terms.

Notation and Semantics

What makes a component? What is a replaceable unit? What is a component composed of?

A *component* is composed of classifiers, or more specifically, is implemented by classifiers. It is an abstraction of the implementing classifiers, but not a grouping element in the sense that the classifiers are contained in the component. Figure 3.32 shows the relationship in the metamodel. The realization relationship from the Dependencies package is extended in the context of components in order to restrict the realization to classifiers.

3.2.2.1

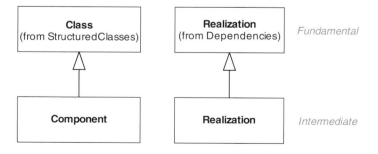

FIGURE 3.31 Arrangement of components and realization relationships.

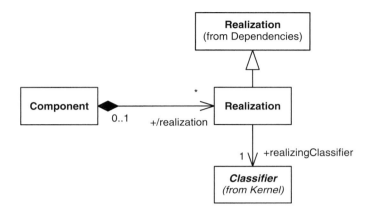

FIGURE 3.32 Section of the metamodel for classifiers that implement components.

A component is a special structured class. Therefore the component can own properties and operations. The internal structure of its properties is modeled in a composite structure diagram. Note that the implementing classifiers of a component do not have to be a property of the component; that is, they cannot be modeled in a composite structure diagram.

The UML 2 notation for components has changed since UML 1.x. In UML 1.x, a component was denoted in the form of a "Lego" building block.

In contrast, UML 2 components inherit the notation from their base class, the (structured) Class. To preserve some recognizable feature of UML 1.x, the old symbol can optionally be denoted in the upper right corner. The keyword *component* is written above the component's name. You can see the notation of a UML 2 component in Figure 3.33.

The notation for the extended realization relationship is a dashed arrow (see Figure 3.34).

3.2.2.2   Alternatively, the classifiers that realize the component can also be represented within the component (see Figure 3.35). This representation is very intuitive. However, looking at it superficially, there is a risk of mistaking it for a composite structure diagram.

FIGURE 3.33 The UML 2 notation for components with interfaces.

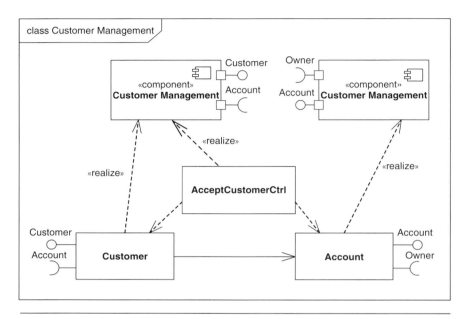

FIGURE 3.34   Notational example of a realization relationship between classifiers and components.

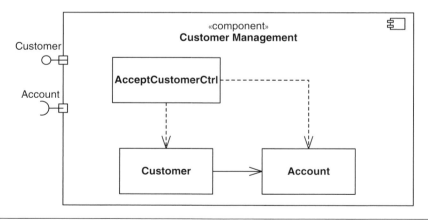

FIGURE 3.35   A structure diagram showing components with realized classifiers.

This alternative representation is called a *structure diagram*. It shows all regular relationships between the realized classifiers (association, generalization, and so on) as well as dependency relationships and can be used for mapping the *external view* (also referred to as *black-box view*) to the *internal view* (also referred to as *white-box view*).

Compared to the structure diagram, however, the composite structure diagram is more expressive because it lets you use parts and connectors. The composite structure diagram is also an internal view of the component.

3.2.2.3   **Usage relationship.** The interfaces provided by a component are implemented either by the component itself or by the realized classifiers, or they are the type of one of the classifiers' ports. Accordingly, requested interfaces either are the type of a port or they are used by the component itself or by one of its realized classifiers, in which case we speak of a *usage relationship*. This means that the interfaces of a component can be derived, a fact shown in the metamodel by a preceding slash,/ (see Figure 3.39).

A more compact representation of a component is the table notation. A *table notation* lists the realized classifiers and the interfaces by compartment with the classifier symbol (see Figure 3.36). In addition, it lists artifacts in a separate compartment (see Section 3.8.2).

What is a component at runtime? How would you implement a component in Java or C++? The answer is that it's impossible to directly implement a component in a common programming language because programming languages don't know anything about the component concept. Their largest building block is a class or object. This shows that UML 2 hasn't been designed solely for software development, but for other things, too, such as systems engineering [Weilkiens2006] and business process modeling [Oestereich2004c].

3.2.2.4   UML 2 offers two variants for component instantiating: direct and indirect instantiation. An *indirectly instantiated component* is represented only by its realized classifiers or their instances at runtime. This corresponds to the implementation possible in programming languages. With a *direct instantiation*, an instance of the component is available in addition to the instances of the realized classifiers at runtime. This cannot be implemented when using one of the common

FIGURE 3.36   A table notation representing a component.

programming languages. The property *isIndirectlyInstantiated* of the component is used to specify which of the two variants is to be applied. The default is *true*; that is, indirect instantiation is used.

A component can also serve as a grouping element. This property is described in the package *PackagingComponents*, but because it is part of the Advanced certification, we won't discuss it further here.

UML 2 defines several standard stereotypes for components. The most impor- *3.2.2.5* tant standard stereotype is "*subsystem*". UML 1.x has a metaclass called *Subsystem* (Figure 3.37), which is a specialization of Package and Classifier. In practice, the UML 1.x subsystem is scarcely used. The practical delimitation to packages and components is unclear, and this point is subject to many discussions.

The metaclass Subsystem no longer exists in UML 2. It has been replaced by a predefined standard stereotype for components. This stereotype describes a component that is a unit of the hierarchical decomposition of a larger system. Large systems are frequently structured in a system-subsystems-components hierarchy. This means that a subsystem is the first hierarchical level below System. However, UML 2 leaves the exact use intentionally open.

In general, a subsystem is indirectly instantiated and divided into specification and *3.2.2.6* implementation elements. This division stems from the definition of the UML-1.x Subsystem. In addition, standard stereotypes have been defined for the two element types, namely, "*specification*" and "*realization*". Note, however, that these two stereotypes refer to classifiers in general rather than being limited to components only.

A specification classifier has only specifications and no implementation. In contrast, a realization classifier has implementing elements. (See Figure 3.38.)

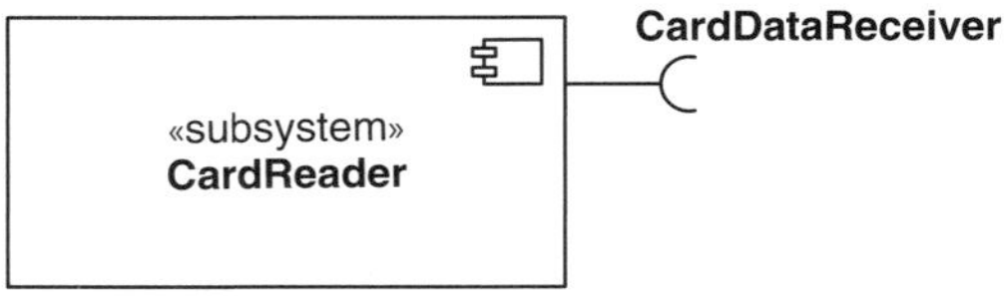

FIGURE 3.37 A subsystem example.

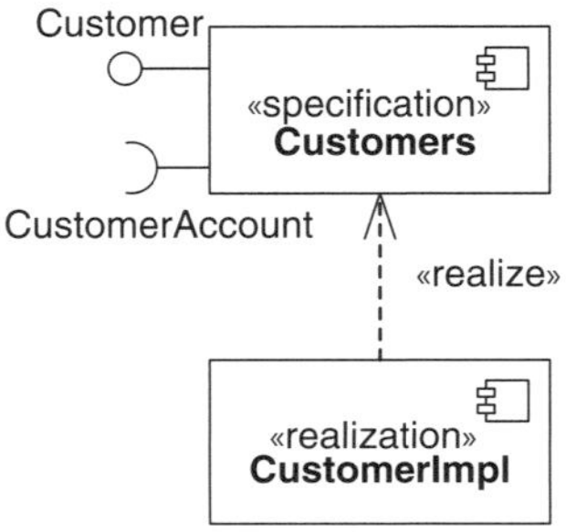

FIGURE 3.38 Specification and realization components.

Metamodel

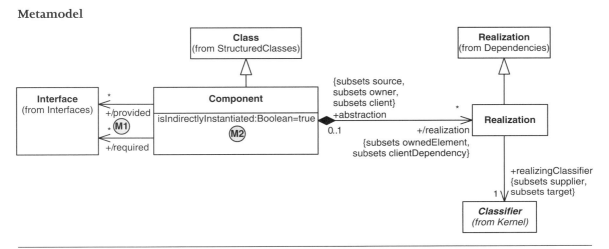

FIGURE 3.39 The metamodel for components.

CHECKLIST: COMPONENTS

- ☐ 3.2.2.1. What is a component composed of?
- ☐ 3.2.2.2. Explain the relationships among a component, a structure diagram, and a composite structure diagram.
- ☐ 3.2.2.3. Explain the relationships among a component, an interface, and a port.
- ☐ 3.2.2.4. Explain the property *isIndirectlyInstantiated* of a component.
- ☐ 3.2.2.5. List the characteristics of a subsystem.
- ☐ 3.2.2.6. Explain the stereotypes "specification" und "realization".

3.2.3   CONNECTORS

This section extends the connector concept described in Section 3.1.3 in the context of components.

Definition

A *delegation connector* is used to connect an externally visible port with the internal part of a component that implements or uses interfaces that are provided or requested.

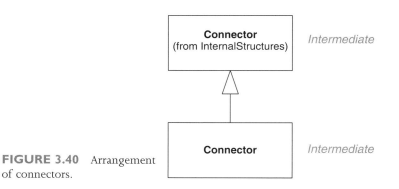

FIGURE 3.40 Arrangement of connectors.

An *assembly connector* is used to connect two components, where one component requests an interface and the other component provides that interface.

Figure 3.40 shows an arrangement of connectors.

Notation and Semantics

A *component* is a special structured class; it can own parts, and the composition of these parts can be specified in composite structure diagrams.

The connector concept has been extended for components. The new metaclass *Connector* is located in the package *BasicComponents*. This metaclass defines two types of connector: a *delegation connector* and an *assembly connector*. The desired connector type is specified in the property *kind* of the metaclass Connector (see Figure 3.43).

A *delegation connector* takes an invocation that arrived at a port and forwards it to the appropriate part of a component. In contrast, invocations of parts are forwarded via the delegation connector to ports and from there to the component's environment. If a delegation connector is connected with more than one subordinated port, requests will be delivered to all of them that support the request.

3.2.3.1

A delegation connector is denoted as a solid arrow from the port to the realizing part or in the opposite direction (see Figure 3.41). The keyword *delegate* is stated near the arrow.

An *assembly connector* links two parts, where one part offers a service and the other part requests that service. The type of service is specified in the interfaces of the pertaining classifiers. The assembly connector can alternatively be modeled between a port and a part.

3.2.3.2

The notation for an assembly connector shows a provided interface and a requested interface that engage with one another. Note that this actually represents one connector rather than two distinct interfaces, as the notation may suggest (see Figure 3.42).

3.2.3.3

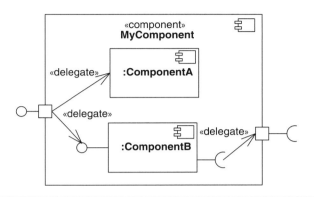

FIGURE 3.41 Notational example of delegation connectors.

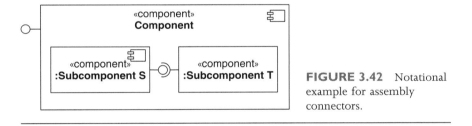

FIGURE 3.42 Notational example for assembly connectors.

Metamodel

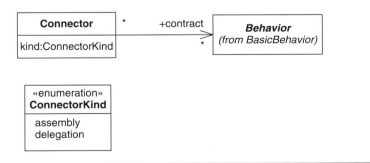

FIGURE 3.43 The metamodel for assembly connectors.

CHECKLIST: ASSEMBLY CONNECTORS

☐ 3.2.3.1.   List the characteristics of a delegation connector. What elements does a delegation connector link?

☐ 3.2.3.2.   List the characteristics of an assembly connector. What elements does an assembly connector link?

☐ 3.2.3.3.   Look at the symbols for a provided interface and a requested interface that engage with one another. How many model elements are there and how are they called?

3.3 BEHAVIOR BASICS

This section discusses the basics for the representation and description of general behavior in UML (see Figure 3.44) to the extent relevant for the Intermediate OCUP test. The following sections explain special aspects of behavior in the context of various diagram types.

3.3.1   EXAMINATION TOPICS

The following topics will be tested in the Intermediate test:

- The *Communications* package
- The *SimpleTime* package

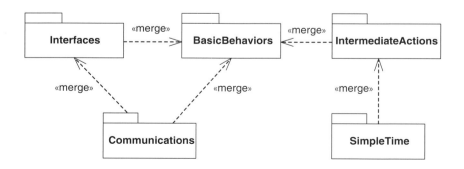

FIGURE 3.44   The CommonBehaviors package structure.

3.3.2 COMMUNICATIONS

The package *Communications* contains concepts used to let objects communicate and to invoke behavior.

Definition and Semantics

3.3.2.1   Behavior in UML is event oriented by definition. The execution of behavior (see Figure 3.45) is always triggered by an event. In turn, new events may happen during each execution of behavior. Two particular events occur always: the *start occurrence* and the *termination occurrence*.

3.3.2.2   Behavior can be started directly, in which case it is called *CallBehaviorOccurrence*, or indirectly by a trigger (*TriggerOccurrence*), for example, when a time event or a signal event is reached, or when a *ChangeEvent* occurs because a value has been changed. In an indirect behavior call, the event is stored in an *EventPool*, which is assigned to the classifier. How these events will eventually be processed depends on the specification of the classifier and the form of behavior description.

UML logically separates the call and the execution of behavior. Upon a call, a *request* object is created and transmitted to the receiver that should execute the behavior. Figure 3.45 shows a schematic view of this scenario. The sender and the receiver can be the same object or different objects. No statement is made as to the form of transmission, its duration, the transmission path, or the sequence in which several requests are to be received.

Upon receipt of a request, the receiver creates a *ReceiveOccurrence*, which can cause a behavior to execute. This behavior is then executed in the context of the receiver (*host*). Information about the sender can be deduced from the request object.

The notation model for behavior calls is shown in Figure 3.46.

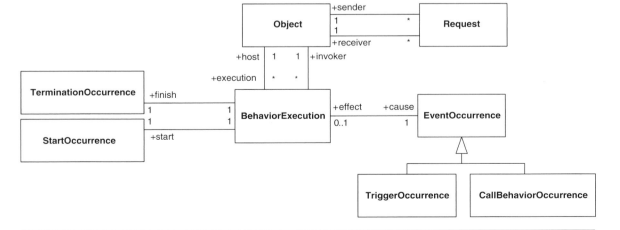

FIGURE 3.45 The notational model for executing behavior.

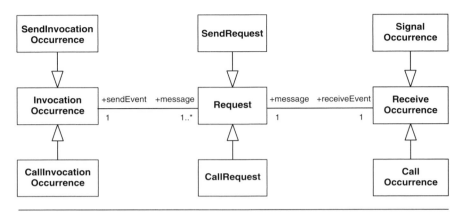

FIGURE 3.46   The notational model for behavior calls.

FIGURE 3.47   The notation for an active class.

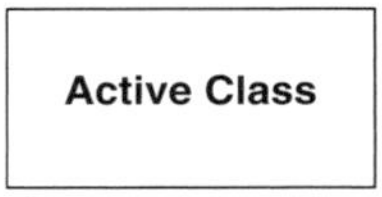

The Class in the package Communications is extended by the property to receive signals. A *signal* is the specification of a communication object, for example, *MouseSignal*, with attribute values for the current screen coordinates, such as "Left key pressed?", and so on. The metaclass Reception is a declaration saying that a classifier is ready to receive signals.

A class that can receive signals is frequently an active class. This means in general that the class has its own *thread of control*.

3.3.2.3

The notation for an active class is shown in Figure 3.47.

The class *Reception* (see Figure 3.48) is a specialization of *BehavioralFeature*, which is extended by the property to specify concurrent executions in more detail (see Figure 3.49). *CallConcurrencyKind* is a class that defines three categories. If the concurrency is not to be managed, you state *sequential*. To specify that the behavioral feature can be executed concurrently, you state *concurrent*; and finally, stating *guarded* means that the behavioral feature can be invoked concurrently, but only one invocation at a time.

Events are also defined in the package Communications. UML knows five types of event, which are briefly explained next. (See Figure 3.50.)

3.3.2.4

AnyReceiveEvent refers to a transition trigger (see Section 3.7.2). This event always occurs when a message is received, provided that this message does not trigger another transition originating from the same state node. (See Figure 3.51.)

A *CallEvent* occurs when the specified operation is invoked.

A *ChangeEvent* occurs when something has changed in the system. The change is formulated by a Boolean expression, which becomes *true* at the specified change.

A *SignalEvent* occurs when the specified signal is received.

TimeEvent refers to an absolute or relative time statement. A relative time event always refers to a trigger, and the time measurement starts from the trigger's activation. The syntax for a relative time statement is `after <expression>`.

An absolute time event is activated as soon as the specified time is reached. The syntax is `at <expression>`.

Metamodel

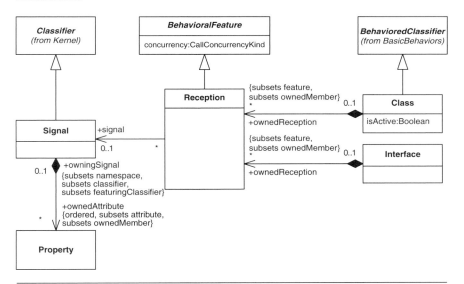

FIGURE 3.48 The metamodel for receptions.

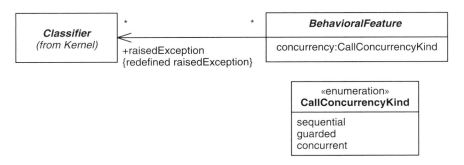

FIGURE 3.49 Extending a behavioral feature.

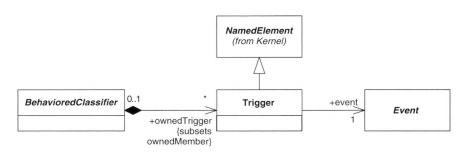

FIGURE 3.50 The metamodel for events.

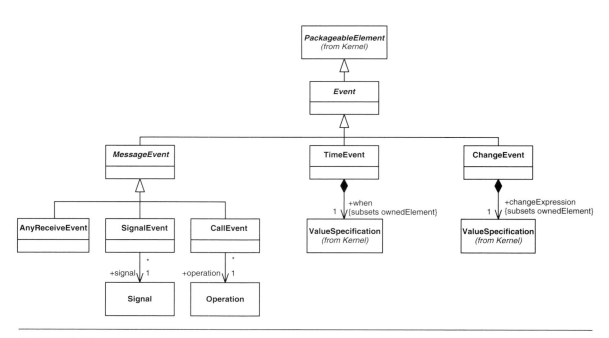

FIGURE 3.51 The metamodel for triggers.

CHECKLIST: COMMUNICATIONS

☐ 3.3.2.1.   How is the execution of behavior triggered?
☐ 3.3.2.2.   What are the two possibilities of invoking behavior?
☐ 3.3.2.3.   What is an active class?
☐ 3.3.2.4.   Explain the different kinds of UML event.

3.3.3   THE SIMPLETIME MODEL

UML keeps the time model simple, not dealing with issues like, for example, clocks with limited resolution. Specific requirements like these have to be supported by UML profiles for the corresponding fields of application (e.g., real-time applications).

Definition and Semantics

The *SimpleTime* model of UML 2 includes elements to describe the time as well as elements for time constraints and time measurements (see Figure 3.52).

3.3.3.1   The central element is *TimeExpression*, which describes an absolute time value. It is a specialization of *ValueSpecification*. The time value can be defined for instance by an implementation-specific character string. Moreover, there is a way to reference an event–the beginning or end of this event is described by the time expression (using the attribute firstTime). Similarly, the duration can also be described.

3.3.3.2   An interval can be described for both elements: *TimeInterval* and *DurationInterval*. Note that the constraints of the time model also refer to these intervals, ensuring a certain interval size.

3.3.3.3   Two actions are used in the time model: *TimeObservationAction* is an action that measures the time, and *DurationObservationAction* is an action that measures a duration.

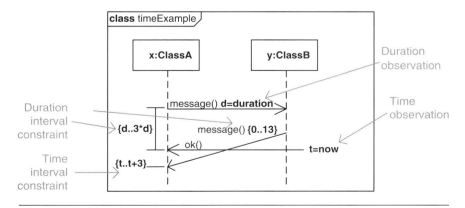

FIGURE 3.52   Example of time observations and time constraints.

Metamodel

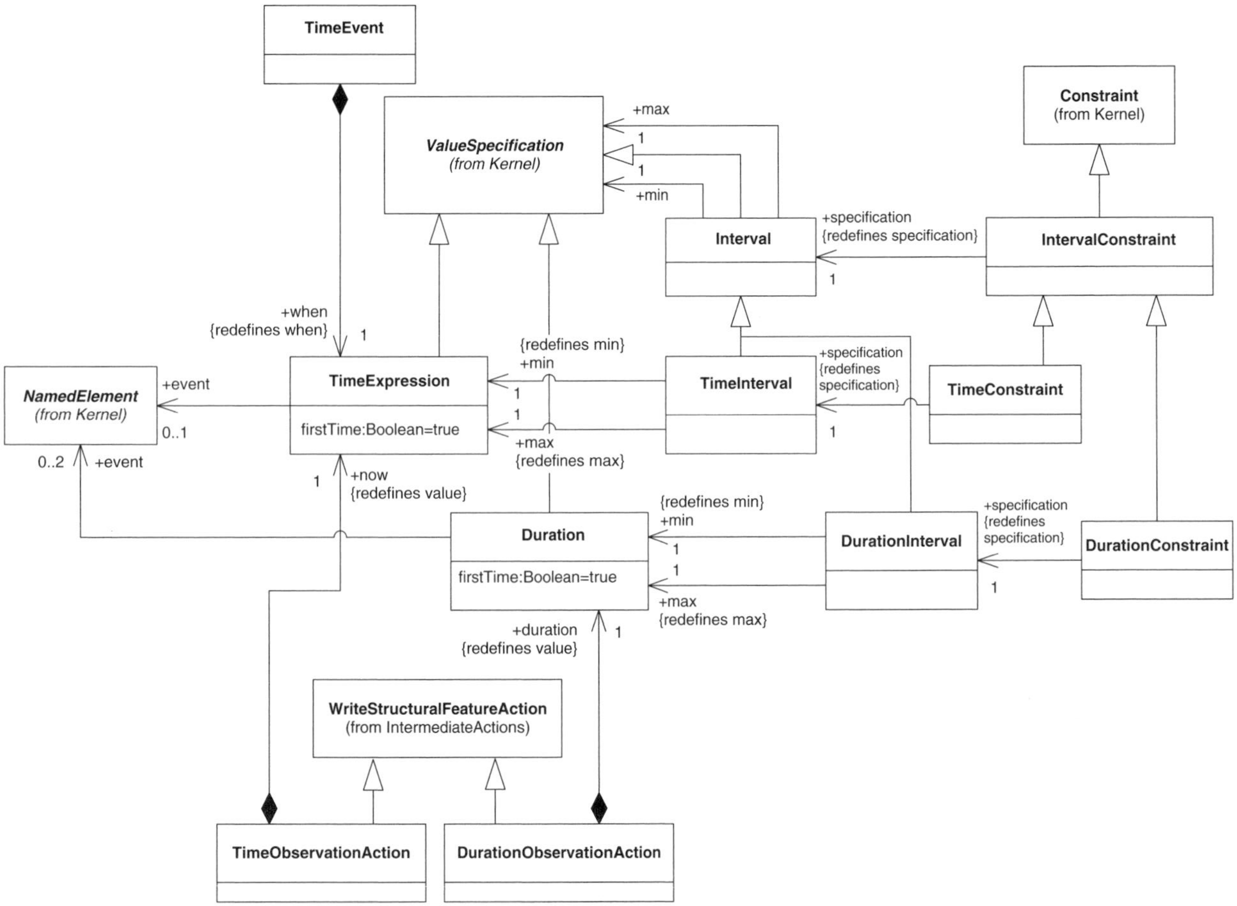

FIGURE 3.53 The metamodel for SimpleTime.

CHECKLIST: THE TIME MODEL

☐ 3.3.3.1.   How is the execution of behavior triggered?
☐ 3.3.3.2.   What time intervals can be specified?
☐ 3.3.3.3.   Explain the actions used in the time model.

3.4 ACTION MODELS

This section discusses action models, which are jointly referred to as *Action Semantic*. The word *diagram* is not used here because, in fact, they are really just models. Action models had been included in the UML 1.5 Specification, but they have enjoyed little attention and use in practice, since no notation had been defined for them.

The action model has been revised in UML 2. In particular, there is now a defined notation for the action model. Actions have been integrated in the activity model. The single actions of an activity are the actions from the action model defined here.

Since the definition of single actions reflects primarily in the metamodel and to a lesser extent in diagrams, we use more figures from the metamodel in this section to better explain actions.

The names of most of the elementary actions are self-explanatory, as you can see in Figure 3.54.

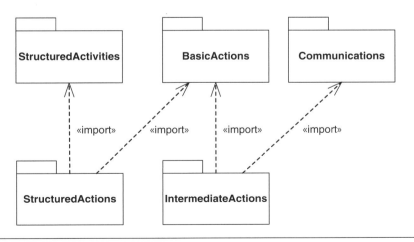

FIGURE 3.54   The package structure for actions.

3.4.1   EXAMINATION TOPICS

The Intermediate test does not cover the full set of actions defined in UML 2. All actions discussed in this section are tested in the Intermediate examination; actions not discussed in this section are part of the Advanced certification.

The package *BasicActions* belongs to the first Compliance Level in UML 2, and parts of it are tested for the Fundamental certification.

The following topics are covered in the Intermediate test:

- *InvocationAction*
- *OpaqueAction*
- *ObjectAction*
- *StructuralFeatureAction*
- *LinkAction*
- *VariableAction*

Other actions from the package *IntermediateActions*

This topic area constitutes 10 percent of the test.

3.4.2   ACTIONS

Actions are actually part of the Fundamental certification. However, since Action is the base class for all actions, it is important to fully understand the concept. For this reason, we revisit the metaclass in this section.

Definition

An *action* is an elementary unit that describes executable behavior (see Figure 3.55).

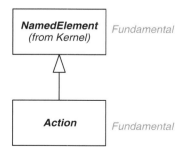

FIGURE 3.55   Arrangement of actions.

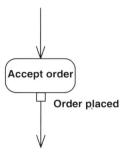

FIGURE 3.56 Example of an action with an output pin.

Notation and Semantics

3.4.2.1   *Action* is the abstract base class for all actions. An action is denoted as a rectangle with rounded corners. Input and output pins are used to specify the input and output arguments for an action. Figure 3.56 shows an action with an output pin, representing a section of an activity. The action shown in this example is a *CallBehaviorAction* (see Section 3.4.3).

Metamodel

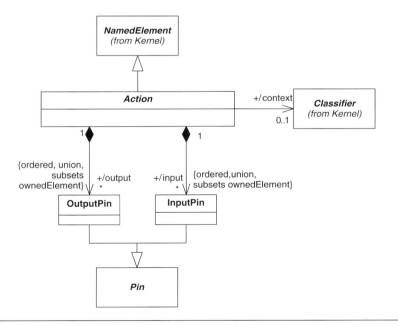

FIGURE 3.57 The metamodel for actions.

CHECKLIST: ACTIONS

☐ 3.4.2.1. List the characteristics and notation of an action.

3.4.3 INVOCATION ACTIONS

Invocation actions (see Figure 3.58) cause behavior to execute. A behavior is either called (by a *CallAction*) or triggered by sending signals or objects.

Definition

InvocationAction is the abstract superclass for actions that invoke behavior or operations or that send signals or objects.

CallAction is the abstract superclass for actions that invoke a behavior or an operation.

CallBehaviorAction is an action that invokes behavior directly. The arguments of the action are passed to the called behavior.

CallOperationAction is an action that invokes an operation at a specified object. The arguments of *CallOperationAction* are passed to the operation.

SendSignalAction is an action that takes the input parameters to create a signal instance, which it then sends to the specified object.

BroadcastSignalAction is an action that takes the input parameters to create a signal instance and then broadcasts this signal instance to many objects.

SendObjectAction is an action that sends an object to the specified object.

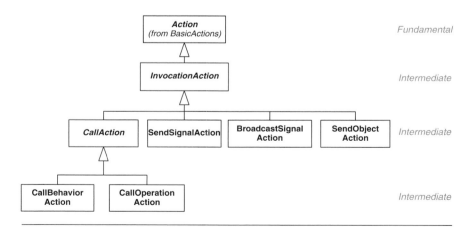

FIGURE 3.58 Arrangement of invocation actions.

Notation and Semantics

3.4.3.1   *InvocationAction* is an abstract superclass, and its only property is to own a set of input pins for input arguments.

3.4.3.2   There is another abstract superclass one hierarchical level below *InvocationAction*: the abstract *CallAction* stands for actions that invoke behavior or an operation directly (see Figure 3.59). A call action can be synchronous or asynchronous, and it owns a set of output pins, which accept the return parameters. An asynchronous call action has no return parameters.

3.4.3.3   *CallBehaviorAction* is a concrete specialization of *CallAction* (see Figure 3.60). It invokes a behavior, for example, an activity or a state machine. In contrast to *CallOperationAction*, which is explained a bit later, this action invokes the behavior directly, without using a behavioral feature, such as an operation.

A call behavior action inherits the notation from its superclass, *Action*. The name of the behavior to be invoked appears in the rounded rectangle (see Figure 3.61).

3.4.3.4   One distinct particularity is the invocation of an activity. In this case, a fork is denoted in the lower right corner. The shape symbolizes a hierarchical structure. When an action that is within an activity invokes that activity, then this is to be

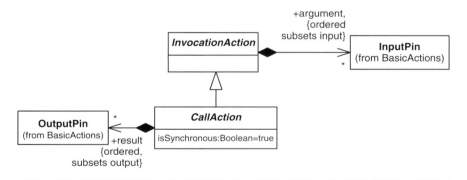

FIGURE 3.59   The metamodel for call actions.

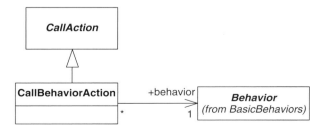

FIGURE 3.60   The metamodel for call behavior actions.

FIGURE 3.61   The notation for call behavior actions.

seen as a kind of decomposition (see Figure 3.62). The notation originated in UML 1.x, where it has a similar meaning.

In contrast to call behavior actions, *CallOperationAction* is an action that invokes a behavioral feature, or more specifically, an operation, rather than invoking behavior directly. A call operation action inherits its property to own input and output parameters from the abstract base class *CallAction*. In addition, a call operation action specifies the operation to be called and obtains the object, at which the operation is called upon execution, via an input pin.

3.4.3.5

The notation for call operation actions (see Figure 3.63) is similar to that of call behavior actions, except that the action symbol shows the name of the operation to be called and perhaps the name of the pertaining classifier, instead of showing a behavior. It is also possible to choose a name for a call operation action that differs from the operation (see Figure 3.64).

The classifier to be specified is the one within the context of which the operation is defined. The object the call operation action receives via the input pin must be of a type compatible with the classifier.

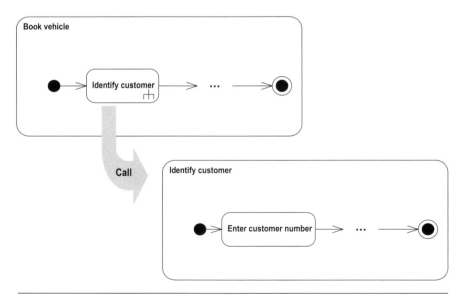

FIGURE 3.62   Invoking an activity.

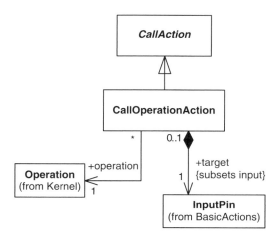

FIGURE 3.63   The metamodel for call operation actions.

FIGURE 3.64   The notation for call operation actions.

Call actions invoke a behavior or an operation directly. The other three invocation actions are different. A behavior is invoked indirectly when a signal or an object is sent. The sender cannot determine the kind of behavior. The receiver is solely responsible for the kind of behavior.

3.4.3.6   *SendSignalAction* is an action that sends a signal object to a specified receiver object. The signal object is created by the send signal action from the input arguments. The receiver object is identified via an input pin (see *target* association end in Figure 3.65). The transmission of a signal is always asynchronous, which means that it has no return parameters.

A send signal action is denoted by an arrow that symbolizes the transmission. The name of the signal is shown inside the arrow (see Figure 3.66). This symbol was used in UML 1.x, which also allows you to send signals in activity models.

3.4.3.7   Rather than send it to one specified receiver object, a *BroadcastSignalAction* broadcasts a signal object to a large number of objects (see Figure 3.67). However, the

3.4.3.8   objects supposed to receive the signal object are not specified. Instead, a *semantic variation point* is used. UML 2 uses several semantic variation points, which means that UML 2 leaves the semantics intentionally open at this point. The interpretation is left up to the environment in which the model is used.

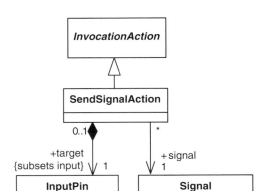

FIGURE 3.65 The metamodel for send signal actions.

FIGURE 3.66 The notation for send signal actions.

FIGURE 3.66 The notation for send signal actions.

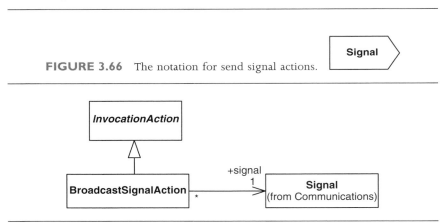

FIGURE 3.67 The metamodel for broadcast signal actions.

A broadcast signal action has no particular notation. It is simply represented like a regular action, in a rounded rectangle.

SendObjectAction is similar to a send signal action. It sends an object to a specified receiver object. It differs from a send signal action in two distinct ways: First, the transmitted object doesn't have to be a signal object; it can be an arbitrary object. Second, the object is not created by the action, but instead it is passed on to the send object action at an input pin (see Figure 3.68).

3.4.3.9

3.4.3.10

There is no particular notation for send object actions. However, there is one exceptional case: If all objects to be sent are signal objects, then the notation for send signal actions may be used. But be careful: In this case, the action looks exactly like a send signal action, and it actually sends signal objects, but these signal objects have to be passed on at the input pin and cannot be created by the action.

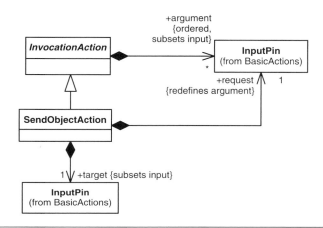

FIGURE 3.68   The metamodel for send object actions.

Metamodel

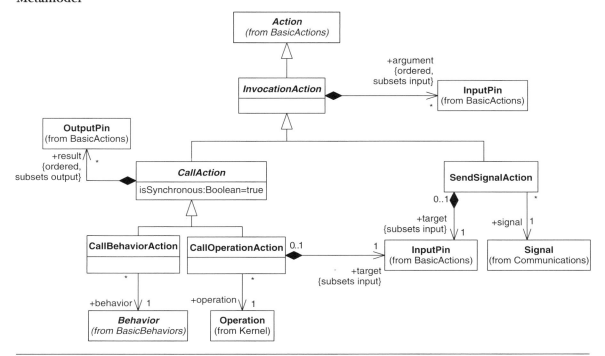

FIGURE 3.69   The metamodel for invocation actions from the BasicActions package.

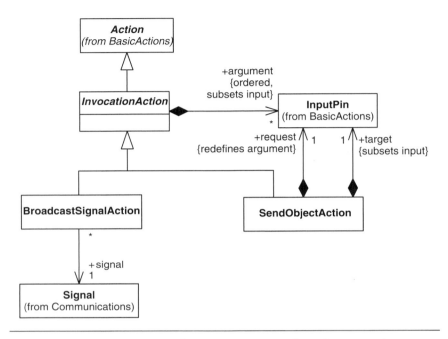

FIGURE 3.70 The metamodel for invocation actions from the IntermediateActions package.

CHECKLIST: INVOCATION ACTIONS

- ☐ 3.4.3.1. List the characteristics of an invocation action.
- ☐ 3.4.3.2. List the characteristics of a call action. Compare it with the UML call model (see Section 3.3.2).
- ☐ 3.4.3.3. List the characteristics of a call behavior action.
- ☐ 3.4.3.4. What does the fork in the notation for a call behavior action mean?
- ☐ 3.4.3.5. List the characteristics of a call operation action.
- ☐ 3.4.3.6. List the characteristics of a send signal action. Compare it with the UML call model (see Section 3.3.2).
- ☐ 3.4.3.7. List the characteristics of a broadcast signal action.
- ☐ 3.4.3.8. Explain the meaning of the semantic variation point in a broadcast signal action.
- ☐ 3.4.3.9. List the characteristics of a send object action.
- ☐ 3.4.3.10. Explain the difference between a send object action and a send signal action.

3.4.4   OPAQUE ACTIONS

Definition

An *OpaqueAction* is an action that executes implementation-specific instructions.

Notation and Semantics

3.4.4.1   An opaque action specifies a set of language-specific instructions, including the language itself (Java, C#, OCL, a natural language, etc.).

This type of action has been introduced to enable the execution of instructions that are implementation specific or to set a temporary placeholder pending the final selection of an action. There is no particular notation for opaque actions.

Note: There is a major change in this area between the final UML 2.0 specification [UML2.0] and the draft version [UML2.0cert] on which the certification is still based. The latter specifies a PrimitiveFunction that describes a function in any language. The function just returns a value and doesn't change the model. The ApplyFunctionAction executes the PrimitiveFunction. This concept is replaced by the OpaqueAction in the final specification.

Metamodel

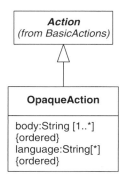

FIGURE 3.71   The metamodel for opaque actions.

CHECKLIST: OPAQUE ACTIONS

☐ 3.4.4.1.   List the characteristics of and the motivation for opaque actions.

3.4.5   OBJECT ACTIONS

Object actions are used to create and destroy objects. Moreover, there are object actions that check object identities and determine the object *self*.

Definition

CreateObjectAction is an action that creates an instance of the statically specified classifier and returns it via the output pin.

DestroyObjectAction is an action that destroys the object passed on via the input pin.

TestIdentityAction is an action that checks two objects to see whether they are identical.

ReadSelfAction is an action that retrieves the object to which the action belongs.

Figure 3.72 shows an arrangement of object actions.

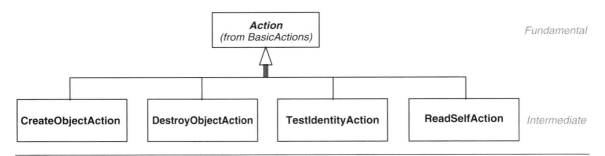

FIGURE 3.72 Arrangement of object actions.

Notation and Semantics

CreateObjectAction is an action that creates an instance of the specified classifier and supplies the result object at the output pin. The classifer may not be abstract. The action has no further impact. No initial values for structural features, such as attributes, are set, and the object does not obtain links (instances of an association), and no behavior is executed. This action cannot be used to create link objects (instances of association classes).   3.4.5.1 / 3.4.5.2

There is no particular notation for create object actions.   3.4.5.3

DestroyObjectAction is an action that destroys the object passed to it via the input pin. The action has no return values.

The two properties *isDestroyLinks* and *isDestroyOwnedObjects* control the behavior of an object as it is destroyed. If *isDestroyLinks* is set to *false* (default), then links in which the object participates won't be destroyed with the object. If this property is set to *true*, then all links are destroyed with the object.   3.4.5.4

Accordingly, objects owned by the object to be destroyed won't be destroyed if *isDestroyOwnedObjects* is set to *false* (default). If *isDestroyOwnedObjects* is set to *true*, then objects owned by the current object via composition will be destroyed with the object.   3.4.5.5

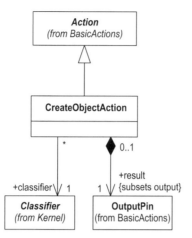

FIGURE 3.73 The metamodel for create object actions.

In contrast to create object actions, destroy object actions can process link objects. Where this is the case, the semantics corresponds to that of destroy link actions (see Section 3.4.7).

There is no particular notation for destroy object actions (See Figure 3.74).

3.4.5.6   *TestIdentityAction* is an action that has exactly two input values. Objects are passed via the two input pins, and the action checks the objects for identity. The Boolean result is supplied via the output pin.

There is no particular notation for test identity actions (see Figure 3.75).

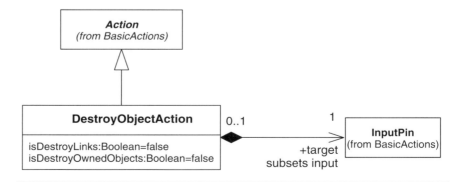

FIGURE 3.74 The metamodel for destroy object actions.

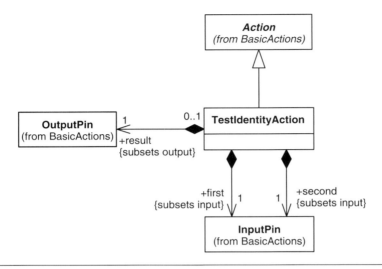

FIGURE 3.75 The metamodel for test identity actions.

ReadSelfAction is an action that retrieves the host object of an action. Each action   *3.4.5.7*
is part of an activity. The activity can be assigned to a classifier (*host classifier*), for
example, as the body of a method or part of a state machine.

A read self action returns the classifier object, if there is one. Otherwise, it   *3.4.5.8*
retrieves the activity object. An activity is a special behavior that, in turn, is a
special class.

There is no particular notation for read self actions (see Figure 3.76).

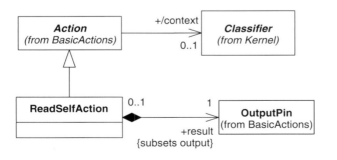

FIGURE 3.76 The metamodel for read self actions.

Metamodel

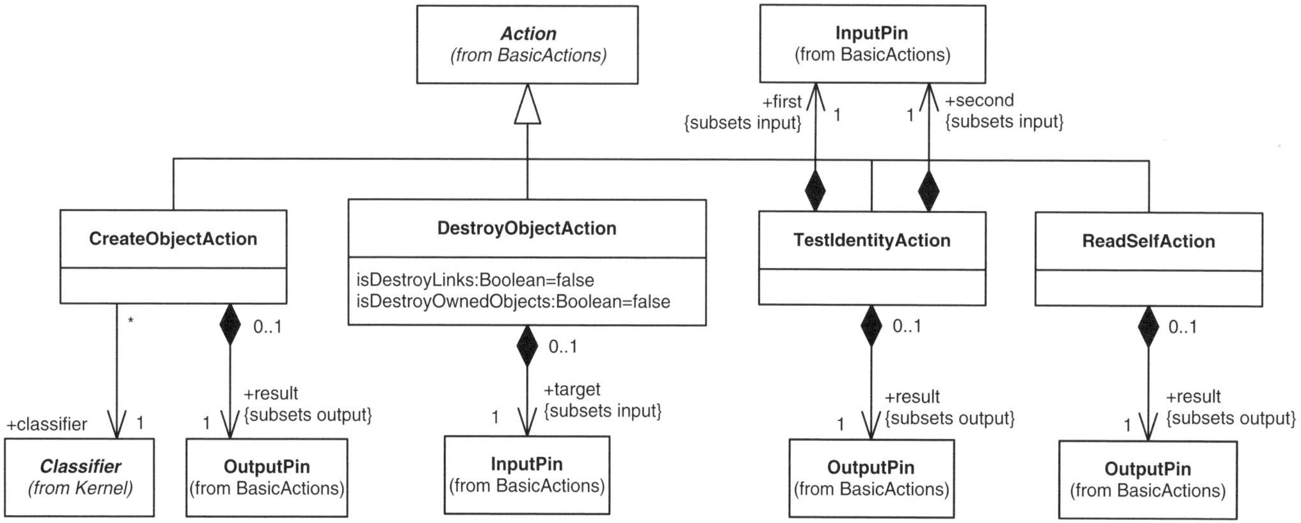

FIGURE 3.77 The metamodel for object actions.

163

3.4.6   STRUCTURAL FEATURE ACTIONS

Structural feature actions are actions used to read, write, and delete structural feature values.

Definition
StructuralFeatureAction is an abstract superclass. It describes actions that operate on static structures of classifiers.

ReadStructuralFeatureAction is an action that reads the value of a structural feature.

ClearStructuralFeatureAction is an action that deletes all values of a structural feature.

WriteStructuralFeatureAction is an abstract superclass for actions that change values of structural features.

AddStructuralFeatureValueAction is an action that adds values to a structural feature.

RemoveStructuralFeatureValueAction is an action that removes a value from a structural feature.

Figure 3.78 shows the arrangement of structural feature actions.

Notation and Semantics
StructuralFeatureAction is an abstract class that combines the common features of structural feature actions. The action is used to directly specify a structural feature. The object that owns this structural feature is passed on via the input pin. Behavior for static structural features is not permitted, and structural features that are not visible for the action are undefined. (See Figure 3.79.)   *3.4.6.1*

ReadStructuralFeatureAction is an action that represents a concrete specialization of *StructuralFeatureAction* (see Figure 3.80). A read structural feature action supplies the value of the specified structural feature. A structural feature can have several values because it is also a special *multiplicity element* (see Figure 3.81), among other things.   *3.4.6.2*

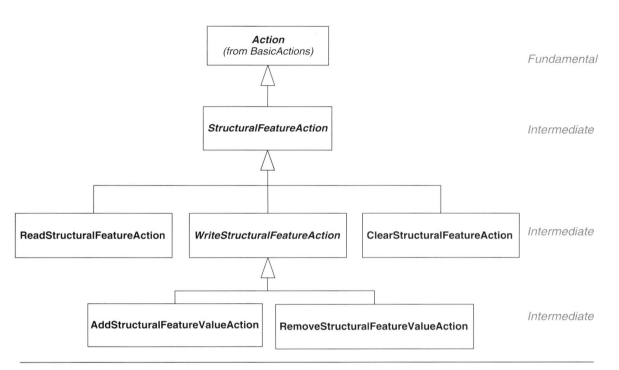

FIGURE 3.78   Arrangement of structural feature actions.

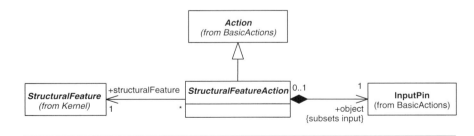

FIGURE 3.79   The metamodel for structural feature actions.

The multiplicity of a structural feature has to match the multiplicity of the output pin of *ReadStructuralFeatureAction*.

There is no particular notation for read structural feature actions.

3.4.6.3   *ClearStructuralFeatureAction* is an action that removes all values from the specified structural feature (see Figure 3.82). If the structural feature is an association end, then the semantics of *ClearAssociationAction* applies (see Section 3.4.7).

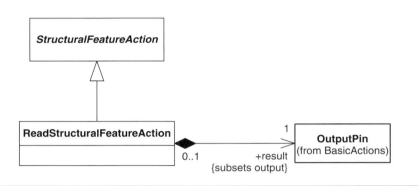

FIGURE 3.80 The metamodel for read structural feature actions.

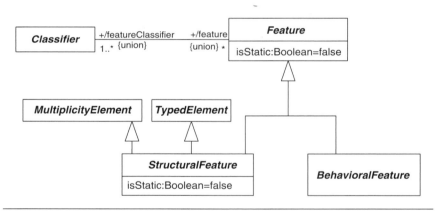

FIGURE 3.81 The metamodel for structural features.

All values of the specified structural feature are deleted, even if it would violate a defined multiplicity minimum, if one was stated.

Just like every action, clear structural feature actions are atomic. There are no intermediate states, even when several values are deleted.

There is no particular notation for clear structural feature actions.

WriteStructuralFeatureAction is an abstract base class for actions that write or delete single values to or from a structural feature. The value to be changed is made available via the input pin. The multiplicity of the input pin must be 1, and the type has to match the type of the structural feature. (See Figure 3.83.)   3.4.6.4

AddStructuralFeatureValueAction is a concrete write structural feature action. It writes   3.4.6.5
a value to the specified structural feature. Since a structural feature can contain

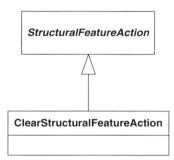

FIGURE 3.82 The metamodel for clear structural feature actions.

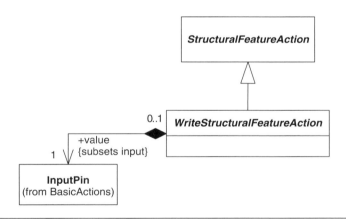

FIGURE 3.83 The metamodel for write structural feature actions.

several (ordered) values, there is a way to state the position of insertion. This position is passed to the add structural feature value action via an input pin.

The Boolean property *isReplaceAll* of the action specifies whether existing values should be deleted before inserting the new value.

There is no particular notation for add structural feature value actions. (See Figure 3.84.)

3.4.6.6 *RemoveStructuralFeatureValueAction* is an action that removes a value from the speci-
3.4.6.7 fied structural feature. In contrast to a clear structural feature action, which deletes

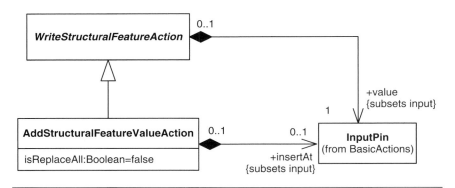

FIGURE 3.84 The metamodel for add structural feature value actions.

all values, this action removes only the value specified at the input pin. Removing a value can violate the specified minimum multiplicity, since this is not considered by the action.

Structural features can contain several ordered values. In this case, we can state the position of the value to be removed at the input pin. The Boolean property *isRemoveDuplicate* can be used to additionally specify whether all values should be removed, if the specified value occurs more than once ({nonunique} property modifier).

There is no particular notation for remove structural feature value actions. (See Figure 3.85.)

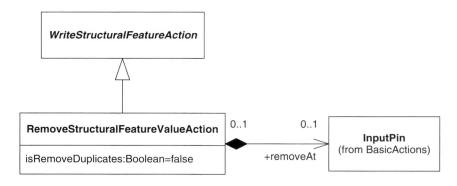

FIGURE 3.85 The metamodel for remove structural feature value actions.

Metamodel

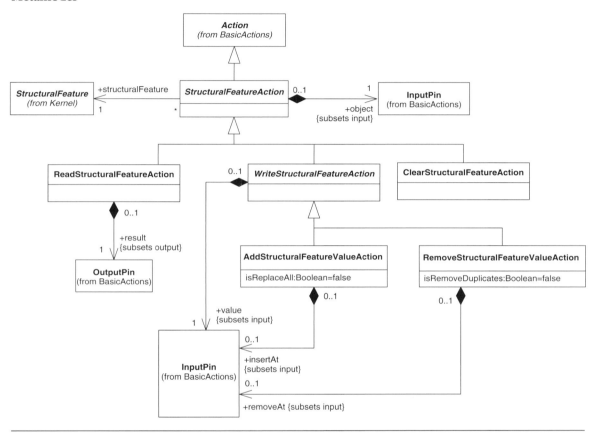

FIGURE 3.86 The metamodel for structural feature actions.

CHECKLIST: STRUCTURAL FEATURE ACTIONS

☐ 3.4.6.1.   List the characteristics of *StructuralFeatureAction*.
☐ 3.4.6.2.   List the characteristics of *ReadStructuralFeatureAction*.
☐ 3.4.6.3.   List the characteristics of *ClearStructuralFeatureAction*.
☐ 3.4.6.4.   List the characteristics and concrete subclasses of
            WriteStructuralFeatureAction.
☐ 3.4.6.5.   List the characteristics of *AddStructuralFeatureValueAction*.
☐ 3.4.6.6.   List the characteristics of *RemoveStructuralFeatureValueAction*.
☐ 3.4.6.7.   Explain the difference between *ClearStructuralFeatureAction* and
            RemoveStructuralFeatureValueAction.

3.4.7 LINK ACTIONS

Link actions are used to read, write, create, and destroy links, that is, instances of associations.

Definition

LinkAction is an abstract superclass for actions that identify links based on the objects at the link ends and the qualifiers.

LinkEndData is not an action, but an element used to identify links.

ReadLinkAction is an action that navigates along an association and returns the object at the other link end.

WriteLinkAction is an abstract superclass for actions that write or destroy links.

CreateLinkAction is an action that creates links.

DestroyLinkAction is an action that destroys links or link objects (instances of association classes).

LinkEndCreationData is not an action, but an element used to identify links, and to support ordered associations when creating new links.

LinkEndDestructionData is an element similar to *LinkEndCreationData*, except that it is used to destroy rather than create links.

ClearAssociationAction is an action that deletes all links of a specified association in which the designated object participates. It also deletes link objects.

Figure 3.87 shows the arrangement of link actions.

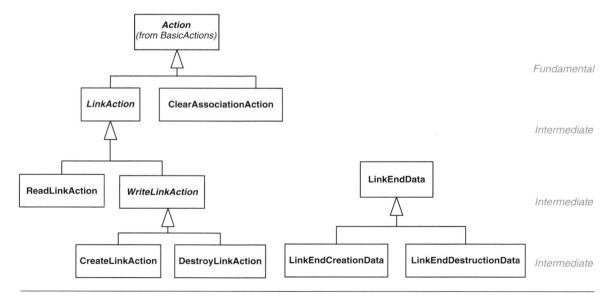

FIGURE 3.87 Arrangement of link actions.

Notation and Semantics

3.4.7.1 *LinkAction* is an abstract base class for actions that use objects at the link ends to identify links. Link actions create, destroy, write, or read links.

3.4.7.2 Since links are not objects that can, for instance, be passed on via input pins, they have to be identified in another way. To identify a link, we use the objects connected to that link. However, it is not sufficient to just state the objects. For example, two objects can be interconnected by several links (see Figure 3.88). For unique identification of a link end, UML 2 defines the metaclass *LinkEndData*. This metaclass is not an action, but merely a structure used for unique description of a link end.

LinkEndData is derived from Element; that is, it does not inherit any particular properties from its base classes. The type of object at the link end is specified via the association to the metaclass Property, emergency doctor's diagnosis or diagnosis must fit to Figure 3.87. The object itself is passed via the input pin *value* (see Figure 3.88).

Depending on the association, a link action has at least two LinkEndData elements, but it can have an arbitrary number, which refers to n-ary associations. (See Figure 3.89.)

3.4.7.3 *ReadLinkAction* is a concrete link action that returns the specified object at a link end. Though LinkEndData is used to specify both link ends, an object is passed only for one LinkEndData via the input pin. ReadLinkAction then returns the object via the output pin at the other end. The end that is not fully specified is also called *open end*.

There is no particular notation for read link actions. (See Figure 3.90.)

3.4.7.4 *WriteLinkAction* is an abstract base class for link actions that create or destroy links. You can easily see in the metamodel shown in Figure 3.91 that WriteLinkAction is more or less just a term that doesn't define new properties. It merely defines a

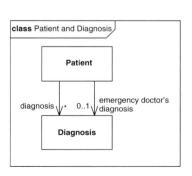
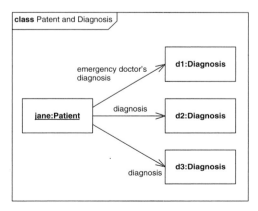

FIGURE 3.88 Example showing a class and object diagram for a hospital information system.

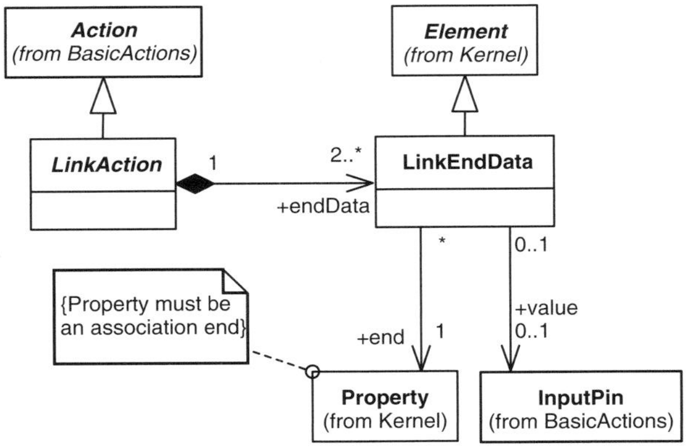

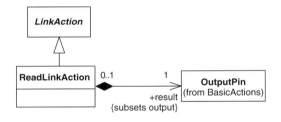

Figure content (Figure 3.89): Action (from BasicActions), Element (from Kernel), LinkAction, LinkEndData, Property (from Kernel), InputPin (from BasicActions), with note {Property must be an association end}, multiplicities 1, 2..*, +endData, *, 0..1, +value, 0..1, +end, 1.

FIGURE 3.89 The metamodel for link actions with LinkEndData elements.

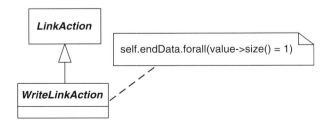

Figure content (Figure 3.90): LinkAction, ReadLinkAction, OutputPin (from BasicActions), multiplicities 0..1, 1, +result {subsets output}.

FIGURE 3.90 The metamodel for read link actions.

Figure content (Figure 3.91): LinkAction, WriteLinkAction, note: self.endData.forall(value->size() = 1)

FIGURE 3.91 The metamodel for write link actions.

constraint in the form of an OCL expression.[1] Each LinkEndData element has to have exactly one input pin. This means that with regard to the multiplicity of the association end *value* in Figure 3.89, only the upper limit 1 is permitted for write link actions.

3.4.7.5   *CreateLinkAction* is a special write link action that creates a link. It can also create link objects, that is, instances of association classes. This action has no return value.

3.4.7.6   CreateLinkAction is an action that uses *LinkEndCreationData* — a specialization of LinkEndData — to support ordered associations. LinkEndCreationData has an additional property, *isReplaceAll*, to let you specify the insertion position. Also, LinkEndCreationData can be used to specify whether existing links should be deleted prior to creating the specified link. The principle is identical with that of AddStructuralFeatureValueAction (see Section 3.4.6).

There is no particular notation for create link actions. (See Figure 3.92.)

3.4.7.7   Similarly to the way CreateLinkAction has taken on the concept of AddStructural FeatureValueAction, the concept of *DestroyLinkAction* is like that of RemoveStructural FeatureValueAction (see Section 3.4.6).

3.4.7.8   *DestroyLinkAction* is a special WriteLinkAction, that is, an action that destroys links
3.4.7.9   and link objects. To identify a link, DestroyLinkAction uses the class *LinkEndDe-structionData* derived from LinkEndData. In addition to the identification, you can specify the exact delete position for n-ary links using the association end *destroyAt*. The removal of duplicates is controlled by the property *isRemoveDuplicates*.

There is no particular notation for destroy link actions. (See Figure 3.93.)

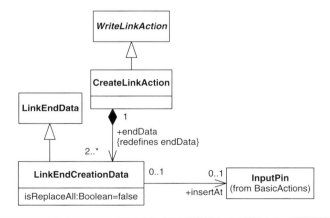

FIGURE 3.92   The metamodel for CreateLinkAction and LinkEndCreationData.

---

[1]   OCL (Object Constraint Language) is a formal constraint language for object networks; it is a topic on the examination for Advanced certification.

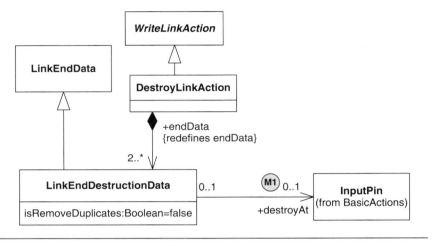

FIGURE 3.93 The metamodel for destroy link actions.

This finalizes our discussion of link actions. However, there is another action in this area. Although it is not a link action, we list it here for the sake of completeness. *ClearAssociationAction* is an action that, rather than single links, deletes all links belonging to a specified association and an object passed via the input pin.

The concept is similar to that of ClearStructuralFeatureAction. One single atomic action deletes all links. There are no intermediate states.

There is no particular notation for clear association actions. (See Figure 3.94.)

3.4.7.10
3.4.7.11

CHECKLIST: LINK ACTIONS

- ☐ 3.4.7.1.   List the characteristics of *LinkAction*.
- ☐ 3.4.7.2.   How are links identified?
- ☐ 3.4.7.3.   List the characteristics of *ReadLinkAction*.
- ☐ 3.4.7.4.   List the characteristics of *WriteLinkAction*.
- ☐ 3.4.7.5.   List the characteristics of *CreateLinkAction*.
- ☐ 3.4.7.6.   List the characteristics of the *LinkEndCreationData* structure.
- ☐ 3.4.7.7.   Explain the concept used to add or delete a value.
- ☐ 3.4.7.8.   List the characteristics of the *LinkEndDestructionData* structure.
- ☐ 3.4.7.9.   List the characteristics of *DestroyLinkAction*.
- ☐ 3.4.7.10. List the characteristics of *ClearAssociationAction*.
- ☐ 3.4.7.11. Explain the difference between *ClearAssociationAction* and *DestroyLinkAction*.

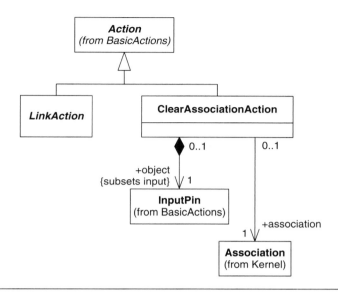

FIGURE 3.94   The metamodel for clear association actions.

Metamodel

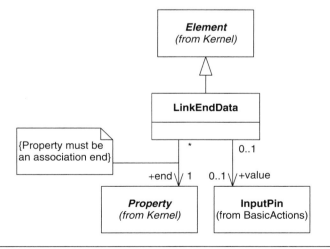

FIGURE 3.95   The metamodel for link identifications.

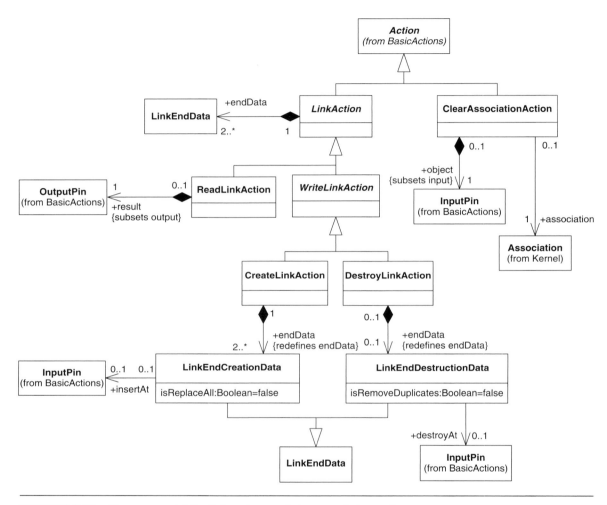

FIGURE 3.96 The metamodel for link actions and clear association actions.

3.4.8   VARIABLE ACTIONS

Before we discuss variable actions, note that "variable" in this context is not the commonly known local variable of an operation. We are talking about a variable in the context of structural nodes in activity diagrams (Section 3.5.5).[2] Actions

3.4.8.1

---

[2]   If the activity is mapped to the implementation of an operation, the variable is in a sense the variable known from common programming languages.

can jointly access variables within a structural node. As they do, there is an indirect data exchange, in contrast to an object flow, which exchanges data directly.

Definition
VariableAction is an abstract superclass for actions that read, write, and delete variables.

ReadVariableAction is an action that reads the content of the specified variable.

WriteVariableAction is an abstract superclass for actions that write or delete variable values.

AddVariableValueAction is an action that adds a value to a variable.

RemoveVariableValueAction is an action that removes a specified value from a variable.

ClearVariableAction is an action that deletes all values of a variable.

Figure 3.97 shows an arrangement of variable actions.

Notation and Semantics
3.4.8.2 *VariableAction* is an abstract superclass for actions that read, write, or delete a statically specified variable. (See Figure 3.98.)

3.4.8.3 *ReadVariableAction* is a concrete variable action that reads the values from the specified variable and returns them via the output pin. Similar to structural features,

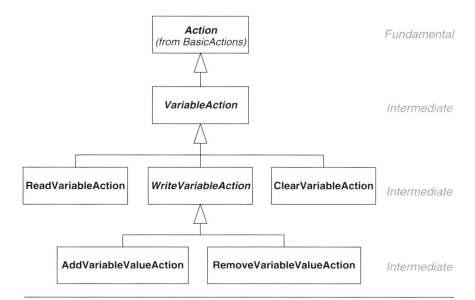

FIGURE 3.97 Arrangement of variable actions.

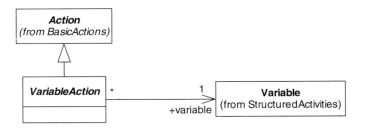

FIGURE 3.98 The metamodel for variable actions.

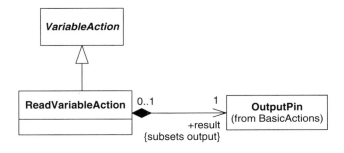

FIGURE 3.99 The metamodel for read variable actions.

variables can also be n-ary. The order in which values are returned corresponds to how they are stored in a variable.

There is no particular notation for read variable actions. (See Figure 3.99.)

WriteVariableAction is an abstract base class for variable actions that write or delete single variable values. Notice that the concept of structure actions and link actions (Sections 3.4.6 and 3.4.7) comes up again here.

3.4.8.4
3.4.8.5

A write variable action specifies an input pin that is used to pass the value to be written or deleted. (See Figure 3.100.)

AddVariableValueAction is a special WriteVariableAction that stores the value passed via the input pin in the specified variable.

3.4.8.6

The insertion position can be specified via the input pin by using the association end *insertAt* for n-ary variables. Moreover, you can use the property *isReplaceAll* to specify whether existing values should be deleted prior to inserting a new value.

There is no particular notation for add variable value actions. (See Figure 3.101.)

RemoveVariableValueAction is an action that removes the specified value from a variable.

3.4.8.7

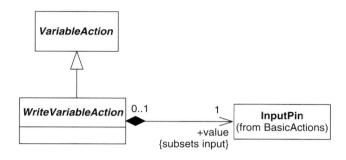

FIGURE 3.100 The metamodel for write variable actions.

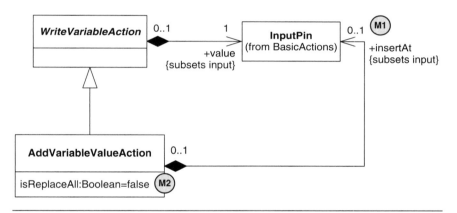

FIGURE 3.101 The metamodel for add variable value actions.

The delete position can be passed as a positive integer for n-ary variables via the input pin. The property *isRemoveDuplicates* can be used to specify whether duplicates should be deleted.

There is no particular notation for remove variable value actions. (See Figure 3.102.)

3.4.8.8   *ClearVariableAction* is an action that removes all values from the specified variable,
3.4.8.9   similarly to ClearStructuralFeatureAction (Section 3.4.6) and ClearAssociationAction (Section 3.4.7). To delete one single value, you would use RemoveVariableValueAction instead.

There is no particular notation for clear variable actions. (See Figure 3.103.)

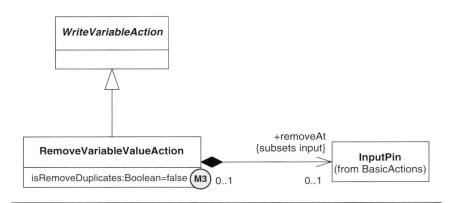

FIGURE 3.102 The metamodel for remove variable value actions.

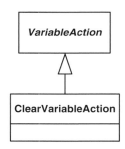

FIGURE 3.103 The metamodel for clear variable actions.

CHECKLIST: VARIABLE ACTIONS

☐ 3.4.8.1. What variables do variable actions refer to?
☐ 3.4.8.2. List the characteristics of *VariableAction*.
☐ 3.4.8.3. List the characteristics of *ReadVariableAction*.
☐ 3.4.8.4. List the characteristics of *WriteVariableAction*.
☐ 3.4.8.5. List the concrete subclasses of *WriteVariableAction*.
☐ 3.4.8.6. List the characteristics of *AddVariableValueAction*.
☐ 3.4.8.7. List the characteristics of *RemoveVariableValueAction*.
☐ 3.4.8.8. List the characteristics of *ClearVariableAction*.
☐ 3.4.8.9. Explain the difference between *RemoveVariableValueAction* and *ClearVariableAction*.

Metamodel

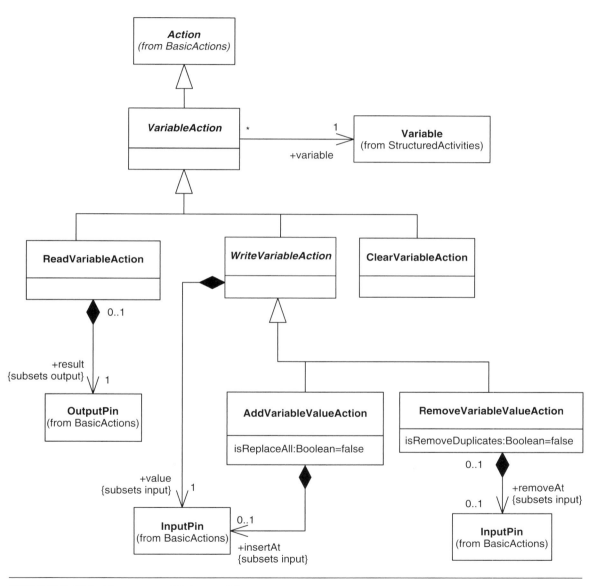

FIGURE 3.104 The metamodel for variable actions.

3.4.9   OTHER ACTIONS

The package *IntermediateActions* includes an area with miscellaneous actions (see Figure 3.105) that are not allocated to specific issues.

Definition
ValueSpecificationAction is an action that evaluates a value specification.

Notation and Semantics
The *value specification* is evaluated as soon as the action is activated. The result is returned at the output pin. There is no particular notation for *ValueSpecificationAction*.

3.4.9.1

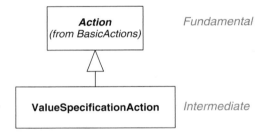

FIGURE 3.105 Arrangement of miscellaneous actions.

Metamodel

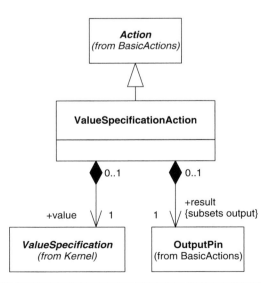

FIGURE 3.106 The metamodel for miscellaneous actions.

3.5 ACTIVITY DIAGRAMS

This section discusses a diagram form that is used to model flows. The activity diagrams of UML 1.x have been widely used in all kinds of domains—business process modeling [Oesterreich2004c], systems engineering [Weilkiens2006], and requirements analyses to algorithms. All these domains have gained much experience in UML-specific diagramming. In particular, problems have been identified and limits have been sounded out. These findings have been introduced in the activity diagrams of UML 2 (see Figure 3.107).

The activity model has been revised considerably. For example, the activities of UML 1.x are a special form of state machines, but the activities of UML 2 no longer relate to state machines. Rather, they correspond to the semantics of Petri nets, supporting a much better flow semantics.

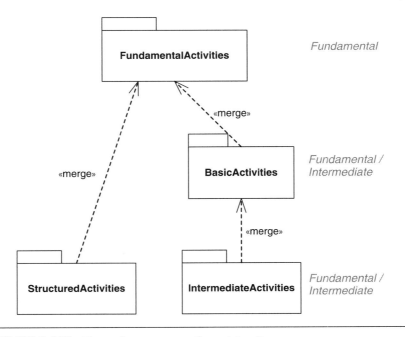

FIGURE 3.107 The package structure for activity diagrams.

3.5.1 EXAMINATION TOPICS

BasicActivities and *IntermediateActivities* are two packages containing elements that are part of the test for the Fundamental certification. The Intermediate test covers the following topics:

- Object nodes
- Control nodes
- Activity partitions
- Structured activity nodes
- Conditional and loop nodes
- Exception handlers

This topic area constitutes 15 percent of the test.

3.5.2 OBJECT NODES

ObjectNode is an abstract superclass for several concrete nodes. For example, *Pin* and *ActivityParameterNode* are concrete object nodes that are part of the Fundamental certification examination. This section discusses another concrete object node: *CentralBufferNode*.

Definition
CentralBufferNode is a special object node for managing flows from multiple sources and destinations that is not connected to an action or an activity. (See Figure 3.108.)

Notation and Semantics
All object nodes have puffer functionality. Pins and activity parameter nodes are special object nodes that are connected directly with an action or activity. In contrast a central buffer node is a special object node that is directly connected with other object or control nodes.

3.5.2.1

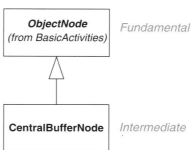

FIGURE 3.108 Arrangement of central buffer nodes.

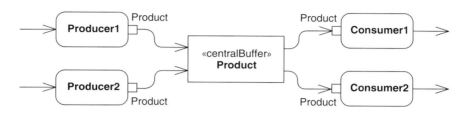

FIGURE 3.109 Example of a central buffer node.

Figure 3.109 shows a producer/consumer pattern. The producers create products that are used by the consumers. The central buffer node decouples the producers from the consumers. Created products are buffered in the central buffer node. The consumers help themselves from the buffer and retrieve the products if available.

3.5.2.2   The incoming and outgoing edges of a central buffer node have a semantic. That means a producer can deliver a product every time independent of the other producer. Inversely only one product is delivered from the buffer to one consumer at a time. The object token traverses to the consumer action as soon as it is available and the action is ready to take it. If both consumers in Figure 3.109 are ready to take a token, it is nondeterministic which one wins the race.

A central buffer is denoted as a rectangle with the keyword *centralBuffer*. The name of the object token that the node can accept appears underneath the keyword. This name is denoted similarly to a pin.

Metamodel

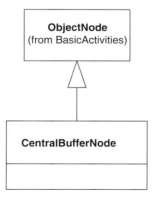

FIGURE 3.110 The metamodel for central buffer nodes.

3.5.3   CONTROL NODES

Control nodes are also part of the test for Fundamental certification. More specifically, the Fundamental examination covers *InitialNode*, *ActivityFinalNode*, *DecisionNode*, and *MergeNode*. The test for Intermediate certification extends this list, adding *ForkNode*, *JoinNode*, and *FlowFinalNode*.

Definition

ForkNode is a special control node that splits an incoming control flow or object flow into several outgoing control flows or object flows.

JoinNode is a special control node that synchronizes several incoming control flows or object flows and has exactly one outgoing control flow or object flow.

FlowFinalNode is a special control node that terminates a flow. Every arriving token will be destroyed.

Figure 3.111 shows an arrangement of these control nodes.

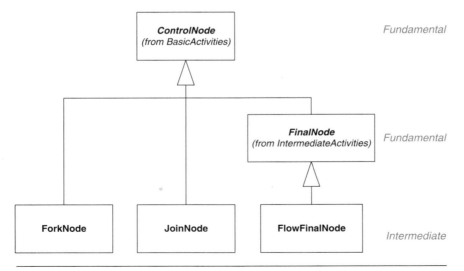

FIGURE 3.111   Arrangement of fork nodes, join nodes, and flow final nodes.

Notation and Semantics

3.5.3.1   Figure 3.112 shows a *ForkNode* that splits one incoming control flow into two outgoing control flows. More specifically, the incoming control token is copied, and a control token is made available at each outgoing edge.

This splitting is denoted as a black bar with one incoming edge and several outgoing edges.

3.5.3.2   Figure 3.113 shows how an object flow can be split. The general flow semantics says that a token won't be forwarded until all edges and target nodes are ready.

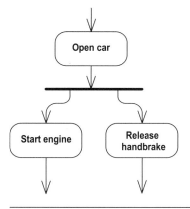

FIGURE 3.112   Example of a fork node.

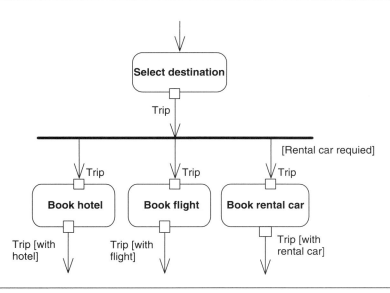

FIGURE 3.113   Example of a fork node with object flow.

In addition, a token must not be waiting at a control node. These rules cause a conflict in the ForkNode semantics: the outgoing flows are independent. You can see in Figure 3.113 that the condition [*Rental car required*] can block the entire fork node.

This conflict is the reason for the two exceptions to the general flow semantics:

1. To ensure that a condition (*guard*) that will be evaluated as *false* won't block the entire splitting, no token will be made available at the edge concerned, while all other edges will be served. In Figure 3.113, both hotel and flight will be booked, but no rental car.
2. Normally, ForkNode isn't be able to forward an object token while the target node is not ready to accept it. In this case, the object token waits at the ForkNode edge concerned. This is an exception to the general rule, which says that a token must not wait at a control node. All other edges will be served. The waiting object token won't get lost, though; it will be forwarded by the FIFO (First In First Out) semantics to the target node as soon as the latter is ready.

JoinNode is a node that has several incoming edges and one outgoing edge. In contrast to MergeNode, a join node synchronizes the flows based on three rules:

3.5.3.3
3.5.3.4

1. Tokens have to be available at all incoming edges in order for a join node to supply tokens at the outgoing edge.
2. If all incoming tokens are control tokens, then exactly one control token will be made available at the outgoing edge.
3. If object tokens and control tokens arrive at the incoming edges, then only the object tokens will be forwarded, and in the sequence in which they arrived at the join node. Object tokens that refer to the same object are combined into one token.

A join node is denoted as a black bar with several incoming edges and one outgoing edge.

It is permissible in a diagram to draw a fork node immediately followed by a join node (or vice versa) as one single black bar with several incoming and outgoing edges (see Figure 3.115). However, there will still be two control nodes in the model.

FlowFinalNode is a node that terminates a single flow. In contrast to an activity final node, which terminates the entire activity when a token arrives, a flow final node destroys only the incoming token. No other token within the activity is impaired.

3.5.3.5

The entire activity is terminated when the last of its tokens reaches a flow end.

A flow final node is denoted as a circle with a cross (Figure 3.116).

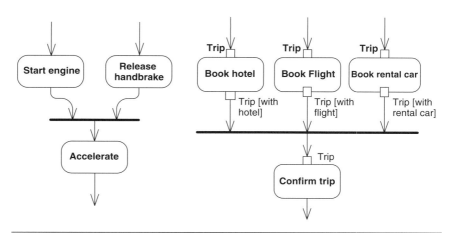

FIGURE 3.114   Section of an activity with a join node.

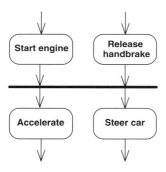

FIGURE 3.115   One single symbol representing a fork node and a join node.

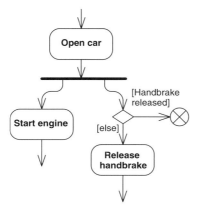

FIGURE 3.116   Section of an activity with a flow final node.

Metamodel

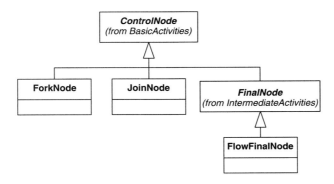

FIGURE 3.117   The metamodel for control nodes.

CHECKLIST: CONTROL NODES

☐ 3.5.3.1.   List the characteristics of *ForkNode*. How many tokens flow after a fork node?
☐ 3.5.3.2.   Explain the token flow semantics of a fork node.
☐ 3.5.3.3.   List the characteristics of *JoinNode*.
☐ 3.5.3.4.   Explain the token flow semantics of a join node. How many tokens flow after a join node?
☐ 3.5.3.5.   List the characteristics of *FlowFinalNode*.

3.5.4   ACTIVITY PARTITIONS

Definition

ActivityGroup is an abstract element that groups a set of nodes and edges of an ctivity.

ActivityPartition is a concrete activity group. Figure 3.118 gives an overview of partitions.

Notation and Semantics

ActivityGroup is an abstract element, which means that it cannot be used directly.   *3.5.4.1*
There is no notation.

Activity groups can be nested; that is, an activity group can contain other activity groups.

The nodes and edges in an activity group all have to belong to the same activity. They can be part of several activity groups, provided that these activity groups are not supergroups or subgroups of one another.

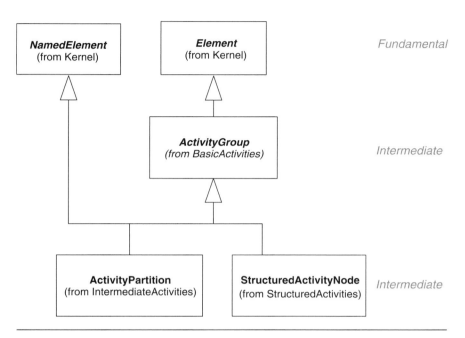

FIGURE 3.118 Overview of partitions.

3.5.4.2   *ActivityPartition* is a specialization of activity group and named element. The latter is important to be able to name the partition. This is a property that activity group doesn't have.

A partition is denoted as a rectangle with a naming area and another area for nodes and edges. A vertical orientation is common, but not mandatory (Figure 3.119).

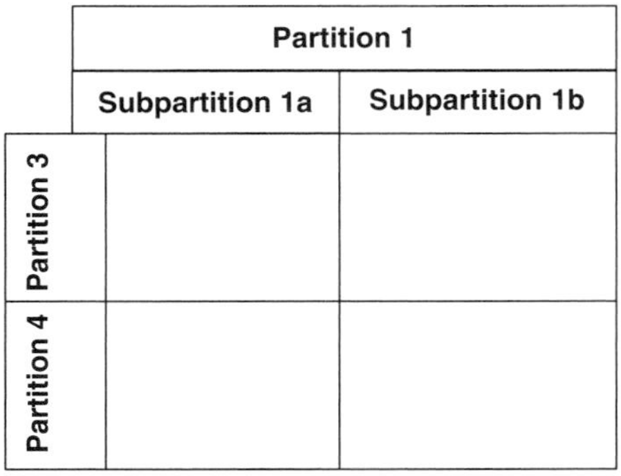

	Partition 1	
	Subpartition 1a	**Subpartition 1b**
Partition 3		
Partition 4		

FIGURE 3.119 The notation for activity partitions.

A partition can have subpartitions, which allows you to model hierarchical structures. In contrast to activity group, nodes and edges must not be present in more than one partition. The only exception is the dimension property.

The common criterion for forming partitions can be modeled explicitly, using the association end *represents*. What is associated is the abstract base class Element. This means that any UML grouping criterion model element can be a partition.

In the diagram, the element can be denoted in a separate area above the partition name. In addition, the name of the pertaining metaclass is stated as a keyword.

The property to be outside of the partitioning focus is a special grouping criterion. The corresponding partition is called *"external"* and used, for example, to model the flow of a use case with an activity. The partition marked *"external"* contains the actions of actors.

A partition can have a *dimension*. Such a partition must not be a subpartition. It appears orthogonally on the top partitions that have no dimension. You can see in Figure 3.120 that the partitions grouped after components have a dimension.

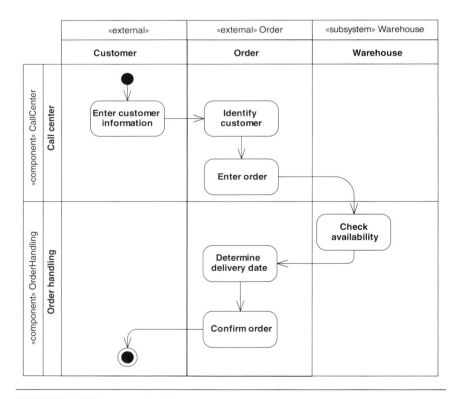

FIGURE 3.120 Example of partitions.

FIGURE 3.121   Alternative notation for partitions.

As an exception to the general rule, nodes and edges can be contained in several partitions, provided they reside in different dimensions.

The paths of a partition represent a considerable restriction of freedom in laying out an activity diagram. For this reason, there is an alternative notation that avoids this restriction. The name of a partition is denoted within round brackets above the action name. Nested partitions are separated by two colons; dimensions are separated by commas (see Figure 3.121).

CHECKLIST: ACTIVITY GROUPS

☐ 3.5.4.1.   List the characteristics of *ActivityGroup*.
☐ 3.5.4.2.   List the characteristics of *ActivityPartition*. What does an ActivityPartition refer to?

Metamodel

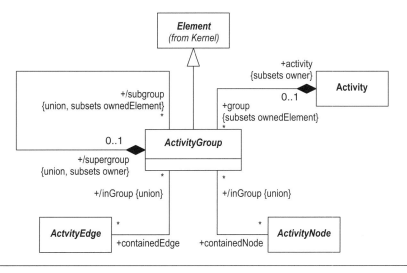

FIGURE 3.122   The metamodel for activity groups.

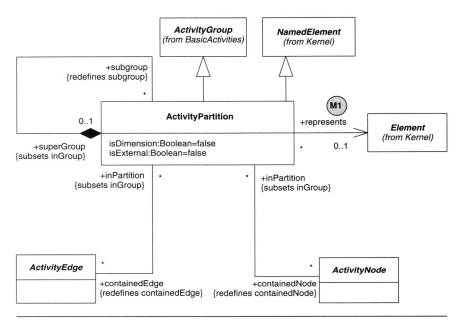

FIGURE 3.123 The metamodel for activity partitions.

3.5.5 STRUCTURED ACTIVITY NODES

Definition

StructuredActivityNode is an executable node and an activity group; that is, it contains other nodes and edges. The elements it contains must not occur in any other structured activity node.

Variable in this context is part of a structured activity node and contains values that can access all actions of that structured activity node.

Figure 3.124 shows an arrangement of structured activity nodes and variables.

Notation and Semantics

In contrast to a single action, which is an atomic executable node, *StructuredActivity Node* represents a non-atomic executable group of actions.

A structured activity node can be compared with an operation in a programming language; a single action would then correspond to a single instruction within that operation. Just as programming language operations can own local variables, you can also define variables within a structured activity node.

A structured activity node can contain *initial nodes* and *activity final nodes*. In the context of a structured activity node, the control flow won't start at an initial node unless the structured activity node executes. Also in the context of a structured

3.5.5.1

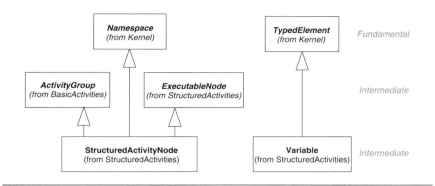

FIGURE 3.124 Arrangement of structured activity nodes and variables.

activity node, the activity final node will terminate only the structured activity node, not the entire activity.

It is not mandatory to state an initial node and an activity final node. When a structured activity node is invoked, the flow starts in the structured activity node at all nodes that have no incoming edges. The same applies to the activity final node in the opposite direction.

3.5.5.2 No flow is started in a structured activity node before the structured activity node executes.

Variable is a typed element that can be accessed by all actions of the pertaining structured activity node. This means that no explicit data exchange is required across object flows. A variable belongs to a structured activity node.

A structured activity node is denoted as a dashed rectangle with rounded corners. The keyword *structured* and the name of the structured activity node appear in the upper area. (See Figure 3.125.)

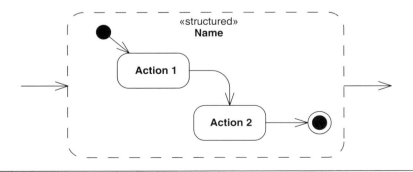

FIGURE 3.125 The notation for structured activity nodes.

Metamodel

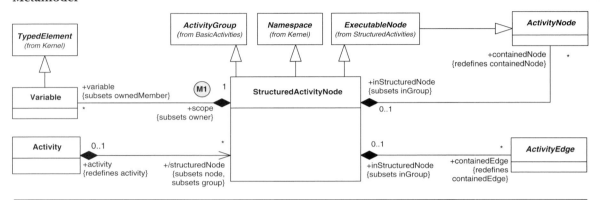

FIGURE 3.126   The metamodel for structured activity nodes.

CHECKLIST: STRUCTURED ACTIVITY NODES

☐ 3.5.5.1.   List the characteristics of *StructuredActivityNode*.
☐ 3.5.5.2.   List the characteristics of *Variable*. What does a variable in this context belong to?

3.5.6   CONDITIONAL NODES, LOOP NODES, AND SEQUENCE NODES

Branches, loops, and sequences are very common patterns in flows. Conditional nodes, loop nodes, and sequence nodes provide useful structures to express these patterns in a compact and easily understandable way within an activity.

Definition

ConditionalNode is a special structured activity node that corresponds to the *if-then-else* semantics.

   Clause is an element that represents a conditional branch that consists of a test section and a body section that is executed if the test is *true*.

   LoopNode is a special structured activity node that maps the *while* or *do-while* semantics.

   SequenceNode is a node that runs executable nodes in sequence.

   Figure 3.127 illustrates these nodes and clauses.

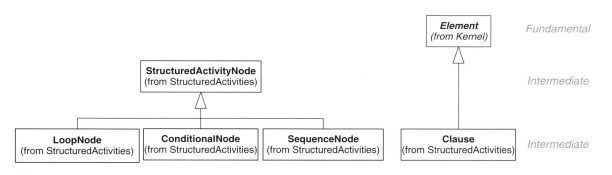

FIGURE 3.127 Arrangement of conditional nodes, clauses, loop nodes, and sequence nodes.

Notation and Semantics

3.5.6.1   A *clause* is a conditional branch that groups a set of nodes, which are divided into two sections: test and body nodes.

Test nodes run a test jointly and produce a Boolean result. One of the test nodes—the *decider*—has to own an output pin that accepts the test result. If the test result is *true*, then the body nodes will be executed. The flow begins at all the nodes that have no incoming edges (*front end nodes*) and ends in the nodes that have no outgoing edges (*back end nodes*).

3.5.6.2   *ConditionalNode* is a node that owns a set of branches. All tests of branches can be executed in parallel, if permitted by the runtime environment of the activity model. The flow is not deterministic if several tests result in *true*. Conditional branches can be ordered by using the association ends *predecessorClause* and *successorClause* to prevent this.

A special conditional branch is the *else* branch. It is the successor of all other branches of a conditional node, and its test always results in *true*.

The property *isAssured*=true ensures that at least one test is evaluated for *true*. The property *isDeterminate*=true ensures that only one body at most will be executed in case there are concurrent evaluations of the test sections.

A conditional node is denoted as a dashed rectangle with rounded corners. It inherits its notation from structured activity node (Figure 3.128).[3]

3.5.6.3   Like a conditional node, *LoopNode* is a special structured activity node. According to the semantics of a loop, the node is composed of three sections: setup, test, and body (Figure 3.129).

----

[3]   The UML specification doesn't specify an official notation for conditional nodes.

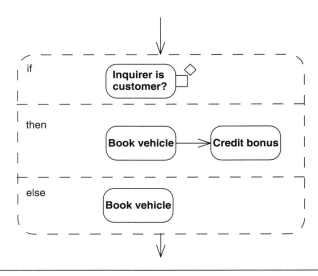

FIGURE 3.128   Notation and example of conditional nodes.

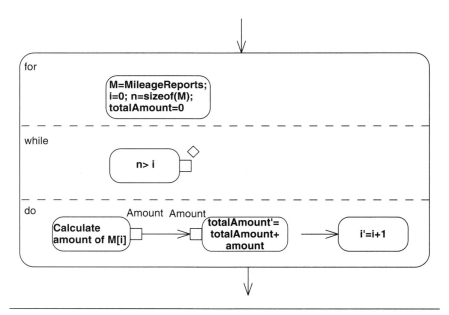

FIGURE 3.129   Notation and example of loop nodes.

Each of the three sections is represented by a set of nodes. One node in the test section—the *decider*—has to own an output pin for accepting the Boolean test result.

3.5.6.4   When executing a loop node, the setup section is run first. If the property *isTestedFirst* is set to *true* (*while-do* semantics), then the test section runs next. If the test result is *true*, then the body executes. Subsequently, the test runs again, and so on, until the test is *false*.

The test-body execution sequence is reversed if the property *isTestedFirst* is set to *false* (*do-while* semantics).

3.5.6.5   *SequenceNode* is a node that points to an ordered list of executable nodes. When a sequence node is activated, the executable nodes run one by one in the specified order. If these nodes are linked with control flows or object flows, then the conditions attached to these flows have to be met for a node to be able to run.

Metamodel

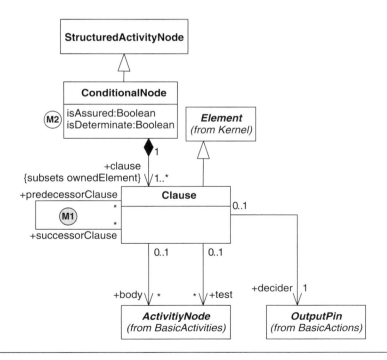

FIGURE 3.130   The metamodel for conditional nodes.

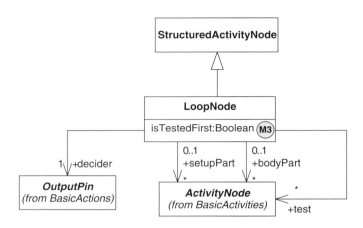

FIGURE 3.131 The metamodel for loop nodes.

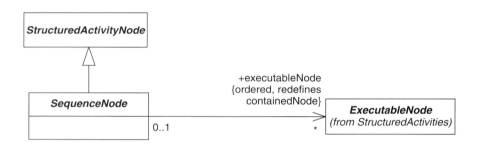

FIGURE 3.132 The metamodel for sequence nodes.

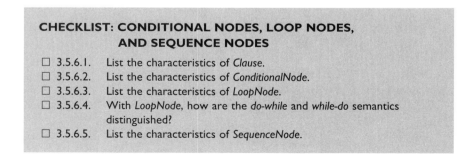

CHECKLIST: CONDITIONAL NODES, LOOP NODES, AND SEQUENCE NODES

☐ 3.5.6.1. List the characteristics of *Clause*.
☐ 3.5.6.2. List the characteristics of *ConditionalNode*.
☐ 3.5.6.3. List the characteristics of *LoopNode*.
☐ 3.5.6.4. With *LoopNode*, how are the *do-while* and *while-do* semantics distinguished?
☐ 3.5.6.5. List the characteristics of *SequenceNode*.

3.5.7   EXCEPTION HANDLING

Definition
ExceptionHandler is an element that specifies an executable node that is invoked if an exception occurs during the execution of a protected node.

ExecutableNode is the abstract base class for nodes that can be executed. The node can be protected by an exception handler.

Figure 3.133 shows exception handlers and executable nodes.

Notation and Semantics
ExecutableNode is the abstract base class for nodes that can be executed.

3.5.7.1   An executable node can own several exception handlers. An exception handler specifies one or more exception types it can catch and handle.

A thrown exception object represents input information on the executable node that uses the association end *handlerBody* to run the exception handler. The node has no incoming or outgoing edges other than the edge over which the exception object arrives. The return values have to comply with the return values of the protected node.

3.5.7.2   Figure 3.134 shows an exception handler's flow: The protected node *Book vehicle* executes, an exception occurs, and the exception handler *Handle database error* starts. After the exception handler's execution, the flow continues along edge *A* with an object token, *Booking*. In this example, *Booking* is the return value of the exception handler.

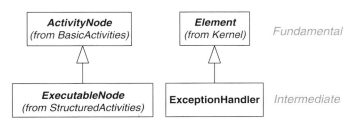

FIGURE 3.133   Arrangement of exception handlers and executable nodes.

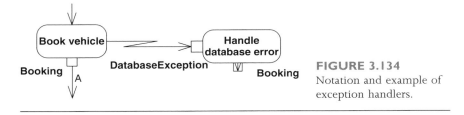

FIGURE 3.134
Notation and example of exception handlers.

An exception handler is denoted as an executable node with an incoming object flow shaped like a lightning flash and an input pin for accepting the exception object.

Metamodel

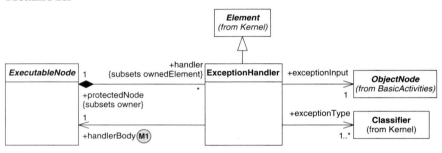

FIGURE 3.135   The metamodel for exception handlers.

CHECKLIST: EXCEPTION HANDLERS

☐ 3.5.7.1.   List the characteristics of *ExceptionHandler*. What does an exception handler protect?

☐ 3.5.7.2.   Explain the flow of *ExceptionHandler*.

3.6 INTERACTION DIAGRAMS

This section discusses a dynamic diagram form that represents interaction among selected elements (see Figure 3.136). The best-known candidate of interaction diagrams is the *sequence diagram*. In addition, there is the *communication diagram*, which was called "collaboration diagram" in UML 1.x, and there are two new diagram forms introduced in UML 2: the *timing diagram* and the *interaction overview diagram*.

Sequence, communication, and timing diagrams represent different views of the same model. The test for Intermediate certification focuses more on the interaction model than on the interaction model notation.

The interaction overview diagram is actually an activity diagram that puts single interaction models into a logical sequence.

The OCUP examination uses mainly sequence diagrams. We briefly discuss the other diagram forms of the interaction model at the end of this section.

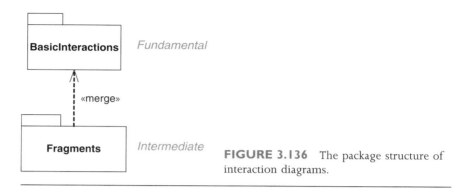

FIGURE 3.136 The package structure of interaction diagrams.

3.6.1 EXAMINATION TOPICS

The basic notions of interaction modeling are topics dealt with in the examination for Fundamental OCUP certification. They are not tested directly, but are assumed as a basis.

The following topics are covered on the Intermediate test:

- Interaction references (*InteractionUse*)
- Interaction operations (*CombinedFragment*)
- Connection points (*Gate*)

This topic area constitutes 15 percent of the test.

3.6.2 INTERACTION REFERENCES

If you have used sequence diagrams in UML 1.x, you are familiar with the fact that even simplest matters can eventually lead to very large diagrams. The reason is that UML 1.x sequence diagrams lack decomposition mechanisms.

One of the outstanding features of UML 2 is that the ways models can be decomposed have been improved considerably. In the field of interaction models, UML 2 introduced interaction references (*InteractionUse*) and lifeline decompositions (*PartDecomposition*).

Definition

InteractionUse is a reference to an interaction. The model is designed such that the reference could be substituted by the referenced interaction.

PartDecomposition is a description of the internal interactions of one lifeline relative to the interaction in which that lifeline is located.

Figure 3.137 shows interaction references and lifeline decompositions.

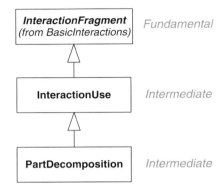

FIGURE 3.137 Arrangement of interaction references (InteractionUse) and lifeline decompositions (PartDecomposition).

FIGURE 3.138 The notation for interaction references (InteractionUse).

Notation and Semantics

InteractionUse can be used to describe parts of interactions from one sequence diagram in a separate sequence diagram. In the sequence diagrams in which the interaction fragment occurs, InteractionUse is then merely used to refer to that fragment (see Figure 3.138).

3.6.2.1

The fragmenting of sequence diagrams into easily manageable sizes is only one of the benefits of interaction references. An even greater benefit is that one single interaction can be referenced in several sequence diagrams. This means that redundancies (i.e., recurring descriptions of the same interaction) can be avoided.

Similarly to a *combined fragment*, an interaction reference is denoted with the interaction operator *ref*. The reference within the interaction operator's frame is written in the following syntax:

```
[attribute=][CollaborationUse.]interaction['('arguments ')']
[:return value]
```

where

- *attribute* is the attribute of an instance that points to one of the lifelines (e.g., *s.status* in Figure 3.139).
- *CollaborationUse* is the name of the collaboration use that binds the interaction's lifelines.

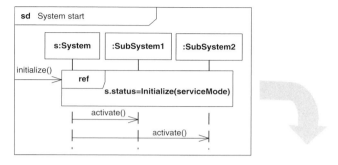

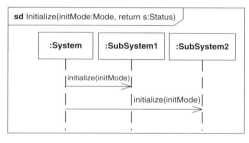

FIGURE 3.139 Example of an interaction reference (InteractionUse).

- *interaction* is the name of the interaction that is referenced. This is a mandatory statement.
- *arguments* are parameters that will be passed to the referenced interaction. An interaction is a special behavior, which means that it has input and output values as well as return values, which are written to *attribute*. The syntax for arguments is a list separated by commas, where an entry is stated in the following syntax:

```
<input argument> | out <output argument>
```

- *return value* is the value that the referenced interaction will return. This value is written to *attribute*.

3.6.2.2   In addition to interaction references, there is another decomposition mechanism: *PartDecomposition* can be used to decompose even a single lifeline. This process can be thought of as a kind of zooming into that lifeline. The reference is denoted in the header of the lifeline beneath the name. The syntax is as follows:

```
ref <interaction> [strict]
```

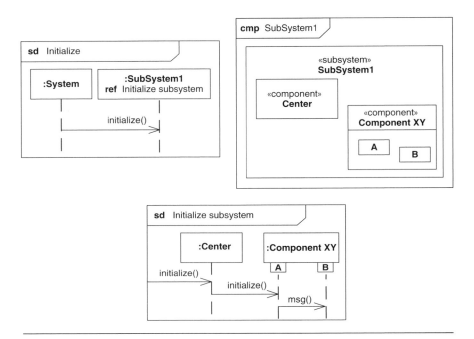

FIGURE 3.140   Example of decomposing lifelines (PartDecomposition).

You can see an example of how a lifeline can be decomposed in Figure 3.140. The referenced interaction, *Initialize subsystem*, belongs to *Subsystem1*. The realizing classifiers of the subsystem are represented in the component diagram.

The sequence diagram, *Initialize subsystem*, contains another lifeline decomposition. But this time, the decomposition is represented directly rather than referencing another interaction. The diagram shows the interaction of two classes, *A* and *B*, which realize *Component XY*.

The word *strict* can be added for inner decompositions to state that all elements on the inner lifelines are subject to a strict order (for a description of the interaction operator *strict* see Section 3.6.3).

**CHECKLIST: INTERACTION REFERENCES AND LIFELINE
      DECOMPOSITIONS**

☐ 3.6.2.1.   List the characteristics of interaction references (*InteractionUse*).
☐ 3.6.2.2.   List the characteristics of lifeline decompositions
         (*PartDecomposition*).

Metamodel

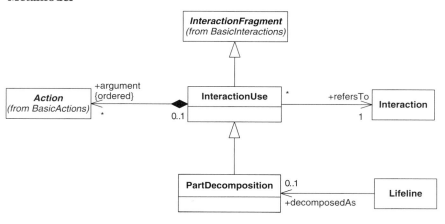

FIGURE 3.141   The metamodel for interaction references (InteractionUse).

3.6.3   INTERACTION OPERATIONS

Sequence diagrams represent a concrete scenario, that is, an interaction between selected elements in a limited situation. In general, loops or conditional branches are not be required. Still, there are cases where they are necessary, for example, to model similar flows within one single interaction. Though UML 1.x supports this kind of constructs, they are hard to understand and can easily lead to misunderstandings. UML 2 improved this area considerably and extended it. For instance, you can now model parallel and invalid flows.

Definition

CombinedFragment is a special interaction fragment that describes an expression of interaction fragments (see Figure 3.142). The expression has an interaction operator and interaction operands and an interaction constraint, if applicable.

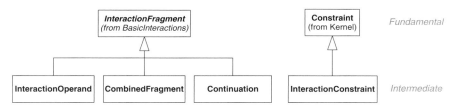

FIGURE 3.142   Arrangement of combined fragments, interaction operands, interaction constraints, and continuation labels.

Continuation is a syntactic way to label the continuation of a conditional combined fragment.

Notation and Semantics

The *operands* of a combined fragment are interaction fragments—generally a set of messages between lifelines. *Interaction operators* cause the conditional execution of operands, loops, or parallel execution and other flows of control variants.

3.6.3.1

A combined fragment is denoted similarly to a diagram frame: a rectangle with solid lines and a small pentagon in the upper left corner. The interaction operator is denoted inside the pentagon. The interaction operands are separated by dashed lines. Depending on the operator, an interaction constraint is stated in addition. If applicable, the interaction constraint is denoted on the right side of the operator outside the pentagon.

Before we take a closer look at each of the operators, let's have a brief look back at a topic from the Fundamental certification, which is significant for the operators discussed here. If you have the Fundamental certification behind you, you will surely remember the sequences of send and receive events. There are normally two events with a message: a send and a receive event. The logical sequence is that the send event occurs before the receive event. The semantics of an interaction is given by a pair, $[P, I]$, where P represents the set of valid sequences and I represents the set of invalid sequences. A sequence is an ordered list of occurring events. For example, $< p!, p*, q!, r!, r*, q* >$ and $< p!, r!, p*, q!, r*, q* >$ are valid sequences in Figure 3.143.

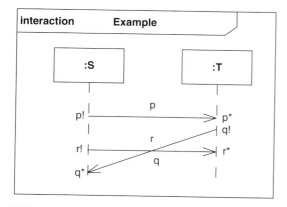

FIGURE 3.143   Example of send and receive events.

FIGURE 3.144   The twelve interaction operators.

TABLE 3.1 The Interaction Operators of the Enumeration
Class and Their Applications

Operators	Application
alt, opt, break	Conditional flows of control
seq, strict, par	Event sequences
loop	Loop
critical, neg, assert, consider, ignore	Valid, invalid, ignored, and critical flows of control

In total there are 12 interaction operators, which are listed in the Enumeration
class *InteractionOperator*, as listed in Figure 3.144. The uses of these operators are
listed in Table 3.1.

3.6.3.2   The interaction operator *alt* (Figure 3.145) is used to describe conditional flows
of control. The operands have conditions (guards). Operands with a condition
that is *true* will be executed. And *true* is assumed if there is no condition. At least
one operand of a fragment is selected.

3.6.3.3   The interaction operator *opt* is semantically equivalent to the operator *alt*, except
that only one operand is admissible.

3.6.3.4   The interaction operator *break* is similar to *opt*. The only difference between the
two operators is that with *break*, the enclosing interaction is terminated as soon as
the *break* operand has been traversed. You can see in Figure 3.146 that the *initialize*()
call doesn't execute when the *break* operand is traversed.

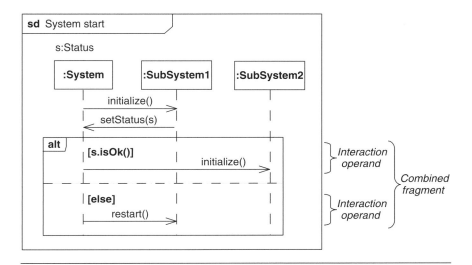

FIGURE 3.145 Example of the interaction operator *alt*.

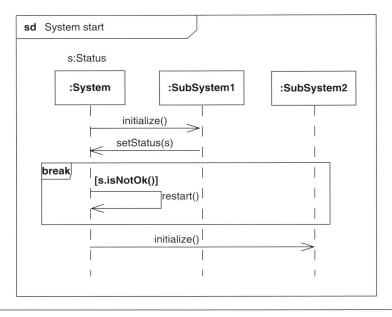

FIGURE 3.146 Example of the interaction operator *break*.

Continuation points (see Figures 3.147 and 3.148) are only significant in connection with conditional fragments and weak sequencing. They appear either at the end of an interaction fragment (property: *setting=true*) or at the beginning (*setting=false*). When a flow of control hits a continuation point at the end of a fragment, the flow of control continues at the continuation point by the same name at the beginning of a fragment.

A continuation point is denoted similarly to a state, but it extends over several lifelines; a state invariant is always on one lifeline only.

A parallel fragment is labeled by the interaction operator *par*. The interaction operands are parallel flows of control. This means that there can be an arbitrary sequence of events between the operands.

In Figure 3.149, message p can be sent any time during the messages q, r, and t. For example, $< p!, p^*, t!, t^*, q!, r!, r^*, q^* >$ and $< r!, p!, t!, t^*, q!, r^*, q^*, p^* >$ would be valid sequences of events.

If there is only one lifeline in a parallel fragment, then we call this a *core-gion* (Figure 3.150). In this case, the notation changes since representing it as a combined fragment would appear overloaded. A coregion is denoted by square brackets on the lifeline. Each interaction fragment within the brackets corresponds to an operand.

3.6.3.5

3.6.3.6

3.6.3.7

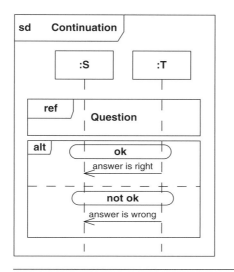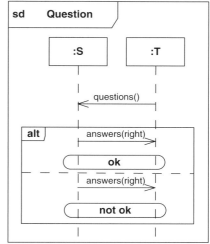

FIGURE 3.147 Example of continuation points.

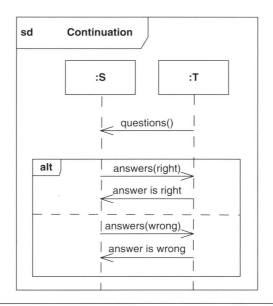

FIGURE 3.148 Interpreting the continuation points from Figure 3.147.

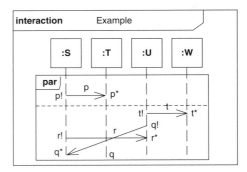

FIGURE 3.149 Example of the interaction operator *par*.

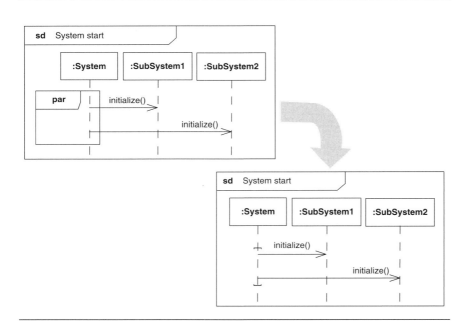

FIGURE 3.150 Example of a coregion.

Weak sequencing is a fragment with the interaction operator *seq* and an arbitrary number of operands (see Figure 3.151). Three rules define the sequencing between send and receive events:

3.6.3.8

1. The sequence of events within an operand is fixed.
2. Events within different operands on different lifelines have no defined sequence.
3. Events within different operands on the same lifeline use the sequence of the operands.

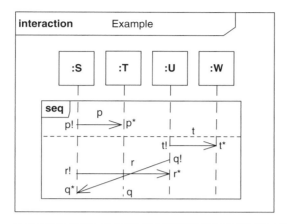

FIGURE 3.151 Example of the interaction operator *seq*.

So, a weak sequence is actually similar to a parallel fragment, with the additional property that the events along a lifeline are ordered. For example, $< p!, p^*, t!, t^*, q!, r!, r^*, q^* >$ and $< p!, t!, t^*, p^*, q!, r!, r^*, q^* >$ in Figure 3.151 would be valid flows of control.

3.6.3.9   *Strict sequencing* defines a fragment with a sequencing that is more rigid than the one defined by the interaction operator *seq*. The interaction operator used here is *strict*. The vertical position of an event determines the sequence, regardless of the lifeline; for example, $< p!, p^*, t!, t^*, q!, r!, r^*, q^* >$ in Figure 3.152 is valid.

3.6.3.10   A *loop* is specified by the interaction operator *loop* (Figure 3.153). You can specify the minimum and maximum number of loop iterations and an abort condition.

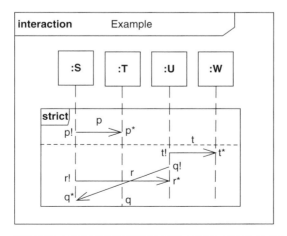

FIGURE 3.152 Example of the interaction operator *strict*.

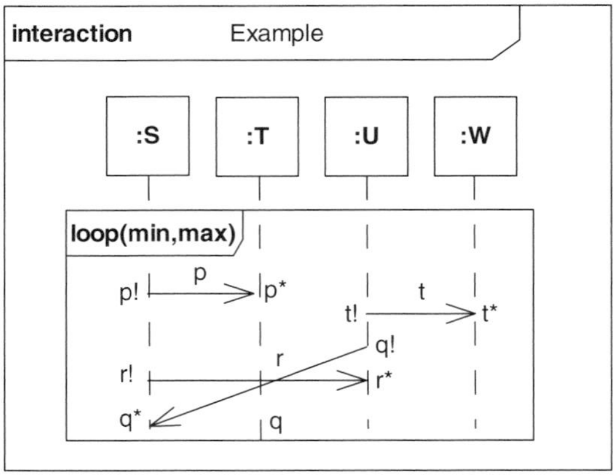

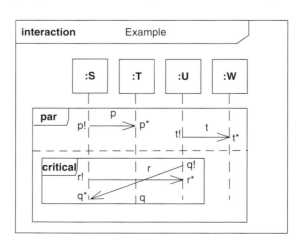

FIGURE 3.153 Example of the interaction operator *loop*.

A loop executes at least <min> times. You can optionally state a condition that will be evaluated after <min> executions upon each iteration and that can lead to an abortion. The maximum number of loop iterations is specified by <max>. If <max> is not stated, then <min>=<max>. If neither <min> nor <max> is stated, then <min>= 0 and <max>= *, that is, infinite. The loop can then be terminated only by the abort condition.

3.6.3.11

A loop has only one operand.

A *critical fragment* is specified by the interaction operator *critical*. The sequence described in the fragment is atomic and has to be fully traversed before new messages can be accepted. A critical fragment defines a sequence of events that cannot be interrupted by any other event. In Figure 3.154, for example,

3.6.3.12

FIGURE 3.154 Example of the interaction operator *critical*.

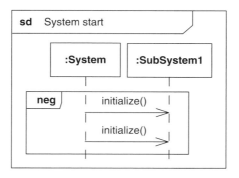

FIGURE 3.155 Example of the interaction operator *neg*.

$<p!, r!, q!, r^*, q^*, p^*, t!, t^*>$ would be a valid sequence, and $< p!, r!, t!, t^*, q!, r^*, q^*, p^* >$ would be an invalid sequence.

3.6.3.13   A fragment with the interaction operator *neg* specifies an invalid sequence of send and receive events (Figure 3.155). In general, you would describe only valid sequences. However, the semantics of an interaction is defined by the (P, I) pair, where P is the set of valid sequences and I the set of invalid sequences. With the interaction operator *neg* UML offers you a way to also define invalid sequences. A negated fragment has only one operand.

3.6.3.14   Since we have started dealing with undesirable things, let's look at the interaction operator *ignore* (Figure 3.156). Immediately behind the interaction operator, the messages to be ignored in the corresponding fragment are denoted within curly brackets. In other words, although these messages may occur, they have no impact whatsoever.

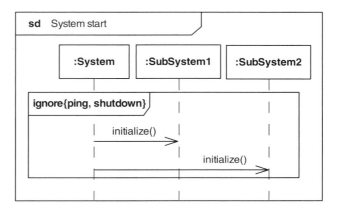

FIGURE 3.156 Example of the interaction operator *ignore*.

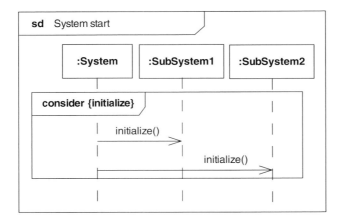

FIGURE 3.157   Example of the interaction operator *consider*.

Returning to more assertive territory, the interaction operator *consider* can be used to specify messages that must be considered inversely in the same way (Figure 3.157). All messages that do not appear in the *consider* operator's list are to be ignored automatically (see description of the interaction operator *ignore*).

3.6.3.15

An interaction describes a limited situation between selected elements. It is not necessary to model all messages that can occur within a scenario. On the other hand, a complete interaction represents an important piece of information. To ensure that an interaction is complete, you can use the interaction operator *assert*, which shows that there are no other valid flows of control within a fragment (Figure 3.158).

3.6.3.16

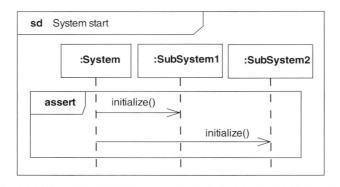

FIGURE 3.158   Example of the interaction operator *assert*.

Metamodel

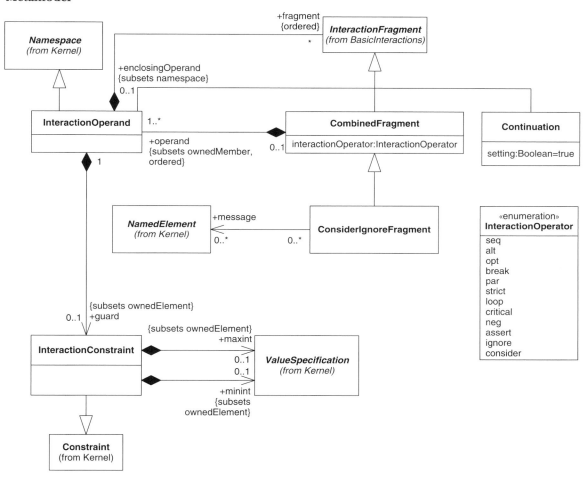

FIGURE 3.159 The metamodel for combined fragments.

CHECKLIST: COMBINED FRAGMENTS

☐ 3.6.3.1. List the characteristics of *CombinedFragment*.
☐ 3.6.3.2. List the characteristics of the interaction operator *alt*.
☐ 3.6.3.3. List the characteristics of the interaction operator *opt*. How does it differ from the interaction operator *alt*?

☐	3.6.3.4.	List the characteristics of the interaction operator *break*. How does it differ from the interaction operator *opt*?
☐	3.6.3.5.	List the characteristics of *Continuation*.
☐	3.6.3.6.	List the characteristics of the interaction operator *par*.
☐	3.6.3.7.	List the characteristics of *Coregion*. How does it relate to the interaction operator *par*?
☐	3.6.3.8.	List the characteristics of the interaction operator *seq*.
☐	3.6.3.9.	List the characteristics of the interaction operator *strict*. How does it differ from the interaction operator *seq*?
☐	3.6.3.10.	List the characteristics of the interaction operator *loop*. How is a loop specified?
☐	3.6.3.11.	How does *loop* behave if no *min* or *max* is stated?
☐	3.6.3.12.	List the characteristics of the interaction operator *critical*.
☐	3.6.3.13.	List the characteristics of the interaction operator *neg*.
☐	3.6.3.14.	List the characteristics of the interaction operator *ignore*.
☐	3.6.3.15.	List the characteristics of the interaction operator *consider*.
☐	3.6.3.16.	List the characteristics of the interaction operator *assert*.

3.6.4   CONNECTION POINTS (GATE)

Definition

Gate is a connection point that connects a message outside an interaction fragment with a message inside that fragment. (See Figure 3.160.)

Notation and Semantics

Consider the example represented in Figure 3.161. It shows a notation commonly used in sequence diagrams to show a message that begins at the diagram frame and ends at an interaction reference (*InteractionUse*).

This representation can be easily understood in the diagram. The diagram maps a model that specifies the message *initialize()*. But what are the start and target points of the message in the model?

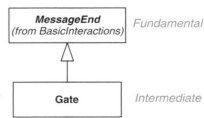

FIGURE 3.160 Arrangement of connection points (Gate).

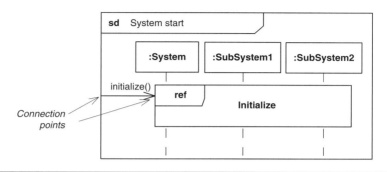

FIGURE 3.161 Example of connection points (gates).

3.6.4.1   In general, the end points of a message are mapped as message ends in the model. *Gate* is a connection point representing a special message end that connects messages outside an interaction fragment with a message inside that fragment.

     A connection point can belong to an interaction, in which case it is called *formalGate*, while *cfragmentGate* is a connection point that belongs to a combined fragment, and *actualGate* is one that belongs to an interaction reference.

3.6.4.2   A connection point is denoted as a point on the frame, which means that it is not explicitly visible. The point can be named; its name is shown next to the point in the diagram.

Metamodel

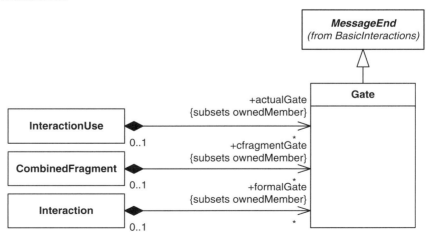

FIGURE 3.162 The metamodel for connection points (gates).

CHECKLIST: CONNECTION POINTS (GATES)

- ☐ 3.6.4.1.   List the characteristics of *Gate*.
- ☐ 3.6.4.2.   Describe the notation for *Gate*.

3.6.5   COMMUNICATION DIAGRAMS

The *communication diagram* in UML 2 is the *collaboration diagram* of UML 1.x. It was renamed because this diagram type represents no collaboration, but a communication between elements.

A communication diagram (Figure 3.163) represents a special view of an interaction model. It shows almost the same information as a sequence diagram, except that the communication diagram emphasizes the topology of the communicating elements rather than the message sequence. The sequence of messages is represented by a numbering scheme.

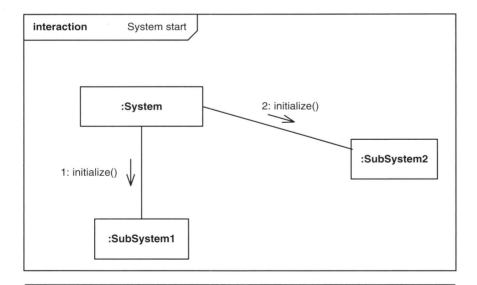

FIGURE 3.163   Example of communication diagrams.

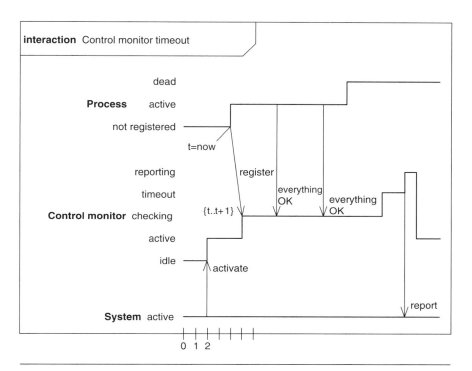

FIGURE 3.164 Example of timing diagrams.

3.6.6 TIMING DIAGRAMS

A *timing diagram* is another diagram type that represents a special view of an interaction model (Figure 3.164). Timing diagrams emphasize time or, more specifically, the states of a lifeline as they change along a real linear time axis. The states correspond to state invariants in the interaction model.

3.6.7 INTERACTION OVERVIEW DIAGRAMS

The interaction overview diagram looks like an activity diagram. In fact it is an interaction diagram that uses the same notation as an activity diagram. The action nodes are interactions or interaction uses. The control nodes are mapped to combined fragments. The diagram describes the sequence of interactions (Figure 3.165).

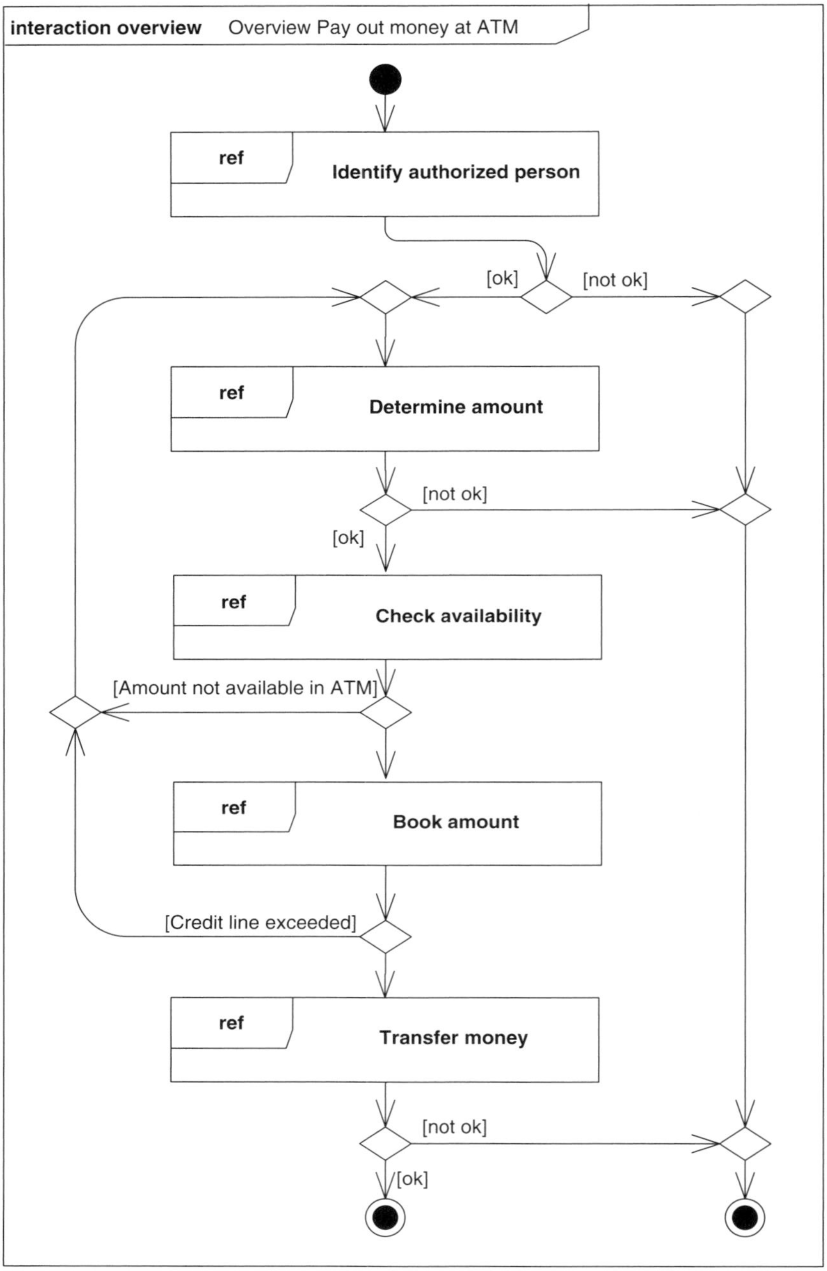

interaction overview   Overview Pay out money at ATM

ref   **Identify authorized person**

[ok]   [not ok]

ref   **Determine amount**

[not ok]

[ok]

ref   **Check availability**

[Amount not available in ATM]

ref   **Book amount**

[Credit line exceeded]

ref   **Transfer money**

[not ok]

[ok]

FIGURE 3.165   Example of interaction overview diagrams.

3.7 STATE DIAGRAMS

This section discusses a form of diagram that is elementary in information technology. *State machine diagrams* are based on the theory of finite machines (Figure 3.166). In his seminal work, David Harel has laid the foundations for their use in (software) system development [Harel1987].

UML 2 hasn't introduced fundamental changes to UML 1.x in this field. So, if you know the state diagrams of UML 1.x, the concepts in this section will be familiar.

3.7.1 EXAMINATION TOPICS

The following topics are covered in the test Intermediate certification:

- State machines
- States and transitions
- Pseudostates

This topic area constitutes 15 percent of the test.

3.7.2 STATE MACHINES

Definition

StateMachine is a special behavior. Behavior is modeled as a traversal of a graph of nodes interconnected by directed edges. The nodes are states or pseudostates and the edges are transitions.

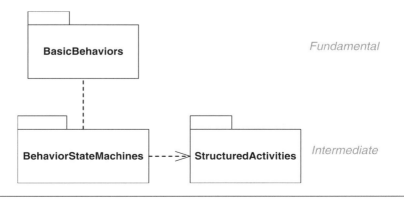

FIGURE 3.166 The package structure for state machines.

A *state* describes a system situation in which an invariant is valid.

FinalState is a special state that indicates that the enclosing region is completed.

Pseudostate is a state that represents a transient node in a state machine.

ConnectionPointReference is a connection point that represents special entry and exit points of a referenced state machine.

Vertex is a state node that represents the base class for all nodes in a state machine.

Transition is a directed relationship between a source and a target vertex.

Region represents a container for transitions and state nodes.

Figure 3.167 shows the arrangement of the state machine model elements.

Notation and Semantics

Figure 3.168 shows a simplified state machine, representing *Time of Day* in a diagram frame. This state machine consists of one single region with an initial state (*pseudostate*), two simple states, *Day* and *Night*, a final state, and four transitions.   *3.7.2.1*

Since behavior is a special class, a state machine as a specialization of behavior can also be specialized (*Generalization*), among other things (see Figure 3.169). Inherited states and transitions are denoted as dashes in the specialized state diagram, unless they are changed (redefined). In the diagram header of a specialized state diagram, {*extended*} is stated after the diagram name. Potential redefinitions during the generalization of state machines are emphasized later in the chapter in Figure 3.185 (see page 237).

A state machine has an *event pool*. From the event pool, events reach the state machine where they can trigger transitions, and where the *run-to-completion* semantics applies. This semantic means that an event is accepted from the event pool if processing of the previous event has been completed.   *3.7.2.2*

States and pseudostates are unified in the abstract superclass *Vertex*. A vertex is part of a region in a graph, and it is linked with incoming or outgoing transitions. The superclass is *NamedElement*. This means that no other properties are inherited.   *3.7.2.3*

A *state* represents a measurable value configuration[4] of the modeled element.   *3.7.2.4*
In contrast, a pseudostate does not represent a value configuration.   *3.7.2.5*

There are four types of state:

- *Simple state* contains no region.
- *Composite state* contains at least one region.
- *Orthogonal state* contains at least two regions.
- *Submachine state* references a state machine.

---

[4] "Value configuration" means a set of possible value combinations from *StructuralFeature*. An example is hour = 16, minute = 23, second = 42 for an object of the class *Time of Day* in Figure 3.168.

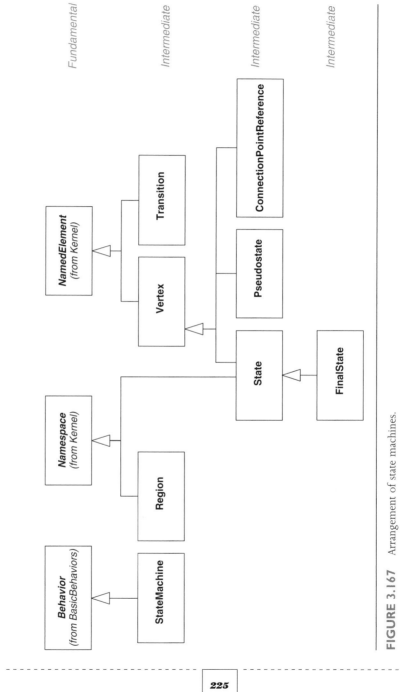

FIGURE 3.167 Arrangement of state machines.

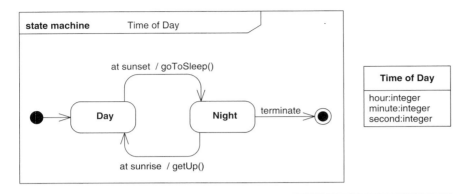

FIGURE 3.168 A simplified state machine, Time of Day, with the pertaining class.

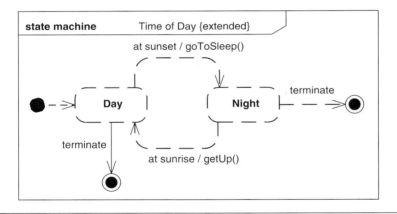

FIGURE 3.169 Generalizing state machines.

The type of state is specified in the derived attributes *isSimple, isComposite, isOrthogonal,* and *isSubmachineState.*

A state is denoted as a rectangle with rounded corners. A state can optionally contain compartments for additional information. In that case, the name of the state may be written in a name tab (see Figure 3.170).

The states shown in the *Time of Day* state machine from Figure 3.168 are simple states.

In Figure 3.170, the state *morning* has no region, and the state *Day* has exactly one region. This means that *Day* is a composite state. The details of a composite state can be hidden. The state will then be represented by a special symbol in the lower right corner, similarly to a simple state. You can see an example in Figure 3.171.

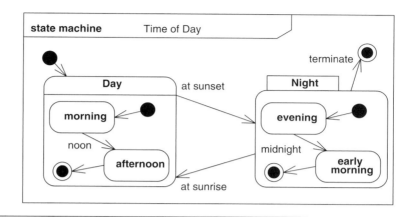

FIGURE 3.170   The Time of Day state machine with a composite state.

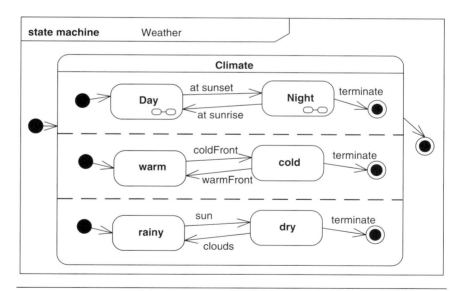

FIGURE 3.171   A state machine, Weather, with an orthogonal state.

Additionally Figure 3.171 shows an orthogonal state, *Climate*. "Orthogonal" means that the regions are independent. We also speak of "parallel" or "concurrent" regions. For example, the state *Climate* is concurrently present in three substates—*Day*, *cold*, and *rainy* in this example. Orthogonal regions are separated by dashed lines. You might have noticed that an orthogonal state is also a composite state.

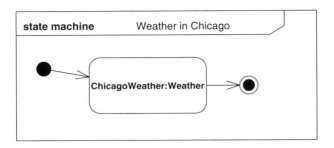

FIGURE 3.172 Example of a state with submachine.

The fourth and last kind of state may appear a little strange at first: a state with a submachine (Figure 3.172). How does this state differ from a composite state? They are both states that, in detail, have substates and transitions themselves. Well, they are nearly identical. They differ only in that a state with a submachine is required if we want to reuse an existing state machine. With a composite state, we can't use an existing state machine.

Figure 3.172 reuses the state machine *Weather* from Figure 3.171 in the state *ChicagoWeather*. The syntax is as follows:

```
<name of state> : <name of state machine>
```

A state can own internal behavior. We distinguish three behavior categories: *3.7.2.6*

- *Entry behavior* executes immediately upon entering a state.
- *Exit behavior* executes immediately before exiting a state.
- *Do behavior* executes while a state is active.

Internal behavior is represented in a separate compartment within the state symbol (see Figure 3.173).

FinalState is a special state. Note that it is not a pseudostate, such as the initial   *3.7.2.7*
state, among others. When a final state is reached, then the pertaining enclosing region is left.

A final state has no outgoing transitions and no internal behavior (*entry, exit,* and *do*), and it cannot own regions.

A *transition* specifies the passage from one state to another state. A state transition   *3.7.2.8*
can be specified in more detail by stating a trigger, a condition (*guard*), and an   *3.7.2.9*
effect (*BasicBehavior::Activity*). If no trigger is stated, the state transition is triggered immediately upon the end of the state's (*do*) behavior, or as soon as the final states of inner regions are reached. In Figure 3.171, for example, the transition leading

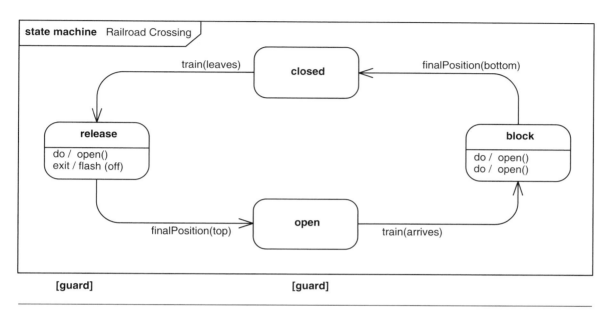

FIGURE 3.173   States with internal behavior.

from the state *Climate* fires as soon as the final states of the three inner regions are reached. "Such a transition is called completion transition."

The following conditions must be valid to fire a transition:

- The source states of the transition must be active.
- The trigger of the transition is occurred.
- The guard condition is true.

3.7.2.10   UML knows four types of event that can trigger a transition:

1. CallEvent
2. ChangeEvent
3. SignalEvent
4. TimeEvent

TimeEvent is an event that, in the context of state machines, is extended by a property. The relative time event (with the keyword *after*) is triggered when the state from which the interesting transition origins has been active over the specified length of time (Figure 3.174).

A transition condition (*guard*) is evaluated when the trigger has been activated or when there is no trigger. A transition will lead to a state transition only if the condition is *true*.

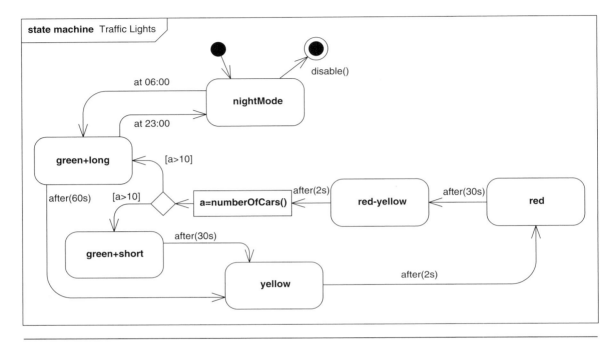

FIGURE 3.174 Example of a transition with a time effect.

An *effect* is an activity that executes upon a state transition. The activity or action sequence can be denoted separately by a slash after the trigger or within a rectangle (see Figure 3.174). Actions that send or receive signals can be represented by using the appropriate symbols discussed in Section 3.4.3.

Similarly to states, transitions are distinguished as simple or compound transitions. A *simple transition* connects two states directly. A *compound transition* consists of several transitions that use one or more pseudostates to link one state with another state (Figure 3.175).

Another classification of transitions can be found in the Enumeration class *TransitionKind*. There are internal, external, and local transitions.

An *internal transition* occurs within a state; that is, the value configuration specified by the state will not be changed. Internal transitions are denoted within the state, like internal activities. Note the difference between internal transitions and recursive transitions. A *recursive transition* is a transition the target state and the start state of which are equal, and both its entry and exit behavior are executed (left side of Figure 3.176). This is not the case with internal transitions (right side of Figure 3.176).

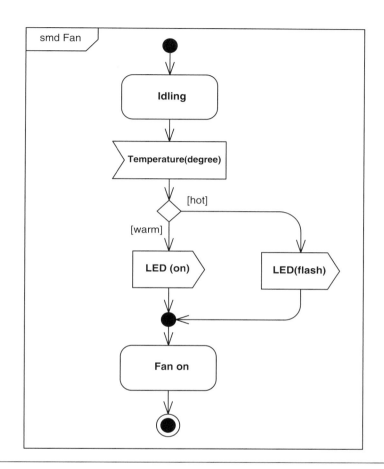

FIGURE 3.175 Example of effects.

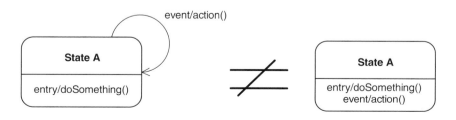

FIGURE 3.176 Recursive versus internal transition.

Local transitions are inside a composite state. External transitions leave a composite state.

In closing this section, let's have a closer look at pseudostates, which we have mentioned several times. There are ten pseudostates (see Enumeration class *PseudostateKind*):

1. Initial state
2. Deep history
3. Shallow history
4. Join
5. Fork
6. Junction
7. Choice
8. Exit point
9. Entry point
10. Terminate

Initial state is a pseudostate that labels the start point of a region. It has only one outgoing transition that leads to the region's default state.   3.7.2.11

There are two types of history state: *shallow history* and *deep history*. To understand history states better, let's first look at the state machine of a hair dryer that doesn't contain history yet (Figure 3.177). As soon as the hair dryer is switched on, it jumps into the default state configurations *cold* and *low*. Unless you are particularly concerned about damaging your hair, you will probably switch the hair dryer   3.7.2.12

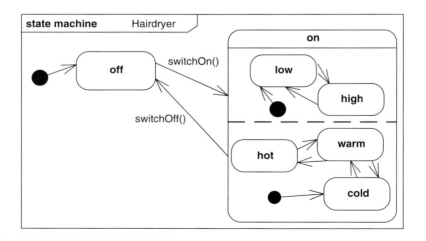

FIGURE 3.177 A state machine, *Hairdryer*.

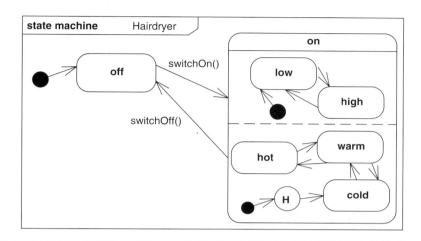

FIGURE 3.178   A state machine, *Hairdryer*, with shallow history.

from *low* to *high* and from *cold* to *hot*. You usually switch the hair dryer off when your hair is dry. The next time you use the hair dryer it will come on in the default state configuration *low* and *cold*. So again, you have to go through the hassle of resetting it to *high* and *hot*. After the third, fourth, or fifth time you do this, you might not want to use that hair dryer every day. This situation can be improved by using a history pseudostate, at least in the model.

In Figure 3.178 you can see that a "bus stop" symbol has been inserted directly after the initial state. This is the notation for *shallow history*. Alternatively the history pseudostate can be drawn without being connected by a transition (see Figure 3.179). The first time you use the hair dryer, you won't notice any difference. However, shallow history causes the last active substate of a region to be stored. If you switch the hair dryer on a second time, when traversing the flat history, the device will read the last active state and activate it directly. This means that the hair dryer will immediately jump into the *low* and *hot* configuration after the second time you use it.

As the name implies, *deep history* has a "deeper" effect than shallow history. To understand better, let's extend our hair dryer example by adding two substates, *regular* and *extreme*, to the state *hot*. As just described, shallow history causes the state *hot* to activate when the hair dryer is switched on again; that is, the state *regular* becomes active in the inner region of *hot*. In contrast, if we use deep history, as in Figure 3.179, the last active state configuration will also be restored in the substates. This means, for example, that the hair dryer will immediately jump into the state configuration *low* and *hot/extreme* as you switch it on.

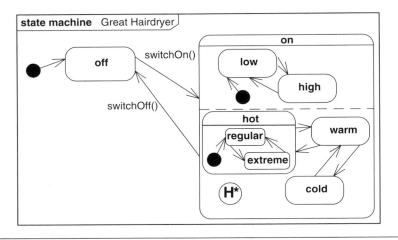

FIGURE 3.179 A state machine, *Hairdryer*, with deep history.

The deep history pseudostate shows an asterisk behind the "H" in addition to the shallow history pseudostate notation.

Junction (static conditional branch) is a pseudostate that joins several transitions into a path. It is possible to join several incoming transitions, or branch transitions, into several outgoing transitions. Static branching has no other semantics. The notation for branching is a black circle (Figure 3.175).   *3.7.2.13*

Choice (dynamic conditional branch) differs from junction in that the conditions can be evaluated on the basis of values that are determined only upon state transition (Figures 3.174 and 3.175). Moreover, choice is not used to join transitions. The notation for choice is a rhombus, like in the activity diagram.   *3.7.2.14*

Terminate is a pseudostate that terminates the behavior described by the state machine without the modeled classifier taking on a new value configuration. Otherwise, rather than terminate, it would be a real new state—the final state. Terminate is denoted as a cross without enclosing circle or rectangle (Figure 3.180).   *3.7.2.15*

Fork is a pseudostate that has an incoming transition and several outgoing transitions. The outgoing transitions lead to different states that appear orthogonally one on top of the other, which means that all target states will be activated. The outgoing transitions must have neither conditions (guards) nor triggers.   *3.7.2.16*

In contrast, *join* is a pseudostate that has several incoming transitions, which come from states appearing orthogonally one of top of the other, and one outgoing transition.

Both splitting (fork) and synchronization (join) are denoted as filled bars. They differ in the context of incoming and outgoing transitions (Figure 3.181).

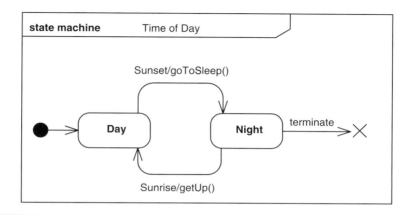

FIGURE 3.180   A state machine with a terminate pseudostate.

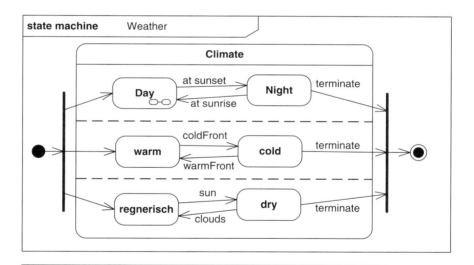

FIGURE 3.181   Example of splitting (fork) and synchronization (join).

3.7.2.17   *Entry point* is a pseudostate that describes an entry point of a state machine. A transition leads from the entry point to a state in every region of the state machine.

Exit point is a pseudostate that terminates a state machine. When a transition in an arbitrary region of the state machine reaches an exit point, then the state machine is terminated and the transition coming from the exit point is activated.

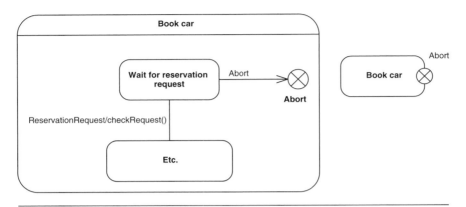

FIGURE 3.182   Notation for an exit point.

An entry point is denoted as a white circle and an exit point is denoted as a circle with a cross (Figure 3.182).

Entry and exit points of statemachines that are referenced by a submachine state are represented by a so-called connection point reference. The notation of a connection point reference is the same as for entry and exit points.   *3.7.2.18*

An entry or exit point can alternatively be denoted in text form at the transition (see Figures 3.183 and 3.184). The syntax is as follows:

```
'( via'name ')'
```

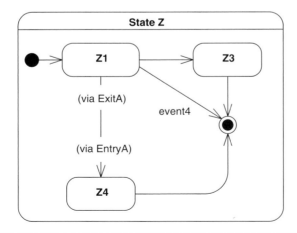

FIGURE 3.183   Alternative notation for an entry or exit point.

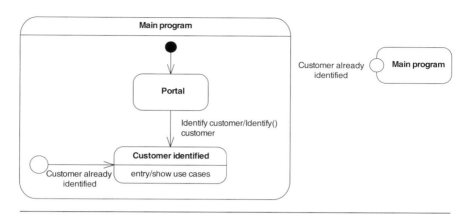

FIGURE 3.184 Example of an entry point.

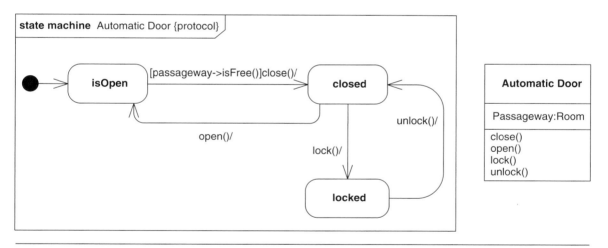

FIGURE 3.185 Example of a protocol statemachine [UML2.0].

The protocol statemachine is a special statemachine that describes the protocol of a classifier. That means it specifies which operations of the classifier can be called under which condition (Figure 3.185). The notation of the transitions in a protocol statemachine has a different meaning than in normal state machines:

```
[precondition] operation / postcondition
```

Metamodel

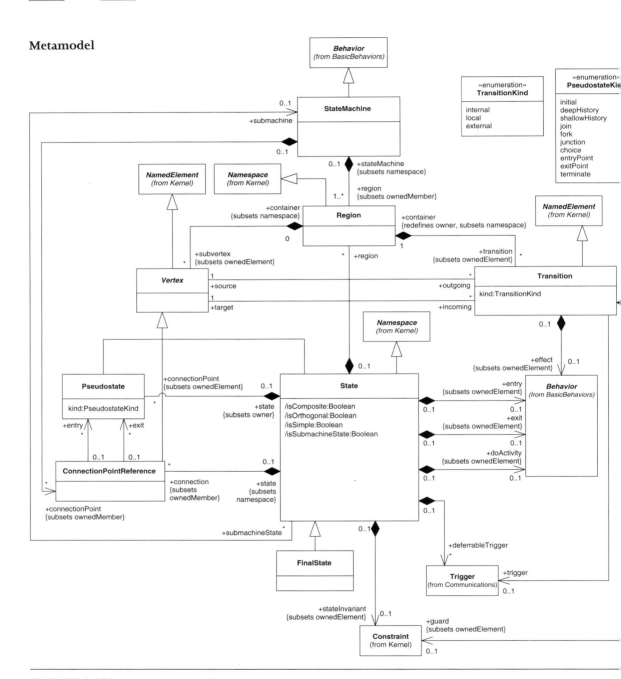

FIGURE 3.186 The metamodel for state machines.

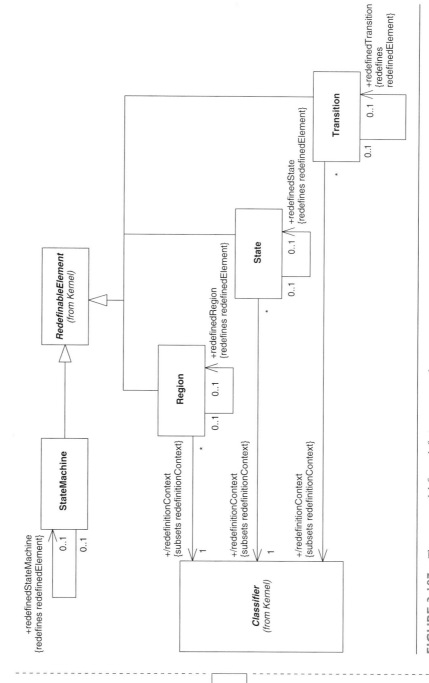

FIGURE 3.187 The metamodel for redefining state machines.

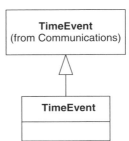

FIGURE 3.188   The metamodel for time events.

CHECKLIST: STATE MACHINES

☐ 3.7.2.1.   Explain the structure of a state machine.
☐ 3.7.2.2.   Explain the *run-to-completion* semantics.
☐ 3.7.2.3.   List the characteristics of the *Vertex* state node.
☐ 3.7.2.4.   List the different kinds of state and their properties.
☐ 3.7.2.5.   Explain the difference between *Pseudostate* and *State*.
☐ 3.7.2.6.   Explain the internal behavior of a state.
☐ 3.7.2.7.   List the characteristics of *FinalState*.
☐ 3.7.2.8.   List the characteristics of *Transition*.
☐ 3.7.2.9.   Explain the functionality of a completion transition.
☐ 3.7.2.10. Explain the triggers possible at a transition.
☐ 3.7.2.11. Explain the functionality of *InitialState*.
☐ 3.7.2.12. Explain the functionality of *history state*. What is the difference between *deep* history and *shallow* history?
☐ 3.7.2.13. Explain the functionality of static branching (*junction*).
☐ 3.7.2.14. Explain the functionality of *choice*.
☐ 3.7.2.15. Explain the difference between *FinalState* and *terminate*.
☐ 3.7.2.16. Explain the functionality of splitting (*fork*) and synchronization (*join*).
☐ 3.7.2.17. Explain the functionality of *entry* and *exit* points.
☐ 3.7.2.18. Explain the functionality of a connection point reference?

3.8 DEPLOYMENT DIAGRAMS

This section discusses *deployment diagrams*—a type of diagram used to model a system's hardware topology and software deployment (see Figure 3.189).

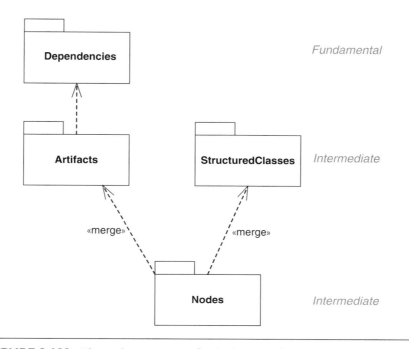

FIGURE 3.189 The package structure for deployment diagrams.

3.8.1   EXAMINATION TOPICS

The topics of the Intermediate test include the description of hardware topologies. A detailed description of software deployment is part of the examination for the Advanced certification.

The following topics are covered on the Intermediate test:

- Artifacts
- Nodes

This topic area constitutes 5 percent of the test.

3.8.2   ARTIFACTS

Definition
An *artifact* is the specification of a physical piece of information that is used or produced by a software development process.

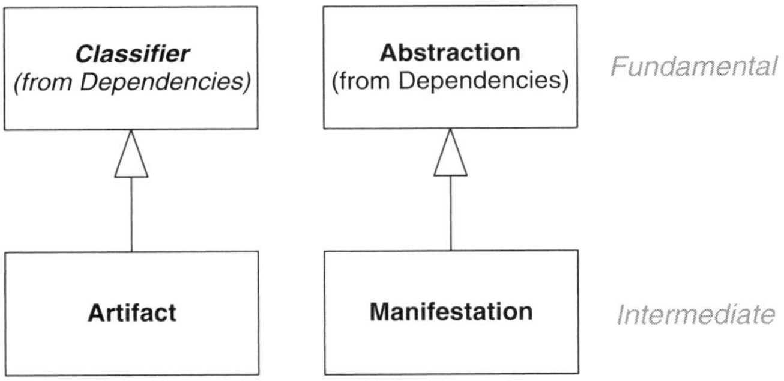

FIGURE 3.190   Arrangement of artifacts and manifestations.

A *manifestation* is the concrete physical rendering of one or more model elements by an artifact.

Figure 3.190 shows artifacts and manifestations.

Notation and Semantics

In general, an *artifact* represents a file. However, a physical piece of information can also be an e-mail or a database table, to name two. The list of standard stereotypes predefined in UML include stereotypes that categorize artifacts, as shown in Table 3.2.

3.8.2.1

An artifact is a special classifier, which means that it inherits the property to own attributes and operations. Moreover, artifacts can be generalized.

TABLE 3.2   UML Artifact Stereotypes

Stereotype	UML Element	Description
"document"	artifact	A file that does not contain source code and cannot be executed.
"file"	artifact	A physical file (but not, for instance, an e-mail or database table).
"library"	artifact	A static or dynamic software library in the form of a file.
"source"	artifact	A file that contains source and can be compiled.

FIGURE 3.191 The notation and examples for artifacts.

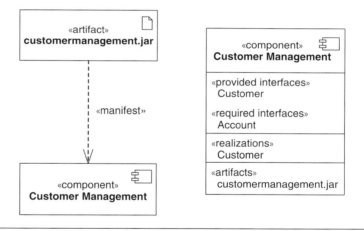

FIGURE 3.192 Notation and example for manifestations.

An artifact also inherits its notation from the classifier. You can additionally use a document symbol in the upper right corner of the rectangle. (See Figure 3.191.)

3.8.2.2
3.8.2.3
3.8.2.4
A manifestation is a special abstraction relationship between an artifact and a packageable model element. The model element does not know anything about its physical representation.

A manifestation is represented as a dashed arrow and the keyword *manifest* (see Figure 3.192). The manifested artifact can also be listed in the table notation of the component.

Metamodel

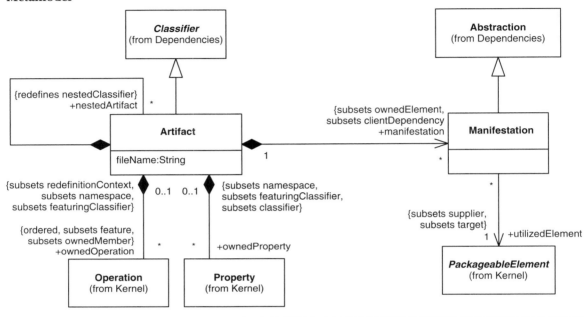

FIGURE 3.193 The metamodel for artifacts.

CHECKLIST: ARTIFACTS

- ☐ 3.8.2.1. List the characteristics of *Artifact*.
- ☐ 3.8.2.2. List the characteristics of *Manifestation*.
- ☐ 3.8.2.3. Explain the relation between *Artifact* and *PackageableElement*.
- ☐ 3.8.2.4. Explain the modeling direction of *Manifestation*.

3.8.3 NODES

A deployment diagram can be thought of as a bridge from a logical model to the physical environment that runs the modeled system. A logical model element can be manifested by an artifact. The artifact, in turn, is assigned to a node. The detailed specification of software deployment (*DeploymentSpecification*) is part of the examination for the Advanced certification.

3.8.3.1

Definition

A *node* is a computational resource upon which artifacts may be deployed for execution.

An *execution environment* is a special node that offers an execution environment for specific types of component that are deployed on it in the form of executable artifacts.

A *device* in this context is a physical computational resource with processing capability upon which artifacts may be deployed for execution.

A *communication path* is an association between two deployment targets, through which they are able to exchange signals and messages.

Figure 3.194 shows nodes, devices, execution environments, and communication paths.

Notation and Semantics

3.8.3.2
3.8.3.3
A node is a concrete model element, but it also serves as a generic term for specializations, such as *Device* and *ExecutionEnvironment*. These specializations are denoted like nodes, using the keywords *device* and *executionEnvironment*, respectively. In addition,

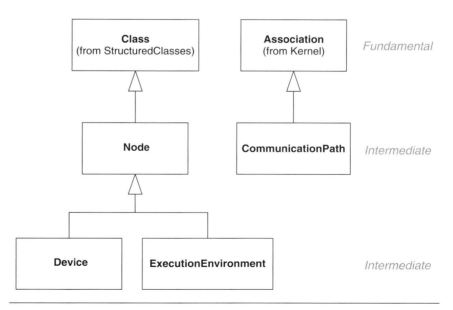

FIGURE 3.194 Arrangement of nodes, devices, execution environments, and communication paths.

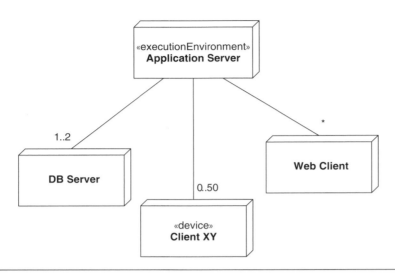

FIGURE 3.195 Example of deployment diagrams.

user-specific stereotypes can be used to define more categories. UML does not predefine standard stereotypes to this end.

Since nodes are special classes, a generalization relationship, among other things, can be used to model them.

A communication path is an association that connects nodes so that they are   *3.8.3.4* able to communicate. Note that this is a special association. Accordingly, it is possible, for instance, to state multiplicities.

The deployment allocates artifacts to a deployment target, for example, nodes. The relationship is shown as a dashed arrow from the artifact to the deployment target with keyword "*deploy*". As an alternative, the artifact may be shown inside the symbol of the deployment target (Figure 3.195).

CHECKLIST: NODES
- ☐ 3.8.3.1.   What does *deployment* mean?
- ☐ 3.8.3.2.   List the characteristics and purpose of a *node*.
- ☐ 3.8.3.3.   List the subclasses of a node and their meanings.
- ☐ 3.8.3.4.   Explain how nodes can communicate.

Metamodel

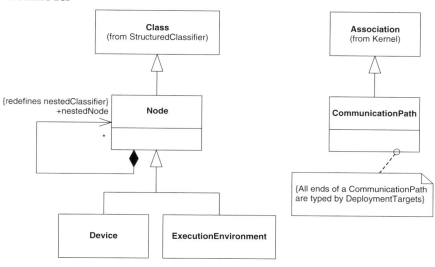

FIGURE 3.196 The metamodel for nodes.

3.9 PROFILES

This section discusses a lightweight extension mechanism (second class extension) of UML: profiles (Figure 3.197). It's called lightweight because it doesn't define new elements in the metamodel of UML. A *profile* is understood as a set of stereotypes. A stereotype extends the UML vocabulary by adding an element. The extension is fully controlled, so that UML cannot be extended arbitrarily in any direction, since this would contradict the standardization thought.

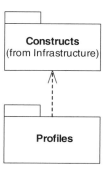

FIGURE 3.197 The package structure for profiles.

The extension mechanism in UML 1.1 is relatively imprecise in the sense that extensions could be made only on the basis of the primitive data type *string*. UML 2.0 lets you use arbitrary data structures for extended elements, which means that more extensive and more precise model extensions are now possible.

To understand the stereotype mechanism better, let's look at the four-layer architecture of UML (Figure 3.198). UML is defined on the level **M2**. The elements that are required to describe the UML metamodel (a pure class model) on level **M2** are defined on the next higher level, **M3**. Level **M1** represents the user's UML model.

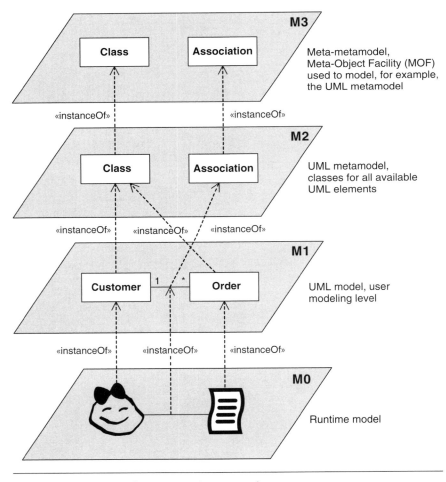

FIGURE 3.198 The four-layer architecture of UML.

The stereotype mechanism is special particularly because it acts in several levels. It is defined in level **M3** to extend elements on level **M2**. But it is also defined in level **M2**, so that new user-specific stereotypes can be specified on level **M1**.

This might be a bit confusing. Stereotypes regularly cause misunderstandings and lengthy discussions, even among the UML Specification Workgroups. But don't worry. You will find an easily understandable explanation of the extension mechanism on the following pages.

3.9.1   EXAMINATION TOPICS

The following topics are covered in the test for the Intermediate OCUP certificate:

- Stereotypes, extensions
- Profiles, profile applications

This topic area constitutes 10 percent of the test.

3.9.2   STEREOTYPES

Definition
A *stereotype* describes how an existing metaclass can be extended; enabling the integration of platform or domain-specific terminology or notation in the modeling language.

A *class* in the context of stereotypes is extended by a derived association for stereotype extension.

A stereotype *extension* is used to indicate that the properties of a metaclass are extended through a stereotype. This is a special binary association.

An *extension end* is used to tie an extension to a stereotype when extending a etaclass.

Figure 3.199 shows stereotypes, classes, stereotype extensions, and extension ends.

Notation and Semantics
The opinion that stereotypes extend the UML metamodel by adding generalization circulates occasionally in specialist circles. After all, the common statement "stereotype XY extends . . . " would actually appear to lead your thoughts in this direction.

This is wrong. Stereotype extension doesn't occur through a generalization relationship in the metamodel (Figure 3.200). And more important, no new

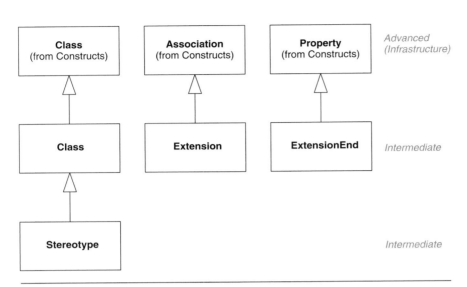

FIGURE 3.199 Arrangement of stereotypes, classes, stereotype extensions, and extension ends.

FIGURE 3.200 Wrong interpretation of stereotype extension.

metamodel element is created. What happens instead is that information is added to an existing metaclass by a stereotype; hence, the name "stereotype."

Information added to a metaclass can represent additional modeling-level properties and constraints. But if constraints are added, they may only be complementing. Constraints for an extended metaclass must not be overwritten or canceled.

A stereotype is a special class, which means that it can have both attributes and operations (see Figure 3.201). The values of stereotype attributes are also called tagged values. This is a common name in the UML world since *TaggedValue* had

3.9.2.1

3.9.2.2

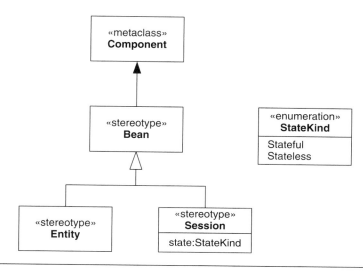

FIGURE 3.201 Example stereotypes [UML2]).

been around for some time as a separate metaclass in UML 1.x. Associations from one stereotype to another stereotype or metaclass are not allowed.

Like any classifier, stereotypes can be generalized. When generalizing a stereotype, however, the rule that a stereotype may generalize or specialize only stereotypes, but no other classifiers, must be observed.

The property *isRequired* that is used in stereotyping specifies whether or not an instance of a stereotype is always tied to an instance of the extended metaclass (*isRequired=true*).

3.9.2.3   A stereotype extension is a special association that connects a stereotype with the metaclass, which is being extended by the stereotype. Note that the metaclass *Class* in Figure 3.203 is not *Class* from the metalevel M2, but *Class* from metalevel M3 (Figure 3.198). Consequently, any UML element can be extended by stereotypes since stereotype extension is not limited to classes.

Figure 3.202 shows a section from the UML data model, also called *repository*, describing how stereotype extension looks in a use case.

There are several alternative notations for stereotyped model elements. The textual notation shows the name of the stereotype in guillemets near the name of the model element. If more than one stereotype is attached, the names of the stereotypes are separated by commas. The decoration notation is a mixture of the UML notation and a user-defined notation for the stereotype. The icon notation shows only the user-defined notation (Figure 3.203).

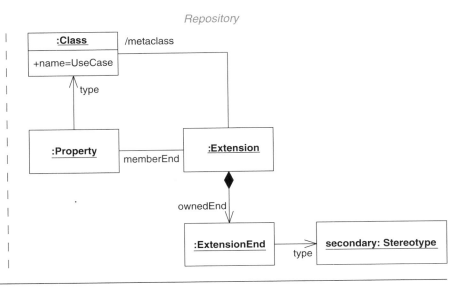

FIGURE 3.202   Repository stereotype extension.

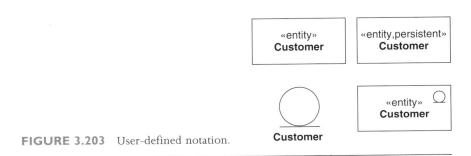

FIGURE 3.203   User-defined notation.

CHECKLIST: STEREOTYPES

☐ 3.9.2.1.   List the characteristics of a stereotype.
☐ 3.9.2.2.   Can stereotypes have attributes? Can they be generalized?
☐ 3.9.2.3.   List the characteristics of *Extension*.

Metamodel

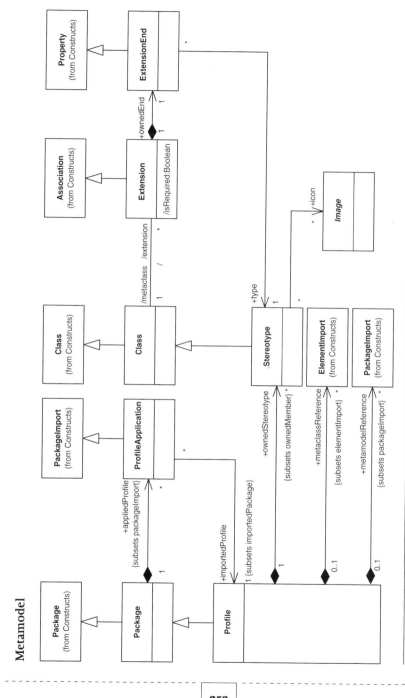

FIGURE 3.204 The metamodel for stereotypes.

3.9.3   PROFILES

Definition

A *profile* is a special package that extends a referenced metamodel by adding stereotypes. These stereotypes are then part of the profile.

A *package* in the context of profiles is extended to enable it to own profile applications.

A *profile application* is a relationship between a package and a profile that allows you to use the stereotypes from the profile in the model elements of the source package.

Figure 3.205 shows profiles, packages, and profile applications.

Notation and Semantics

You will seldom see one stereotype on its own; they usually come in bunches. In fact, domain-specific extensions in UML generally consist of a large number of stereotypes. For example, when using UML for business process modeling, you would normally need stereotypes like "business use case" or "business process".

A group of related stereotypes forms a profile. A profile is a special package   *3.9.3.1* that contains stereotypes. A profile is denoted with the keyword *profile*, similarly to a package. (See Figure 3.206.)

A profile application serves to import the stereotypes of a profile to a package,   *3.9.3.2* allowing you to use these stereotypes for model elements in the package. The association between a profile and *ElementImport* references model elements that are

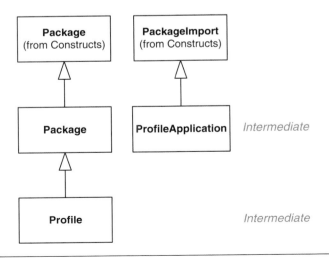

FIGURE 3.205   Arrangement of profiles, packages, and profile applications.

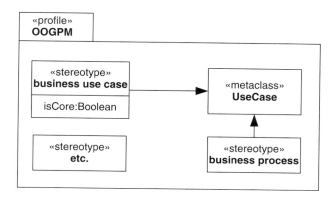

FIGURE 3.206 Example profile for business process modeling (section).

to be extended by stereotypes from that profile. Moreover, the association between a profile and *PackageImport* references packages containing the model elements that are to be extended by stereotypes from the profile.

A profile application is denoted as a dashed arrow pointing in the direction of the profile and the keyword *apply* (see Figure 3.207).

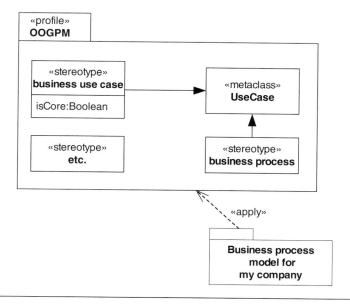

FIGURE 3.207 Example of profile applications.

Metamodel

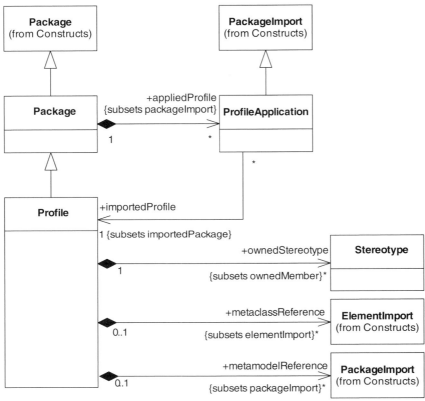

FIGURE 3.208 The metamodel for profiles.

CHECKLIST: PROFILES

☐ 3.9.3.1. List the base class and the properties of *Profile*.
☐ 3.9.3.2. Describe how a profile is used.

3.10 STANDARD STEREOTYPES

This section discusses standard stereotypes predefined in UML. The appendix of the UML specification [UML2a] defines several stereotypes. The list is divided into three sections according to the compliance points: *Basic*, *Intermediate*, and *Complete*.

3.10.1   EXAMINATION TOPICS

3.10.1.1
3.10.1.2
In contrast to the basic standard stereotypes, which are part of the examination topics for the Fundamental certification, the intermediate standard stereotypes do not officially belong to the examination topics for the test for Intermediate certification. However, the list includes not more than ten stereotypes, so that it is easily manageable; also, some stereotypes, such as "subsystem", are important in the context of the other examination topics. We will, therefore, show this list with a brief description (Table 3.3).

TABLE 3.3   Standard UML Stereotypes

Stereotype	UML Element	Description
"document"	Artifact	A file that does not contain source code and cannot be executed.
"file"	Artifact	A physical file (but not, for instance, an e-mail or database table).
"library"	artifact	A static or dynamic software library in the form of a file.
"source"	artifact	A file that contains source code and can be compiled.
"realization"	classifier	A classifier that contains implementation and generally realizes a specification (see "specification").
"specification"	classifier	A classifier that does not contain implementation and only represents a specification. Such a classifier is generally implemented by a "realization" classifier.
"entity"	component	A component that contains persistent data.
"process"	component	A component that does not contain persistent transactions.
"service"	component	A component that is stateless and provides functions.
"subsystem"	component	A special component for the hierarchical decomposition of a large system. A subsystem can be divided into a specification and a realization section (see also Section 3.2.2).

CHECKLIST: STANDARD STEREOTYPES

☐ 3.10.1.1.   Explain how the two stereotypes «specification» and «realization» relate.

☐ 3.10.1.2.   Describe the use of the «subsystem» stereotype.

A

APPENDIX

STUDY QUESTIONS

The purpose of this appendix is to show you how the real test looks and the types of questions it contains. The questions here are not taken from the OCUP examination but they are typical of the questions that appear on the test. The questions here cover parts of the fundamental exam but do not cover every topic and do not address the intermediate exam, which has the same style of questions as the fundamental exam. Some questions have more than one correct answer. In the real test, you will be informed of the number of correct answers to each question. You can check the answers in the next section.

1. Which of the following diagram types are defined in UML?
   a) Composite structure diagram
   b) Message sequence chart
   c) Data flow diagram
   d) Activity diagram

2. The use case diagram is a
   a) behavior diagram.
   b) interaction diagram.
   c) structure diagram.
   d) context diagram.
   e) requirements diagram.

3. What is a relationship? Select the best answer.
   a) Relationship is an abstract concept that specifies the kind of relationship between elements.
   b) Relationship is an arrow between two elements.

c) Relationship is an abstract concept that specifies some kind of relationship between two elements.

d) Relationship defines an association between elements.

4. Which statement(s) about DataTypes is/are correct?

a) A DataType has no attributes.

b) A DataType has no operations.

c) Instances of a DataType are different even if their attribute values are equal.

d) A DataType is a specialized class.

e) An instance of a DataType has no identity.

5. Which primitivetypes are defined in UML?

a) Boolean

b) Integer

c) Real

d) UnlimitedNatural

e) Double

f) String

6. Which is the correct notation for the PrimitiveType Integer?

a)
| «primitive» |
| **Integer** |

b) No notation

c) ☐

d) Integer

7. Which statements are correct?

a) The import relationship between Q and P is an ElementImport.

b) B is known in Q.

c) B is known in A.

d) B is known in C.

e) P is known in C.

f) It's possible to define an alias at the import relationship between Q and P.

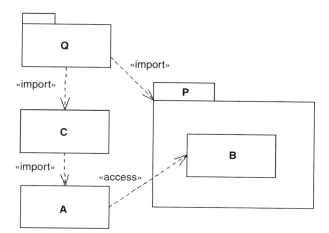

8. Which of the following are valid multiplicities?
   a) 0,1
   b) *
   c) 0..*
   d) 23..42
   e) 9..1
   f) 1
   g) −5..0

9. Which properties can be defined by a MultiplicityElement?
   a) Lower and upper values
   b) Iterator
   c) Ordering

10. What is a constraint? Select the best answer.
   a) An expression that is always true
   b) A condition expressed in natural language text or in a machine-readable language for the purpose of declaring some of the semantics of an element
   c) A structured tree of symbols that denotes a (possibly empty) set of values when evaluated in a context
   d) A boolean expression that restricts the values of an attribute

11. Which statements about an InstanceSpecification are true?
    a) InstanceSpecification is an object.
    b) InstanceSpecification represents an instance in a modeled system.
    c) InstanceSpecification represents an entity at a point in time.
    d) InstanceSpecification has a set of slots that contain the values of the structural features.

12. Which elements may be annotated by a comment?
    a) Class
    b) Operation
    c) Diagram
    d) Comment
    e) Association

13. StructuralFeature is a/an specialized
    a) NamedElement
    b) SuspectElement
    c) PackageableElement
    d) TypedElement
    e) Element
    f) Namespace

14. A class is a specialized
    a) NamedElement
    b) SuspectElement
    c) PackageableElement
    d) TypedElement
    e) Element
    f) Namespace

15. Which of the following statements are true?
    a) A NamedElement is a specialized PackageableElement
    b) A PackageableElement is a specialized NamedElement
    c) A TypedElement is a specialized NamedElement
    d) An Element is a specialized NamedElement
    e) A PackageableElement is a specialized TypedElement

16. What is a BehavioredClassifier?
    a) A classifier that can have operations.
    b) A classifier with behavior that is described by a state machine.

    c) A classifier that can have behavior specifications in its namespace.

    d) A classifier that classifies instances that have operations in common.

17. A generalization is a relationship between... (There is more than one correct answer.)

    a) Classifiers

    b) UseCases

    c) an Actor and a UseCase

    d) DataTypes

18. The instance of an association is called a/an

    a) Object

    b) Link

    c) LinkObject

    d) LinkSpecification

    e) ObjectLink

19. Which of the following statements about dependency relationships are true?

    a) A change in the supplier requires an update of the client.

    b) The client is incomplete without the supplier.

    c) The client sends data to the supplier.

    d) The supplier sends data to the client.

    e) The client requires the supplier for its specification or implementation.

20. Which statements about usage relationships are true?

    a) A change in the supplier requires an update of the client.

    b) The client is incomplete without the supplier.

    c) The client requires the supplier for its implementation.

    d) The supplier sends data to the client.

    e) The client requires the supplier for its specification or implementation.

21. Which of the four solutions shows the following interface configuration?

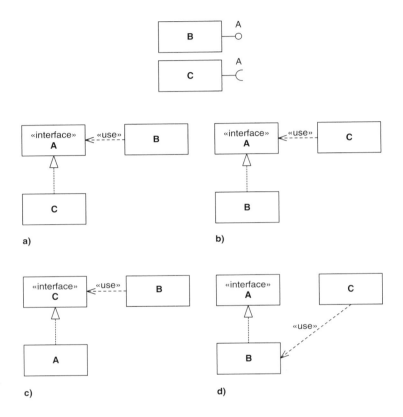

22. What kind of ActivityNodes are defined in UML?
    a) ObjectNode
    b) SleepNode
    c) SuspendNode
    d) ControlNode

23. An activity has an ActivityFinalNode with two incoming edges. When does the activity terminate?
    a) One token arrives at the ActivityFinalNode.
    b) Two tokens arrive at the ActivityFinalNode.
    c) The terminate condition evaluates to true.
    d) The user has pressed the stop button.

24. A token
    a) is a label in the activity diagram.
    b) contains an object or focus of control and is present in the activity diagram at a particular node.
    c) is a state that is valid while an activity is active.
    d) is a condition to trigger activity edges.

25. A MergeNode has three incoming edges. Which statement(s) is/are true?
    a) The MergeNode maps the incoming edges to one or more outgoing edges.
    b) The MergeNode waits for tokens at all incoming edges and offers a token to the outgoing edge.
    c) The MergeNode offers all tokens from the incoming edges to the outgoing edge.
    d) The MergeNode offers tokens to outgoing edges depending on a condition.

26. An interaction is
    a) a communication between two objects.
    b) a call of an operation.
    c) a unit of behavior.
    d) a set of messages.
    e) described by a sequence diagram.

27. A message in an interaction could be
    a) asynchronous.
    b) concurrent.
    c) synchronous.
    d) iterative.

28. A message in an interaction
    a) is a call of an operation.
    b) defines a communication between lifelines.
    c) must be defined in an interface.
    d) executes an action for sending a signal.

29. What kind of events can occur in an interaction?
    a) Send events
    b) Receive events
    c) Flow events

d) Destruction events

e) Creation events

f) Decision events

30. The GeneralOrdering relationship

    a) defines an order between two or more message events.

    b) is a special call of an operation.

    c) defines an order between lifelines.

    d) defines an order between two message events.

31. Which traces are valid for the interaction shown here?

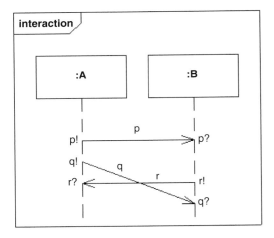

    a) <p!,p?,q!,r?,r!,q?>

    b) <p!,q!,r?,p?,r!,q?>

    c) <p!,p?,q!,r!,r?,q?>

    d) <p!,p?,r!,q!,r?,q?>

    e) <p?,r!,q?,p!,q!,r?>

    f) <p!,r!,p?,q!,r?,q?>

32. What describes a UseCase best?

    a) A UseCase is an ordered list of actions.

    b) A UseCase is the specification of a set of actions performed by a system.

    c) A UseCase describes an interaction between a user and a system.

    d) A UseCase is a specialized operation.

33. What describes an actor best?

    a) An actor is a user of a system.

    b) An actor is a user or any other system that interacts with the subject.

    c) An actor specifies a role played by a user or any other system that interacts with the subject.

    d) An actor is an object that may execute its own behavior without requiring method invocation.

34. An include relationship is a specialized

    a) dependency.

    b) DirectedRelationship.

    c) relationship.

    d) association.

    e) element.

ANSWERS

1. a, d
2. a
3. a
4. e
5. a, b, d, f
6. a
7. b, c
8. b, c, d, f
9. a, c
10. b
11. b, c, d
12. a, b, d, e
13. a, d, e
14. a, c, e, f
15. b, c
16. c
17. a, b, d
18. b
19. b, e
20. b, c
21. b
22. a, d
23. a
24. b
25. c
26. c, e
27. a, c
28. b
29. a, b, d, e
30. d
31. c, d
32. b
33. c
34. b, c, e

GLOSSARY

The definitions of terms in this glossary correspond to the original definitions in the UML 2.0 specification. We have divided this glossary into two sections according the level at which you are likely to find them on the examinations.

FUNDAMENTAL

Abstraction (dependencies) A relationship that relates two elements or sets of elements that represent the same concept at different levels of abstraction or from different viewpoints. In the metamodel, an abstraction is a dependency in which there is a mapping between the supplier and the client.

Action (BasicActivities) An executable activity node that is the fundamental unit of executable functionality in an activity, as opposed to control and data flow among actions.

Activity (BasicActivities) The specification of parameterized behavior as the coordinated sequencing of subordinate units whose individual elements are actions.

ActivityEdge (BasicActivities) An abstract class for directed connections between two activity nodes.

ActivitiyFinalNode (BasicActivities) A final node that stops all flows in an activity.

ActivityNode (BasicActivities) An abstract class for points in the flow of an activity connected by edges.

Note: Definitions of UML terms reprinted with permission of Object Management, Inc. Copyright © OMG, 2006.

ActivityParameterNode (BasicActivities) An object node for inputs to and outputs from activities.

Actor (UseCases) A role played by a user or any other system that interacts with the subject.

Association (Kernel) A set of tuples whose values refer to typed instances. An instance of an association is called a link (see also **InstanceSpecification**).

Behavior (BasicBehaviors) Specification of how its context classifier changes state over time.

BehavioralFeature (Kernel) A feature of a classifier that specifies an aspect of the behavior of its instances.

BehavioredClassifier (BasicBehaviors) A classifier can have behavior specifications defined in its namespace. One of these may specify the behavior of the classifier itself.

Class (Kernel) A set of objects that have the same specifications of features, constraints, and semantics.

Classifier (Kernel) A classification of instances; it describes a set of instances that have features in common.

Comment (Kernel) A textual annotation that can be attached to a set of elements.

Constraint (Kernel) A condition or restriction expressed in natural language text or in a machine-readable language for the purpose of declaring some of the semantics of an element.

ControlFlow (BasicActivities) An edge that starts an activity node after the previous one is finished.

ControlNode (BasicActivities) An abstract activity node that coordinates flows in an activity.

DataType (Kernel) A type whose instances are identified only by their value. A data type may contain attributes to support the modeling of structured data types.

DecisionNode (BasicActivities) A control node that chooses between outgoing flows.

Dependency (Dependencies) A relationship signifying that a single, or a set of model elements, requires other model elements for their specification or implementation. This means that the complete semantics of the depending elements is either semantically or structurally dependent on the definition of the supplier element(s).

DirectedRelationship (Kernel) A relationship between a collection of source model elements and a collection of target model elements.

Element (Kernel) A constituent of a model. As such, it has the capability of owning other elements.

ElementImport (Kernel) Identifies an element in another package and allows the element to be referenced using its name without a qualifier.

Enumeration (Kernel) A data type whose values are enumerated in the model as enumeration literals.

EnumerationLiteral (Kernel) A user-defined data value for an enumeration.

EventOccurrence (Interactions) Represents moments in time to which actions are associated. EventOccurrence is the basic semantic unit of interactions. (Note: This element has been transferred to the MessageEvent concept in the final UML 2.0 Specification.)

ExecutableNode (Kernel) An abstract class for activity nodes that may be executed. It is used as an attachment point for exception handlers.

ExecutionOccurrence (Interactions) An instantiation of a unit of behavior within the Lifeline. (Note: This element has been renamed to ExecutionSpecification in the final UML 2.0 Specification).

Expression (Kernel) A structured tree of symbols that denotes a (possibly empty) set of values when evaluated in a context.

Extend (UseCases) A relationship from an extending use case to an extended use case that specifies how and when the behavior defined in the extending use case can be inserted into the behavior defined in the extended use case.

Extension (Profiles) Indicates that the properties of a metaclass are extended through a stereotype and gives the ability to flexibly add (and later remove) stereotypes to classes.

ExtensionPoint (UseCases) Identifies a point in the behavior of a use case where that behavior can be extended by the behavior of some other (extending) use case, as specified by an extend relationship.

Feature (Kernel) Declares a behavioral or structural characteristic of instances of classifiers.

FinalNode (BasicActivities) An abstract control node at which a flow in an activity stops.

Generalization (Kernel) A taxonomic relationship between a more general classifier and a more specific classifier. Each instance of the specific classifier is also an indirect instance of the general classifier. Thus, the specific classifier inherits the features of the more general classifier.

GeneralOrdering (Interactions) A binary relation between two occurrence specifications to describe that one of these two occurrence specifications must occur before the other in a valid trace.

Implementation (Interfaces) A specialized realization relationship between a classifier and an interface. The implementation relationship signifies that the realizing classifier conforms to the contract specified by the interface. (Note: This element has been renamed to `InterfaceRealization` in the final UML 2.0 Specification).

Include (UseCases) A relationship defining that a use case contains the behavior defined in another use case.

InitialNode (BasicActivities) A control node at which flow starts when the activity is invoked.

InputPin (BasicActivities) An object node that receives values from other actions through object flows.

InstanceSpecification (Kernel) A model element that represents an instance in a modeled system. An instance specification of a class is called *object*; an instance specification of an association is called *link*.

InstanceValue (Kernel) A value specification that identifies an instance.

Interaction (Interactions) A unit of behavior that focuses on the observable exchange of information between connectable elements.

InteractionFragment (Interactions) An abstract notion of the most general interaction unit. An interaction fragment is a piece of an interaction. Each interaction fragment is conceptually like an interaction by itself.

Interface (Interfaces) A kind of classifier that represents a declaration of a set of coherent public features and obligations. An interface specifies a contract; any instance of a classifier that realizes the interface must fulfill that contract.

Lifeline (Interactions) An individual participant in an interaction.

LiteralSpecification (Kernel) Identifies a literal constant that is being modeled.

MergeNode (BasicActivities) A control node that brings together multiple alternative flows. It is not used to synchronize concurrent flows but to accept one among several alternative flows.

Message (Interactions) Defines a particular communication between the lifelines of an interaction.

MessageEnd (Interactions) An abstract named element that represents what can occur at the end of a message.

MultiplicityElement (Kernel) A definition of an inclusive interval of nonnegative integers beginning with a lower bound and ending with a (possibly infinite) upper bound. A multiplicity element embeds this information to specify the allowable cardinalities for an instantiation of this element.

NamedElement (Kernel) A element in a model that may have a name.

Namespace (Kernel) An element in a model that contains a set of elements that can be identified by name.

ObjectFlow (BasicActivities) An activity edge that can have objects or data passing along it.

ObjectNode (BasicActivities) An abstract activity node that is part of defining object flow in an activity.

OpaqueExpression (Kernel) An uninterpreted textual statement that denotes a (possibly empty) set of values when evaluated in a context.

Operation (Kernel) A behavioral feature of a classifier that specifies the name, type, parameters, and constraints for invoking an associated behavior.

OutputPin (BasicActivities) An object node that delivers values to other actions through object flows.

Package (Kernel) Used to group elements and provides a namespace for the grouped elements.

PackageableElement (Kernel) Indicates a named element that may be owned directly by a package.

PackageImport (Kernel) A relationship that allows the use of unqualified names to refer to package members from other namespaces.

PackageMerge (Kernel) Defines how the contents of one package are extended by the contents of another package.

Parameter (Kernel) A specification of an argument used to pass information into or out of an invocation of a behavioral feature.

Permission (Dependencies) A grant of access rights from the supplier model element to a client model element. (Note: This element is no longer included in the final UML 2.0 Specification.)

Pin (BasicActivities) An object node for inputs and outputs to actions.

PrimitiveType (Kernel) A predefined data type without any relevant substructure (i.e., it has no parts). A primitive data type may have an algebra and operations defined outside of UML, for example, mathematically.

Property (Kernel) A structural feature. A property related to a classifier by ownedAttribute represents an attribute, and it may also represent an association end. It relates an instance of the class to a value or collection of values of the type of the attribute. A property related to an association by memberEnd or its specializations represents an end of the association. The type of property is the type of the end of the association.

Realization (Dependencies) A specialized abstraction relationship between two sets of model elements, where one set represents a specification (the supplier) and the other represents an implementation of the latter (the client).

RedefinableElement (Kernel) An element that when defined in the context of a classifier can be redefined more specifically or differently in the context of another classifier that specializes (directly or indirectly) the context classifier.

Relationship (Kernel) An abstract concept that specifies some kind of relationship between elements.

Slot (Kernel) An entity modeled by an instance specification that has a value or values for a specific structural feature.

StateInvariant (Interactions) A runtime constraint on the participants of an interaction. It may be used to specify a variety of constraints, such as values of attributes or variables, internal or external states, and so on.

Stop (Interactions) An event occurrence that defines the termination of the instance specified by the lifeline on which the stop occurs. (Note: This element has been renamed to DestructionEvent in the final UML 2.0 Specification.)

StructuralFeature (Kernel) A typed feature of a classifier that specifies the structure of instances of this classifier.

Substitution (Kernel) A relationship between two classifiers signifying that the substituting classifier complies with the contract specified by the contract classifier.

Type (Kernel) Constrains the values represented by a typed element.

TypedElement (Kernel) An element that has a type.

Usage (Dependencies) A relationship in which one element requires another element (or a set of elements) for its full implementation or operation. In the metamodel, a usage is a dependency signifying that a client requires the presence of a supplier.

UseCase (UseCases) A specification of a set of actions performed by a system, which yields an observable result that is, typically, of value for one or more actors or other stakeholders of the system.

ValuePin (BasicActivities) An input pin that provides a value to an action that does not come from an incoming object flow edge.

ValueSpecification (Kernel) The specification of a (possibly empty) set of instances, including both objects and data values.

INTERMEDIATE

ActivityGroup (BasicActivities) An abstract class for defining sets of nodes and edges in an activity.

ActivityPartition (IntermediateActivities) A kind of activity group for identifying actions that have some characteristic in common.

AddStructuralFeatureValueAction (IntermediateActions) A write structural feature action for adding values to a structural feature.

AddVariableValueAction (StructuredActions) A write variable action for adding values to a variable.

ApplyFunctionAction An action that invokes a primitive predefined function that computes output values based only on the input values and the function. (Note: This element has been replaced by the `OpaqueAction` in the final UML 2.0 Specification.)

Artifact (Artifacts) The specification of a physical piece of information that is used or produced by a software development process or by deployment and operation of a system.

BroadcastSignalAction (IntermediateActions) An action that transmits a signal instance to all the potential target objects in the system, which may cause the firing of state machine transitions or the execution of associated activities of a target object.

CallAction (BasicActions) An abstract class for actions that invoke behavior and receive return values.

CallBehaviorAction (BasicActions) A call action that invokes a behavior directly rather than invoking a behavioral feature that, in turn, results in the invocation of that behavior.

CallOperationAction (BasicActions) An action that transmits an operation call request to the target object, where it may cause the invocation of associated behavior.

CentralBufferNode (IntermediateActivities) An object node for managing flows from multiple sources and destinations.

Clause (StructuredActivities) An element that represents a single branch of a conditional construct, including a test and a body section.

ClearAssociationAction (IntermediateActions) An action that destroys all links of an association in which a particular object participates.

ClearStructuralFeatureAction (IntermediateActions) A structural feature action that removes all values of a structural feature.

ClearVariableAction (StructuredActions) A variable action that removes all values of a variable.

Collaboration (Collaborations) A structure of collaborating elements (roles), each performing a specialized function, that collectively accomplish some desired functionality.

CollaborationOccurrence (Collaborations) The application of the pattern described by a collaboration to a specific situation involving specific classes or instances playing the roles of the collaboration. (Note: This element has been renamed to CollaborationUse in the final UML 2.0 Specification).

CombinedFragment (Fragments) An expression of interaction fragments. A combined fragment is defined by an interaction operator and corresponding interaction operands.

CommunicationPath (Nodes) An association between two deployment targets, through which they are able to exchange signals and messages.

Component (Components) A modular part of a system that encapsulates its contents and whose manifestation is replaceable within its environment.

ConditionalNode (StructuredActivities) A structured activity node that represents an exclusive choice among some number of alternatives.

ConnectableElement (InternalStructures) An abstract metaclass representing a set of instances that are owned by a containing classifier instance.

ConnectionPointReference (BehaviorStateMachines) A usage (as part of a submachine state) of an entry/exit point defined in the state machine reference by the submachine state.

Connector (InternalStructures) A link that enables communication between two or more instances. This link may be an instance of an association or it may represent the ability of the instances to communicate since their identities are known by virtue of being passed on as parameters, held in variables, created during the execution of a behavior, or because the communicating instances are identical.

ConnectorEnd (InternalStructures) An endpoint of a connector that attaches the connector to a connectable element.

Continuation (Fragments) A syntactic way to define continuations of different branches of an alternative combined fragment. Continuation is intuitively similar to labels representing intermediate points in a flow of control.

CreateLinkAction (IntermediateActions) A write link action for creating links.

CreateObjectAction (IntermediateActions) An action that creates an object that conforms to a statically specified classifier and puts it on an output pin at runtime.

DestroyLinkAction (IntermediateActions) A write link action that destroys links and link objects.

DestroyObjectAction (IntermediateActions) An action that destroys objects.

Device (Nodes) A physical computational resource with processing capability upon which artifacts may be deployed for execution.

EncapsulatedClassifier (Ports) Extends a classifier with the ability to own ports as specific and type checked interaction points.

ExceptionHandler (ExtraStructuredActivities) An element that specifies a body to execute in case the specified exception occurs during the execution of the protected node.

ExecutableNode (StructuredActivities) An abstract class for activity nodes that may be executed. It is used as an attachment point for exception handlers.

ExecutionEnvironment (Nodes) A node that offers an execution environment for specific types of components that are deployed on it in the form of executable artifacts.

Extension (Profiles) Indicates that the properties of a metaclass are extended through a stereotype and gives the ability to flexibly add (and later remove) stereotypes to classes.

ExtensionEnd (Profiles) Ties an extension to a stereotype when extending a metaclass.

FinalState (BehaviorStateMachines) A special kind of state signifying that the enclosing region is completed.

FlowFinalNode (IntermediateActivities) A final node that terminates a flow.

ForkNode (IntermediateActivities) A control node that splits a flow into multiple concurrent flows.

Gate (Fragments) A connection point for relating a message outside an interaction fragment with a message inside the interaction fragment.

InteractionConstraint (Fragments) A boolean expression that guards an operand in a combined fragment.

InteractionOccurrence (Fragments) Refers to an interaction. A shorthand for copying the contents of the referred interaction where the interaction occurrence is. (*Note:* This element has been renamed to InteractionUse in the final UML 2.0 Specification.)

InteractionOperand (Fragments) Contained in a combined fragment. Represents one operand of the expression given by the enclosing combined fragment.

InteractionOperator (Fragments) An enumeration designating the different kinds of operators of combined fragments.

InvocationAction (BasicActions) An abstract class for the various actions that invoke behavior.

JoinNode (IntermediateActivities) A control node that synchronizes multiple flows.

LinkAction (IntermediateActions) An abstract class for all link actions that identify their links by the objects and qualifiers at the ends of the links.

LinkEndCreationData (IntermediateActions) Not an action. It is an element that identifies links. It identifies one end of a link to be created by `CreateLinkAction`.

LinkEndData (IntermediateActions) Not an action. It is an element that identifies links.

LinkEndDestructionData (IntermediateActions) Not an action. It is an element that identifies links. It identifies one end of a link to be destroyed by `DestroyLinkAction`.

LoopNode (StructuredActivities) A structured activity node that represents a loop with setup, test, and body sections.

Manifestation (Artifacts) The concrete physical rendering of one or more model elements by an artifact.

Node (Nodes) A computational resource on which artifacts may be deployed for execution.

PartDecomposition (Fragments) A description of the internal interactions of one lifeline relative to an interaction.

Port (Ports) A structural feature of a classifier that specifies a distinct interaction point between that classifier and its environment or between the (behavior of the) classifier and its internal parts.

PrimitiveFunction Not an action. It is the signature of a function that produces output values from input values for use with `ApplyFunctionAction`. (*Note*: This element has been replaced by the `OpaqueAction` concept in the final UML 2.0 Specification.)

Profile (Profiles) Defines limited extensions to a reference metamodel with the purpose of adapting the metamodel to a specific platform or domain.

ProfileApplication (Profiles) Shows which profiles have been applied to a package.

ProtocolStateMachine (ProtocolStateMachines) Always defined in the context of a classifier. It specifies which operations of the classifier can be called in which state and under which condition, thus specifying the allowed call sequences on the classifier's operations.

Pseudostate (BehaviorStateMachines) An abstraction that encompasses different types of transient vertex in the state machine graph.

ReadLinkAction (IntermediateActions) A link action that navigates across associations to retrieve objects on one end.

ReadSelfAction (IntermediateActions) An action that retrieves the host object of an action.

ReadStructuralFeatureAction (IntermediateActions) A structural feature action that retrieves the values of a structural feature.

ReadVariableAction (StructuredActions) A variable action that retrieves the values of a variable.

Region (BehaviorStateMachines) A region is an orthogonal part of either a composite state or a state machine. It contains states and transitions.

RemoveStructuralFeatureValueAction (IntermediateActions) A write structural feature action that removes values from structural features.

RemoveVariableValueAction (StructuredActions) A write variable action that removes values from variables.

SendObjectAction (IntermediateActions) An action that transmits an object to the target object, where it may invoke behavior, such as the firing of state machine transitions or the execution of an activity.

SendSignalAction (BasicActions) An action that creates a signal instance from its inputs and transmits it to the target object, where it may cause the firing of a state machine transition or the execution of an activity.

State (BehaviorStateMachines) Models a situation during which some (usually implicit) invariant condition holds.

StateMachine (BehaviorStateMachines) Can be used to express the behavior of part of a system. Behavior is modeled as a traversal of a graph of state nodes interconnected by one or more joined transition arcs that are triggered by the dispatching of a series of (event) occurrences. During this traversal, the state machine executes a series of activities associated with various elements of the state machine.

Stereotype (Profiles) A stereotype defines how an existing metaclass may be extended and enables the use of platform- or domain-specific terminology or notation in place of, or in addition to, the ones used for the extended metaclass.

StructuralFeatureAction (IntermediateActions) An abstract class for all structural feature actions.

StructuredActivityNode (StructuredActivities) An executable activity node that may have an expansion into subordinate nodes as an activity group.

StructuredClassifier (InternalStructures) An abstract metaclass that represents any classifier whose behavior can be fully or partly described by the collaboration of owned or referenced instances.

TestIdentityAction (IntermediateActions) An action that tests if two values are identical objects.

Transition (BehaviorStateMachines) A directed relationship between a source vertex and a target vertex.

Variable (StructuredActivities) Elements for passing data between actions indirectly.

VariableAction (StructuredActions) An abstract class for actions that operate on a statically specified variable.

Vertex (BehaviorStateMachines) An abstraction of a node in a state machine graph.

WriteLinkAction (IntermediateActions) An abstract class for link actions that create and destroy links.

WriteStructuralFeatureAction (IntermediateActions) An abstract class for structural feature actions that change structural feature values.

WriteVariableAction (StructuredActions) An abstract class for variable actions that change variable values.

REFERENCES

[Gamma 2004] E. Gamma, R. Helm, R. Johnson, and J. Vlissides. *Design Patterns.* Addison-Wesley, Boston.

[Harel 1987] D. Harel. Statecharts: A Visual Formalism for Complex Systems. *Science of Computer Programming,* 8, 231ff.

[Oestereich 2004a] B. Oestereich. *Objektorientierte Softwareentwicklung, Analyse und Design mit der UML 2.0* (*Object-Oriented Software Development, Analysis and Design with UML 2.0*). Oldenbourg Wissenschaftsverlag, Munich.

[Oestereich 2004b] B. Oestereich. *Die UML 2.0 Kurzreferenz für die Praxis—kurz, bündig, ballastfrei* (*The UML 2.0 Short Reference for Practical Work*). Oldenbourg Wissenschaftsverlag, Munich.

[Oestereich 2004c] B. Oestereich, C. Weiss, C. Schröder, T. Weilkiens, and A. Lenhard. *Objektorientierte Geschäftsprozessmodellierung mit der UML* (*Using UML for Object-Oriented Business Process Modeling*). dpunkt.verlag, Heidelberg.

[UML1] OMG Unified Modeling Language, 2005—http://www.omg.org/uml, formal/04-07-02.

[UML2.0] OMG Unified Modeling Language, 2005—http://www.omg.org/uml, formal/05-07-04.

[UML2.0cert] OMG Unified Modeling Language, Adopted Specification, 2003—http://www.omg.org/uml, ptc/03-08-02.

[UML2.1] OMG Unified Modeling Language, 2006—http://www.omg.org/uml, ptc/06-01-02.

[UML-oose] Miscellaneous information on UML—www.oose.de/uml.

[Weilkiens 2004] T. Weilkiens, and B. Oestereich. *UML-2-Zertifizierung* (*Fundamental*). dpunkt.verlag, Heidelberg.

[Weilkiens 2006] T. Weilkiens. *Systems Engineering mit SysML/UML* (*Using SysML/UML for Systems Engineering*). dpunkt.verlag, Heidelberg.

Note: You can find an updated and more detailed list of references at *http:// www.oose.de/bibliographie*.

INDEX